Enterprise Sales and Operations Planning

Synchronizing Demand, Supply and Resources for Peak Performance

George E. Palmatier
with Colleen Crum

J.ROSS
PUBLISHING

APICS.
THE EDUCATIONAL SOCIETY
FOR RESOURCE MANAGEMENT

Copyright ©2003 by J. Ross Publishing, Inc.

ISBN 1-932159-00-2

Printed and bound in the U.S.A. Printed on acid-free paper.
10 9 8 7 6 5

Library of Congress Cataloging-in-Publication Data
Catalog information may be obtained from the Library of Congress

Direct all inquiries to J. Ross Publishing, Inc., 6501 Park of Commerce Blvd., Suite 200, Boca Raton, Florida 33487.

Phone: (561) 869-3900
Fax: (561) 892-0700
Web: www.jrosspub.com

DEDICATION

To Valerie (1971–2000)
Lost to Breast Cancer at Age 29

Little did Valerie know that she would influence so many people and companies around the world with her message: "The secret to success in business is *to just do what you say you are going to do.*"

TABLE OF CONTENTS

FOREWORD

The desire of all companies is to grow — to increase sales revenue and profits while maintaining a strong competitive position. When most companies reach a certain level in their growth, the factors that enabled their success (particularly communications) become harder to manage.

Departments begin to look at their roles as being more important than the success of the total organization. They tend to act and operate independently of each other, even though it is far more advantageous for departments to operate in a coordinated manner. Internally oriented departments (i.e., finance, engineering, manufacturing, and supply) begin to allow their own priorities to take precedence over the market and customers they are supposed to serve. Externally oriented departments (i.e., sales, marketing, service, and customer care) tend to disregard the realities and constraints of the internal organizations while focusing only on market and customer needs without regard to impact.

This independent-mindedness generally results in a dysfunctional organization which has no clear picture of why there is a loss of revenue, loss of customers, and reduced market share. The person who heads the company or organization, whether president, chairman, or general manager, rarely gets a view of the organization as a whole or the full implication of the problems that restrict the company's growth. Decisions of how to best achieve goals are made without fully understanding the implications on the organization as a whole.

Motorola has had a rich history of being ahead of the curve in developing new technologies and bringing them to market, of putting the customer first, and of ensuring that processes and products were driven by rigorous quality standards. Yet, over the last few years, we developed a tendency to make decisions as independent functional groups, ignoring the functional interdependency of the organization. As a senior executive in the Personal Communications Sector, I in fact operated with my peers in this dysfunctional manner.

Despite all of our collective efforts, we were chronically late with products, which in turn affected our market performance, profits, customer satisfaction, and market share. It was only after reading about sales and operations planning, talking to many other companies engaged in the process, and convincing the people I worked with and for that we needed to change our approach and processes that we were able to begin altering the behavior which got us in trouble.

By adopting a sales and operations planning process, along with other changes in the business sector, we were able to become a more synchronized organization. Each functional area of the business began to understand the implications of its actions on other functional areas, the business as a whole, our markets, and our customers. Our senior leaders began moving away from wishful thinking and a brute-force management style to a more functional interactive management approach. As the sales and operations planning disciplines began taking hold, the senior leaders began working together to understand the implications of what was happening to our business — how our markets and customers were changing and what our internal abilities were to serve those markets and customers. This improved understanding enabled us to better prioritize customers and products to serve those customers.

George Palmatier, Colleen Crum, and a small Oliver Wight team, along with four Motorolans, assisted me greatly in implementing a monthly sales and operations planning process across the four regions of the world serving the cellular business as well creating a centralized review with our sector president and his staff. I am pleased that George has been able to convert the ideas he brought to us into a clear and concise book.

This book provides the business context of synchronized decision making and an integrated business management process. When you look at the problems and opportunities from the view of the business as a whole, it prevents short-sighted decisions based on only one or two functional views.

Additionally, this book shows how companies can gain a competitive advantage by looking forward, eighteen months or more. That forward view can allow management to understand where gaps exist in its planning processes — whether those gaps are in developing sales revenue, delivering new products to the market, fulfilling expected customer orders, or in achieving profit goals.

When those gaps become visible in a forward planning process as provided in sales and operations planning, actions can be taken to affect the results. Companies can more effectively determine the best strategies and tactics to ensure that the gaps are reduced or eliminated. It is much easier — and much more effective — to anticipate the strategies and actions that will be required in the future as opposed to trying to respond to what happened last month or today.

You may think that everything I have written about is common sense. And you're right. However, applying common sense to the management of an organization is not easy if you do not have a structured approach that is inclusive of the entire organization.

This book shows how to develop that structure in your company. Ironically, this common sense approach is not expensive to implement or time consuming for managers to utilize once it is established and becomes a part of the organizational culture. At Motorola, we did not have to invest in any major new software tools to support the sales and operations planning process. Senior managers spent less than three hours per month in utilizing the process in order to understand where they should more effectively focus their energies during the coming month(s). That's because the process effectively pointed out the weaknesses that needed to be addressed in order to help get us back on the road to profitability.

My final thought is that sales and operations planning is a never-ending management process. The process evolves as senior management becomes more skilled in utilizing it. Once things are moving in the right direction again, there will be a temptation to want to stop the process or assign it to lower levels in the organization "because everything is now fixed." My caution is *don't*. This process can only be effective with senior management engagement. It is the participation of senior management which ensures that markets are being served and customer as well as shareholder expectations are being met. It is this process which *enables* the senior management of the company or organization to be responsive to its markets.

At Motorola, it helped us begin to get ahead of the curve. I hope that it will have that same benefit at your company as well.

> *Jim Haleem*
> *Corporate Vice President*
> *and Director (Retired)*
> *Personal Communications Sector*
> *Motorola*

PREFACE

I have never known a manufacturing executive who did not want to become a more effective manager. I have never known a manufacturing executive who did not feel the need to help improve his or her company's performance. The issue is not a lack of desire; the issue is *how* to better manage the business to improve performance.

In a quest to improve business performance, executives have turned to technology, particularly information technology. They also have turned to process reengineering or what is sometimes derisively referred to as "alphabet soup," including programs such as enterprise resource planning (ERP), total quality control (TQC), agile manufacturing, and just-in-time (JIT) inventory management, to name just a few.

No doubt about it, planning and controlling the resources of a company is a fundamental need, as is a high quality of products and services. Inadequate planning and control inevitably leads to poor customer service, higher costs, high inventories, late new product introductions, less than optimum financial performance, and a host of other ills.

In my more than twenty years of experience in manufacturing management, I have frequently asked myself what the difference is between companies that successfully deploy process improvements and those that fail.

I have found that the most sophisticated reengineering efforts and technological tools alone do not ensure success. What ensures success is *people using the appropriate operating principles and processes with diligence and discipline.*

This book is primarily about the fundamental operating principles that are required to successfully deploy manufacturing management — and one such practice in particular, known as sales and operations planning.

The benefits of utilizing sales and operations planning have been profound for many companies. At first, use of this methodology leads to improved operational performance, including on-time customer deliveries, reduced inventory, improved quality, and increased profits. As companies gain more experience and proficiency with the process, they begin to improve their strategic performance, which in turn leads to improved business performance for all the company's stakeholders. In short, the management team becomes more effective at managing the business.

This book focuses on the people aspect of successfully using sales and operations planning. It presents fundamental operating principles, the logic behind the principles, and how to apply these principles in a manufacturing business environment.

In communicating this information, I have created a fictional company. The information is presented from the viewpoint of the company's management team.

This is an effective technique for conveying the reasons behind the operating principles and application methodology. I find that company executives are often quick to grasp concepts, but their shortcoming is applying the concepts and bringing them to fruition. If managers cannot relate the concept to the personal day-to-day challenges and struggles of operating the business, it is difficult to make a commitment to change the way one manages.

I know, because that's how it was for me when the company for which I worked began implementing sales and operations planning. It gives me great pleasure to share my experience with you. I hope this book will help spur you and your company to greater success.

George E. Palmatier

ACKNOWLEDGMENTS

As an educator and consultant for more than fifteen years, I have had the opportunity to learn from many clients and companies. It has been a privilege to work with talented people in well-managed companies — representing both large, global companies and very small, privately owned firms that make everything from soup to satellites. I have learned from so many people that it is not possible to single out those individuals who have influenced me the most. I am grateful for the many opportunities I have had over the years to help clients improve their operations and, in turn, thank my clients for a willingness to learn and share that learning within their organizations.

I owe an acknowledgment to Donald E. Bently and the management team of the Bently Nevada Corporation (now a part of General Electric). I was a member of Bently Nevada's executive management team during the implementation and operation of a Class A sales and operations planning process. This experience set the stage for my second career as an educator and consultant.

A special acknowledgment goes to the Oliver Wight Companies as a whole for providing me with an environment conducive to continuous learning and knowledge sharing. I especially would like to thank Walter Goddard, Chairman Emeritus, for his early encouragement on this book and his detailed review and direction. Roger Brooks will undoubtedly recognize some of the principles and practices he shared with me over the years. The sales and operations planning education team of John Schorr, Pete Skurla, and Tom Gillen contributed to the evolution of a number of the key elements of sales and operations planning and thus have influenced this book. I am also grateful to Oliver Wight Europe for its continued efforts to evolve the education model for sales and operations planning.

Recent client engagements working with Oliver Wight consultant Rob Tearnan have helped me to keep the fundamentals of sales and operations planning in perspective. Marc Bergeron, as a member of the Oliver Wight team, put life into the implementation of sales and operations planning through his contribution to process improvement and to the Oliver Wight sales and operations planning template. Clearly, others within the Oliver Wight organization have helped to shape the message of this book, and I am very grateful for their generous contributions.

Without Colleen (Coco) Crum, this book would still be a draft. Coco not only has a deep understanding of sales and operations planning and demand planning, but she also has the ability to take what I write and turn it into something that more clearly and distinctly says what I mean. I truly thank her for her content contributions and her considerable work in editing this book.

I also owe thanks for a critical review to Jim Haleem, Senior Vice President of Motorola. Jim provided an excellent practitioner's perspective and influenced considerable changes to an early draft of this book.

To my wife, Nadine, I say thank you for graciously putting up with all my time at the computer — at home and on vacations, always stealing some of our time together. Without her patience, this book would still be but an idea, something I wished I would write.

George E. Palmatier

THE AUTHORS

George E. Palmatier, a consultant and educator with the Oliver Wight Companies since 1986, is recognized as a leading expert in integrated sales and operations planning. He helped to pioneer one of the first applications of sales and operations planning as vice-president of marketing at Bently Nevada Corporation, now part of General Electric. Based on this experience, he co-authored a book, *The Marketing Edge: The New Leadership Role of Sales and Marketing in Manufacturing.* The premise of the book — that sales and marketing have an essential role to play in developing manufacturing strategies — has helped to drive an increasing number of companies toward using sales and operations planning as an integrated management process.

George has transferred his knowledge to hundreds of companies that produce or market all types of products, from services to soups to satellites. It is this experience as a practitioner, educator, and coach that is imparted in this book.

Colleen Crum is a consultant and educator with the Oliver Wight Companies. She has assisted many companies in implementing sales and operations planning, demand management, and forecasting.

Colleen has been involved in the food industry's supply chain management effort. She participated in the development of *ECR: Road Map to Continuous Replenishment,* published by Canadian food industry trade groups in 1995. The publication documented the best continuous replenishment practices in Canada, addressing logistics, distribution, transportation, and resource planning.

She is currently writing a book with co-author George Palmatier on demand management to be published by J. Ross Publishing.

ABOUT OLIVER WIGHT

Throughout the world, the Oliver Wight name is synonymous with many widely adopted operational methodologies. Oliver Wight is a global firm of consultants and educators who specialize in planning and control and change management for businesses and professionals in the fields of manufacturing, procurement, logistics, and distribution. Since 1969, Oliver Wight has been a thought leader in manufacturing — creating the disciplines of Material Requirements Planning and Manufacturing Resources Planning and pioneering the use of Class A Business Excellence and Sales and Operations Planning.

As part of its commitment to help organizations achieve operational excellence, Oliver Wight began publishing best practice standards and criteria in the form of what is known as the ABCD checklist. Due to popular demand, Oliver Wight decided to expand its publishing program, which has been in operation for more than 20 years. Many of the books are now considered classics and seminal works in their field. Oliver Wight's commitment to help companies through consulting, educational courses, books, and other media still continues today.

Oliver Wight has maintained its leadership role at the forefront of change with the creation of new methodologies and the introduction of best practices that fit the needs of today's — and tomorrow's — companies. Oliver Wight consultants and educators are located throughout the world. Company offices are located in New London, New Hampshire, USA; Gloucester, United Kingdom; and Sydney, Australia.

Oliver Wight previously introduced the mechanics of sales and operations planning and demand management in the best-selling and ground-breaking books entitled *Orchestrating Success: Improve Control of the Business with Sales and Operations Planning* and *The Marketing Edge: The New Leadership Role of Sales and Marketing in Manufacturing*. The sales and operations planning and demand management processes are now best practices that are becoming basic management fundamentals necessary for success in today's business climate. Experience has shown that operational excellence requires a blend of people, process, and tools — in that order. Software alone cannot be the sole driver of a company's success. Today's technology tools are dependent on strong processes, and an effective sales and operations planning and demand management process is essential to the successful implementation of any integrated management system such as enterprise resources planning and supply chain management.

Oliver Wight and J. Ross Publishing are pleased to introduce the Integrated Business Management Series of best practices and innovations. *Enterprise Sales and Operations Planning: Synchronizing Demand, Supply and Resources for Peak Performance* and *Demand Management Best Practices: Process, Principles and Collaboration* are the first two books in this new series. These books demonstrate how to successfully implement these processes to achieve the operational performance required to remain competitive today and in the future. The series is dedicated to the pioneering efforts and innovative spirit of the late Oliver Wight and his mission of helping companies achieve new levels of operational excellence that yield competitive advantage and superior profits. Additional information on these and future titles in the Integrated Business Management Series is available on the J. Ross Publishing web site at www.jrosspub.com.

ABOUT APICS

APICS — The Educational Society for Resource Management is a not-for-profit international educational organization recognized as the global leader and premier provider of resource management education and information. APICS is respected throughout the world for its education and professional certification programs. With more than 60,000 individual and corporate members in 20,000 companies worldwide, APICS is dedicated to providing education to improve an organization's bottom line. No matter what your title or need, by tapping into the APICS community you will find the education necessary for success.

APICS is recognized globally as:

- The source of knowledge and expertise for manufacturing and service industries across the entire supply chain
- The leading provider of high-quality, cutting-edge educational programs that advance organizational success in a changing, competitive marketplace
- A successful developer of two internationally recognized certification programs, Certified in Production and Inventory Management (CPIM) and Certified in Integrated Resource Management (CIRM)
- A source of solutions, support, and networking for manufacturing and service professionals

For more information about APICS programs, services, or membership, visit www.apics.org or contact APICS Customer Support at (800) 444-2742 or (703) 354-8851.

THE COMPANY
AND PLAYERS

The Company

Universal Products, division of Global Products and Services, Inc.

The Players

Jack Baxter	President, Global Products and Services, Inc.
Susan Callahan	Planning Manager, Universal Products
Anita Cooper	Purchasing Manager, Universal Products
Nolan Drake	Consultant, Effective Management, Inc.
Ray Guy	Final Assembly Manager, Universal Products
Peter Newfeld	Product Development/Engineering Director, Universal Products
Janis Novak	Controller, Universal Products
Mike O'Brien	Customer Service/Contract Administration Manager, Universal Products
Ross Peterson	Lead Consultant, Effective Management, Inc.
Justin Roberts	Marketing Manager, Universal Products
Mark Ryan	General Manager, Universal Products
Cheryl Ryan	Mark's wife
Chad Ryan	Mark and Cheryl's son
Jim Simpson	Manufacturing Director, Universal Products
Sheri Waterman	Administrative Assistant to Mark Ryan
Sam Wente	Sales Director, Universal Products

OUT OF CONTROL

It's 3:24 a.m., and Mark Ryan is wide awake. That darn digital clock. It glows brightly in the dark and displays the time to the nearest minute.

Since Mark's laser surgery, he no longer has to put on glasses to see the clock in the middle of the night. He wonders how he lived without this technology.

It is not surprising that Mark is having another sleepless night. Ever since his promotion nine months ago to general manager of Universal Products, a division of Global Products and Services, Inc., Mark feels like he is in over his head. He has never failed at anything that he seriously attempted, but he is failing now.

Universal Products makes a wide range of products. Some are made to stock for quick delivery to customers, some are made to order with a wide range of options, and others are engineered specifically for individual customers. The division has been under significant pressure from its customers to improve on-time delivery and to shorten delivery lead times. Key customers are also pressuring Universal Products for lower prices, and the competition is nipping at the division's heels for every major account. Most troubling to Mark is that the division has not been hitting its sales and profit budgets for the year.

Of course, the customers and the competition are not really to blame. We haven't been helping ourselves, Mark observes as he rearranges the pillow in hopes of catching at least a few more winks before sunrise. Since he took over as general manager, customer lead times have actually gotten longer. And, as customers continually point out, the division is extremely unreliable when it comes to meeting promised ship dates. To make matters worse, manufacturing costs are higher than plan.

If only we could hit the numbers, Mark says to himself. Although everyone tells him they will hit their numbers, that has rarely happened.

No matter how hard he tries, Mark can't seem to get the division on track, and he knows that things have actually gotten worse since he took over. Now he dreads reading his e-mail in the morning. Yesterday, he had twenty-seven new messages from customers, members of his staff, suppliers, and yes, corporate management. And none of the e-mails were positive.

The most upsetting e-mail was from Jack Baxter, president of Global Products and Services, Inc. and Mark's boss. Jack hired Mark into the corporation fifteen years ago, and Mark has been working for Jack through his promotions and division moves.

Mark has never let Jack down, but he knows that Jack is starting to question his ability to lead the division. He overheard Jack on the phone during his last visit to Colorado, and he used the phrase "the Peter Principle." Lord knows what phrases Jack uses when I am out of earshot, Mark says to himself.

All Mark knows for sure as he tosses and turns in bed is that he is running out of time. "I have to get this division improving or I am gone. I feel like I have been given a chance at bat and already have two strikes against me. The rule is three strikes and you're out!" Mark says as he punches the pillow one more time.

■ ■ ■

Despite lack of sleep, Mark is looking forward to the new day. He likes the sunrise and pulls open the curtains to see it emerge over the mountainscape. It is quiet. The early birds have not yet begun their singing, but Mark knows that in a few minutes, the air will be full of the sounds of the morning.

While watching the sun come up, Mark feels happy to be living in the Denver area. He likes living within walking distance from work, even though he doesn't actually walk to work as often as he could. Living less than two miles from work beats the seventy-five-minute commute he put up with before moving to the eastern slope of the Rockies.

His only regret is that he won't be able to move his family until after the school year. His son, Chad, graduates this year, and there was no way he would consent to being uprooted from his classmates, friends, and studies. As always, Mark's wife, Cheryl, has not complained about the sacrifices required by another corporate move, especially being apart from Mark. She is anxious to move to Colorado. She much prefers to be in the mountains with the clean, dry air.

The whole family enjoys the majesty of the mountain peaks, the smell of pine, and the mountain wildflowers, but for Cheryl, mountain living is a passion. When she was a college student, she worked summers in the high country in Yosemite. Living in the flat, humid East Coast has not been easy for her. While they enjoyed the past six years on the eastern seaboard, Cheryl would point out from time to time that "it's still not the West!"

It will only be a few more months now before we are all here as a family, assuming I am still here, Mark says to himself.

Even though it is going to be a sunny day, Mark knows that the temperature is not expected to rise above freezing. That is a good excuse to drive to work.

As he pulls into the parking lot, Mark sees that Ray Guy, the final assembly manager, is already at work. Mark knows he has really been putting the pressure on him. He told Ray yesterday, and the week before, and the week before, "If we don't get shipments up, we won't even hit last year's numbers, much less the 15 percent growth I promised to deliver when we did the annual plan!"

If I can only hit and exceed last year's numbers, Jack will give me a shot at another year, Mark thinks. But the prospects do not look good.

What frustrates Mark is that much of the current situation is out of his control. Nobody told him that last year's numbers were achieved by giving special deals as incentives to customers to make their purchases last year instead of this year. And, of course, no one changed the sales budget to reflect the lower sales this year as a result of the early orders. Nobody also told him that the division was burdened with excess, old, and obsolete inventory that was the result of the accumulated sins of the four division general managers before him. And nobody told him that the executive "team" wasn't a team at all. Mark's first staff meeting almost ended in a fistfight!

When Jack approached Mark about becoming the general manager, he told Mark that he would be moving into a division "under control and poised for growth." On the surface, that appeared to be true.

Universal Products' plant and division headquarters are relatively new, attractive, and comfortable. The facility is designed for a combination of flow manufacturing and job shop production, which makes sense for manufacturing a mix of high-volume, medium-volume, and one-of-a-kind products. The division has a good reputation for solid technology and high quality.

In reality, Mark has found that nothing is as it seemed on the surface. Under control is actually under water, and poised for growth turns out to be poised for disaster.

Every day, Mark is confronted with a new set of surprises, and he doesn't like surprises. Even the pleasant surprises are a symptom of being out of control.

As he walks into the plant, Mark mumbles under his breath, "They said I should not have any problem with the organization. I just had to manage the growth. Right!"

Mark has taken to entering the building each morning through the shipping and receiving area. He purposely walks through shipping and receiving and then the assembly area to observe where there may be problems. It is usually obvious. He can tell by where groups of assembly workers, supervisors, and a manager or two have gathered. There are two such groups this morning.

Mark doesn't stop to hear what they are talking about. He is anxious to put his briefcase in his office, pour a cup of coffee, and get started on a new tack. Today is the first day of his "company correction" sessions with key individuals in the division.

The purpose of these private, one-on-one sessions is to finally get to the bottom of the problems within the division. Mark has heard all sorts of complaints from managers, customers, and Jack and others in the corporate offices. He knows that complaints are generally symptoms of a deeper problem. He also knows that he must get to the cause of the problem and then implement the solution.

What baffles Mark in particular is that the division implemented many different operational improvement initiatives over the years. Those improvements seem to him to have resulted in higher costs and lower performance. Why? What is the key? What is the secret? What would the truly modern, yet experienced general manager do? Hell, what am *I* going to do? he asks himself as he sets his briefcase on his desk and trudges down the hall, coffee cup in hand, to the cafeteria.

■ ■ ■

Mark Ryan and Ray Guy, the final assembly manager, sit down for the first of Mark's one-on-one interviews. Mark starts the conversation. "Thanks for coming in, Ray," he says. "I saw that you were here early again this morning. Is the final assembly area making any progress? I already had two e-mails and two phone calls regarding the Anderson job this morning. Are we getting close to shipping it?"

Ray's face reddens. He is noticeably upset. "Quite frankly, I don't know for sure," he replies. "Every time I think it is under control, something else happens. We would have had it out last week except that planning came in with that must-ship Lucas order last Wednesday. We had to stop work on the Anderson job, and we had to take some of the completed parts from the Anderson job to ship the Lucas order. If you would just get Susan Callahan in planning to clean up her act, we could make the shipments. Every day is a surprise. Every day I come in wondering what fire we will need to put out. We had the whole crew here on the weekend only to find that manufacturing didn't give us all the parts. Mark, give me the parts, and I will make the product and make shipments. Jim Simpson in manufacturing didn't have his people in here on Saturday even though he knew they owed us the parts. You keep preaching teamwork. Where is it? Working twelve-hour days and on weekends only to find I don't have what I need to build the orders is crazy."

Ray pauses for a moment, letting his fingers brush through his close-trimmed salt-and-pepper beard.

"I appreciate your comments," Mark says.

Ray holds up a hand to signal Mark to stop. "Mark, I'm not through," he says. "I'm glad you asked for this private session. My people are busting their butts. They work long, hard hours, and it's not just for the overtime. They want to feel good about their jobs. They want to feel like they have done what the company wants done, but all they ever hear is how they're screwing up. They know our on-time delivery to customers is in the low 80 percent range. They know seventeen out of every hundred orders are late or not filled completely. They also know costs are up due to all the overtime and that quality is suffering because of the pressure to ship late jobs. What they don't know is what you are doing to fix the problem. Planning is out of control, and Jim in manufacturing just doesn't deliver us the parts we need when we need them. Mark, I know that Susan in planning is your person of choice, but what has she done since she came on board? Things are worse now than before when Dave was here. When are you going to fix that, Mark? The problem is not me or my crew — it's the rest of the organization. They work for you."

Ray realizes he might have gone too far with his last points. He takes a deep breath and leans back in his chair. "I'm sorry to come on so strong. I'm just frustrated," he says. "By the way, how is your family? When are your wife and son going to move out here?"

Stung by Ray's comments, Mark thinks a little cooling off is in order. "Thanks for asking. Cheryl and Chad will be moving here the end of May," he replies. "I sure am getting tired of only seeing Cheryl every other week, even if it is for a long weekend. And flying across the country is not much fun anymore."

Mark decides to end the conversation. He does not think it will be any more fruitful. Ray obviously is frustrated and not in a frame of mind for problem solving. "Ray, thanks for your input," he says. "I appreciate your being open, honest, and frank. I will get back to you."

■ ■ ■

Susan Callahan, the planning manager, strides confidently into Mark's office. She is one of the new managers Mark brought on board to help solve Universal Products' problems. She is in charge of the planning organization, which was formerly called production and inventory control.

Mark and Susan chitchat easily about the Colorado weather, getting settled into their homes, and what they do with their free time now that they don't have long commutes to and from work. Then Mark decides to get down to business. "Susan, you know why we are having this session," he says. "The division is not performing, and the heat is on."

Not wanting to have a repeat of the Ray Guy conversation, Mark decides to set some boundaries. "I want your view of the situation," he says, "but first let me talk for a bit." He explains to Susan that he hired her six months ago with high expectations. The planning organization had been decimated as a result of one of the previous rightsizing initiatives, and the division was out of control.

"You assured me that you had solid experience and could build the planning organization into a truly professional team," Mark says. "I just finished getting an earful from Ray Guy, and he had nothing good to say about the planning organization. He, in essence, said that our plans are not coming together, are not in sync. What's happening?"

Susan bristles. She pushes her short black hair back and plants both feet on the floor. "Let me first say that I don't appreciate the cheap shots from Ray," she responds. "My planners are working very hard to produce valid plans and schedules. They are here early, and they stay late. As you know, all but one in my organization is certified by the American Production and Inventory Control Society, the professional organization. You know it as APICS. If the division is in trouble, it is not because of the planners. I have turned that organization from virtually nothing into a showcase group. The problem is that no one here builds to schedule. We create great schedules, but nobody follows them. Manufacturing is the worst. They make whatever they choose whenever they choose. Jim Simpson is from the old school, where the only things that count in manufacturing are productivity and efficiency. Everything is done for lower costs — unless, of course, somebody from Mahogany Row puts the pressure on him to make a particular shipment. Why, just last week you went straight to manufacturing and told them to stop what they were working on and finish the Lucas job. If my people give schedules to manufacturing and you tell manufacturing to ignore the schedules, what kind of message is that? No, Mark, the problem isn't with my planners. The problem is that no one will follow the schedules."

Susan has more to say. "And another thing. Purchasing is as bad if not worse than manufacturing. I think purchasing must tell its suppliers to deliver at their convenience. It amazes me how we can have so much inventory yet can't ship product because purchasing didn't get the parts from our suppliers. Give me that group, and I will turn it around in a hurry. I'd start by outlawing the three-martini lunch."

Mark knows he hit a nerve with Susan. She has high standards and is perceived as being a very thorough professional. He decides she needs reassurance, but first he needs some answers.

"You know I respect the work you have done, Susan," Mark says, "but if your plans are so good, why doesn't the organization follow them? It can't just be everybody else's fault. Where are you helping?"

Susan sighs. "Mark, I am glad you asked. Here's the situation. We put in place schedules that have valid dates and balance demand and supply. But then sales sells products not in the schedule for immediate delivery. The people in sales only know one word, and that word is *yes*. I know Sam Wente has been here a long time and has strong relationships with our customers, but someone has to represent the supply side of the business in negotiations. You know, Mark, anybody can get an order if all they ever have to say is yes. You want it when? No problem. You want a special feature made out of unobtainium? No problem. You want a discount? No problem. You want us to keep a three-month supply of inventory? No problem. People who only know how to say yes do not know how to sell. Anyway, these unplanned orders come in for immediate delivery and everyone in the company says yes. All the previous schedules immediately go out the window."

Mark cannot help chuckling. Susan always has a way with words. He will remember "unobtainium."

Susan is not finished, however. "And one more thing," she says. "We identified a capacity constraint in the testing area months ago, and you continue to say *no* to the capital equipment requisition needed to increase the capacity. Our schedules were based on getting the new equipment. So again, even *you* are causing us to miss schedules. Ray Guy tells me that every time he brings you the requisition, you ask for more justification. Mark, quite frankly, some of us think you are afraid to make the necessary decisions to get things done."

Now Mark bristles, and his face turns red. "Well, Susan, nobody told me that the equipment was needed to make schedule! How should I know?"

"Do you think your staff is just making the capital equipment requests for the hell of it?" Susan replies. "I am amazed. We do have a problem here, Mark, don't we?"

Mark feels chagrined. "So what are you suggesting I do, Susan?"

"Start by telling your staff to hit the schedules. The schedule is king. We must begin using dates as our priorities, not whoever has the most political influence. Stop everyone from going around the planning organization when they want something. Give me the purchasing organization. Tell the sales group to stop selling stuff we can't deliver. And you had better act soon. All these schedule changes are causing inventory to go up even more. We're in a situation where we have most of what it takes to ship most of the products, but not all of what is required to ship hardly any of them. That means lots of work in process and raw material inventory. And stop blaming planning when inventory goes up and shipments are late!"

Mark and Susan sit quietly for a moment. Mark decides he has learned enough from Susan. "I appreciate your candor, Susan," he says. "However, I would like you to be sensitive to the fact that many people in this organization do not have the same opinion of your schedules. Rumor has it that I am favoring you and am letting you get away with a less than sterling performance. When I finish this review process, we will need to speak again."

Susan pushes right back. "And when we do speak again, I also need to talk to you about engineering change control. Engineering change control here is an oxymoron. It is out of control."

Mark would like to tell Susan that engineering change control is one of his last priorities. He is concerned about hitting the numbers and shipping product on time but figures that would be a futile conversation, plus he's ready for a break. He thanks Susan for her time and is grateful for a few minutes alone in his office.

Mark is disappointed. He expected these one-on-one sessions to reveal answers. He does not feel any better now than when he came to work this morning. What is clear is that everyone perceives the problem as someone else's problem.

He has heard only one answer so far: "It's *their* fault. *They* are the problem." What happened to the total quality and teamwork training the company spent so much money on about eighteen months ago? Every person in the company went through that training. Didn't it take? What a waste of money.

Mark picks up his coffee cup and heads for the cafeteria. Sheri Waterman, his administrative assistant, is hard at work at her desk. Mark stops for a moment. "If Jim Simpson shows up, Sheri, tell him to make himself comfortable. I will be back in a few minutes," he says.

While walking to the cafeteria, he stops muttering. He doesn't want people to think he has lost his mind. But his mind is whirling. This is an ominous start, he observes. Ray blames Susan. Susan blames purchasing, sales, manufacturing, and even me! Where did I ever come up with the bright idea of these "company correction" sessions?

■ ■ ■

Jim Simpson, the manufacturing director, is waiting in Mark's office when he returns with coffee in hand. As he sets his coffee cup on the round conversation table, Mark realizes that he does not know as much about Jim's background as he should. "How long have you lived in this area?" Mark asks.

"Almost twenty years," Jim replies. Jim started his career with an aerospace company. The end of the Cold War brought major defense budget cuts and downsizing. Jim saw it as an opportunity to leave the hustle and bustle of southern California and move to a less crowded area where he could hike, camp, and fish in his spare time. "There are only a few places better than Colorado for outdoor activities. But even Denver is getting more crowded each year," Jim laments.

Mark switches subjects to the business at hand and hopes that Jim is not in a blame-the-other-guy frame of mind. "Jim, you seem to run a pretty tight ship out in the shop. What is your view as to why we can't seem to regularly and routinely make and ship product on time, on quality, on cost?"

Jim hesitates before replying. "I appreciated having some time to prepare for this conversation. I've done a lot of thinking, and I've talked to my people. I'm not sure you are going to like what I am about to say."

Mark braces himself. "I've asked all my staff to be open and honest. I will not shoot the messenger. Please continue."

"I appreciate your comment about my running a tight ship," Jim says, "but the truth is it's the people on the shop floor who are running the tight ship." He explains that the total quality classes and teamwork skills training have helped the factory people tremendously. The shop is organized for production flow through cellular manufacturing, using kanbans where they are most applicable. The total quality training motivated the shop floor people to clean up the shop, and now people are proud of their work environment. "It's a different shop than it was eighteen months ago," Jim states.

In preparing for this one-on-one session, Jim asked the people on the shop supervision team for their views. He specifically asked what needs to happen to improve their performance. "Mark, here's a summary of what they told me," Jim says. "First, supervisors believe that engineering has to better understand how the products are made and assembled. We have manufacturing teams, but with very little engineering participation."

He explains that engineering requirements have tolerances that can't be held on the manufacturing equipment. When this fact is pointed out to the engineering organization, the reply is, "Just do your best." Doing their best results in not meeting the tolerances, which means that manufacturing spends precious time making scrap.

"And when this occurs," Jim says, "the planning group tells us we have to work overtime to get back on schedule. Mark, this is an outdoor community, and the manufacturing people want to have a life outside of the factory. We can't keep them working overtime on evenings and weekends, which they believe shouldn't have been necessary to begin with."

Jim has more to say about engineering. "We seem to get an inordinate number of engineering changes, and the notices come late. We'll have the products partially completed and then receive notification of an engineering change, which, of course, means we have to start over, and we have just made more scrap."

"Making scrap is not what gives manufacturing people job fulfillment, and it threatens employee retention," he continues. "We're lucky to have the skilled people we have. This may be a nice place to live, but there are not a lot of manufacturing professionals knocking on our door to be hired. We need to keep our people satisfied with their jobs. Quite frankly, we can't afford to lose them."

The telephone rings. Mark is irritated. He picks up the phone. "Sheri, I asked you to hold my calls. What is it?" he says sternly.

Sheri, as usual, is unflappable. "Mark, I thought I had better interrupt. It is Jack Baxter on the phone. He said it was important and urgent."

Mark calms down. "Thanks, Sheri. You did the right thing."

He turns to Jim. "This may be a long phone conversation, but I want to finish our discussion. Can you come back in fifteen minutes?"

"I'll be in the cafeteria getting some coffee," Jim replies.

Mark takes a deep breath. These days, he dreads getting calls from Jack, who is both the corporate president and his boss. Phone calls are more unpleasant than e-mails. He picks up the phone and uses his most confident voice. "Jack, hello. How are you? What's so urgent?"

Jack does not waste time with niceties. "Mark, I don't know what is going on out there, but when major customers feel they have to call the president of the corporation to get service, something is not right. Jackson Smith, the president of Anderson, called me to see what I could do to get his order shipped. Anderson is in a bind, and Jackson says we are the cause. I don't have any order number for reference, but it is an order that was supposed to ship from your facility three weeks ago. It still hasn't shipped even though we have made multiple promises that it would. What's going on?"

Mark is glad he knows the status of the Anderson order. "I have been following the Anderson order, Jack. One thing after another has kept it from shipping. I know it is dangerously close to shipping as we speak. Do you want me to call you back or call Jackson Smith with the ship date?"

"Mark, just make it ship," Jack says firmly. "Tell your normal contacts at Anderson the details, and send me an e-mail with the facts. I will call Jackson Smith myself."

Jack is not finished speaking and cuts Mark off as he starts to reply. "The last time we talked, you said you were going to get to the bottom of the problems. What have you found out?"

"I was in a session with Jim in manufacturing when you called. I'm meeting individually with all the key players here to figure this thing out."

"When will you have an answer?" Jack asks gruffly.

"This is getting my full attention. I will give you a call later this week and tell you what I've learned," Mark responds.

"I can send someone in there to help if you need it," Jack says.

"Jack, please don't do that just yet. Give me a little more time. If I can't figure it out, I will ask you for the help. You know I want the division to succeed."

Jack softens a little. "Okay, Mark, but the sooner the better. Understand?"

"I understand, Jack," Mark replies. "I'll talk to you later this week. So long."

Mark hangs up the phone and immediately buzzes Sheri. "Please get Susan Callahan from planning and Mike O'Brien from customer service in here right away. Page Jim and tell him I have a fire to fight. I will call him when I am ready to continue our conversation."

■ ■ ■

Within five minutes, Susan and Mike are seated in Mark's office. "What's up?" Susan asks.

Mark brushes her off. "Susan, you and I had a brief conversation about the Anderson job this morning."

He turns to Mike, the customer service manager, a burly man with a build that shows he regularly lifts weights. He is the opposite of the trim, petite Susan.

"Mike, with all the attention, emphasis, effort, and management direction put on the Anderson job, it still has not shipped," Mark says. "I want you and Susan to pull out all the stops and get that job out the door." Mark goes on to explain that the president of Anderson has called Jack Baxter and asked him to expedite the order. "Jack is not pleased," Mark adds.

He instructs Mike to give Sheri the details of when and how the order will be finished and shipped. He wants an answer in one hour. "If you cannot find a solution in an hour," Mark says, "I want a report on what or who the problem is so that I can take action as required. Do you understand?" Mike nods his head.

Mark continues. He wants Mike to phone and send an e-mail to Anderson through normal channels. Mark will handle Jack. Once the product is shipped, he wants a "who shot John" report on this latest issue.

This time Mike does not nod his head in acquiescence. He asks cautiously, "Suppose it is impossible to ship the order in the next couple of days?"

Mark is not in the mood for hypotheticals. "There is no such thing as impossible. I know you two can make it happen. Now make it happen!" he barks.

Susan intervenes, but carefully. "We understand the need to satisfy Anderson, Mark, but do you know what you just directed us to do? You directed us to potentially change every priority in the entire operation without understanding the consequences. Are you sure you want to do that?"

Susan's comment surprises Mark. He respects her planning and business acumen but does not want to be distracted from the problem at hand. "Normally, I know this is not the right thing to do, but I believe that under the circumstances it is the necessary thing to do. As I see it, I don't have a choice," he says firmly.

Susan opens her mouth to reply, but thinks better of it. She stands to leave, and Mike follows suit. "We'll be back to you in an hour," she says.

■ ■ ■

Jim Simpson, the manufacturing director, sits down again in Mark's office. "I'm sorry for the interruption, Jim," Mark says. "Now where were we? Oh, by the way, I may have just authorized the changing of schedules in your shop. I just got a call from Jack Baxter about the Anderson job. Seems he received a call from the president of Anderson complaining about the delivery, or lack of it, from us."

Mark decides to address the issue head-on. "In fact, I have a question, Jim," he says. Final assembly worked over the weekend on that job. Ray Guy said it couldn't be shipped because he had not received the parts from your area. His team was upset because they were here working and no one in your group worked this past weekend."

These comments clearly agitate Jim. "Mark, this is an example of what I was trying to tell you about," he responds. "We would love to have given final assembly its parts, but engineering put a hold on those parts. I didn't have the right specifications to build the parts for the Anderson job. We asked engineering when the hold would be released and were told no one knew. The fact is our team worked late both Thursday and Friday, but because of the engineering hold, we didn't have anything that could be manufactured this past weekend."

Mark opens his mouth to speak, but Jim has more to say. He poses a volley of questions: Why did final assembly work overtime on something that could not be shipped? Why wasn't he told the parts would be delayed? Where was Susan and her "great" planning group?

Mark doesn't attempt to respond. He listens intently.

"Mark, we regularly work overtime to make parts that then sit on the shelf for days," Jim continues. "It doesn't make sense. I know you are being criticized for carrying too much inventory, but making wrong stuff or making it early builds inventory. Why do we do that?"

I don't know, Mark silently says to himself.

Jim is not finished, however. He tells Mark that lack of proper support from purchasing continues to hinder the manufacturing team. Raw materials are not delivered on time, which stops assembly. Jim proposes a solution. "We think we could do a better job of purchasing," he says, "so we would like to add that responsibility to the manufacturing teams. We are confident we won't do any worse, and we can expedite the items we *really* need."

Jim poses another question. Why do the customer service and project management people come onto the manufacturing floor every day to ask when their parts are going to be done? "It certainly doesn't improve productivity," Jim says. "And to make things worse, the project management people keep telling my people to make products with a different priority than what is in our planning system! Mark, some of these people are powerful within the organization, and the shop people are afraid to tell them no. So we often change priorities without telling planning or anybody else, for that matter. We just do what the last project manager told us to do."

Mark shakes his head just enough for Jim to notice.

Jim concludes his monologue by saying, "We believe our single biggest problem is lack of communication and consistency of direction. It seems anything can be changed by anyone, and it happens all the time. And whenever a change is arbitrarily made, it comes as a surprise to the rest of the organization."

Jim looks Mark directly in the eye and says, "That's a good chunk of the bad news. The good news is the shop is running as well as it ever has and generally speaking our people have a good attitude and just want to perform."

Mark and Jim sit in silence for a moment. Mark decides not to address any of the issues Jim has brought up. He needs to gather more information from others in the organization and stay in listening mode.

"Thank you, Jim. I appreciate your candor," Mark says. "I may want to talk to you again later after I have talked to the other managers."

Jim turns to leave, but stops at the door. "Mark, the people in the shop were pleased that you were interested in their opinion, so thank *you*."

Mark calls after Jim. "Oh Jim, one last thing," he says. "Would you check on the Anderson job for me? Get with Susan and Mike to make sure we make it ship."

■ ■ ■

Mark thinks about his next interview as he waits for Anita Cooper, the purchasing manager, to arrive. Anita is generally recognized as a good purchasing manager. In her mid-thirties, she has spent her entire professional career at Universal Products, most of it in the purchasing organization. When others in the company criticize the purchasing group, they do not criticize Anita personally. They direct their criticism at the lack of performance by the buyers Anita manages.

Anita steps into Mark's office looking a bit frazzled, but dressed smartly in a deep blue pantsuit. "Sorry I'm late," she greets Mark. "We were trying to expedite more raw materials for the Anderson parts that have to be rebuilt because of engineering changes."

This news is not music to Mark's ears, but he decides not to bring up the Anderson fiasco. He wants to stick to the purpose of the interview.

He offers Anita a chair at the round table and starts the conversation. "Anita, as you know, I am interviewing each of the managers to learn their perspectives on why we can't seem to achieve our goals of customer service, sales growth, and profit growth. What is your perspective?"

Anita does not hesitate to answer. She is obviously well prepared for this conversation. "I'm glad to have the opportunity to present my opinion," she says. "It seems that in purchasing, we continue to be asked to do the impossible. We are asked to reduce the price of our raw materials, but we consistently are asked to order most everything inside our suppliers' normal lead times. Have you ever tried to negotiate lower prices while you are asking for special deliveries? Our buyers work extremely hard to minimize the number of extra charges from our suppliers. They should be commended. Instead, mostly what I hear are complaints about lack of performance."

"Why are you ordering so frequently with less lead time than our suppliers request?" Mark asks. "Surely planning knows the lead times. We spent a great deal of money on a computerized planning and control system to communicate such things. Is planning doing its job?"

Given the opportunity to pass the blame to planning, Anita surprisingly does not take up that mantle. "Planning is doing its job," she says. "If you ask me, the problem is that the sales forecast is unreliable."

"How so?" Mark asks.

Anita is happy to explain. The planning group generates plans that support the orders and the forecast, but the sales group does not seem to understand the importance of forecasting. Sam Wente, the sales director, brags about how his salespeople are bringing in the big-buck orders, but they make unrealistic promises to customers.

"Don't get me wrong," Anita says. "I'm pleased that sales is booking the business. It just seems that sales continues to sell products with a shorter customer lead time than the time it takes us to buy raw materials and then build the product. And Sam doesn't seem to understand or care about providing improved visibility to the rest of the company in the form of a forecast. All we hear from Sam are complaints. Quite frankly, Mark, I don't think Sam understands what it means to be a truly professional sales manager in a manufacturing company."

Mark is no longer surprised by what he is hearing. The blame has again been moved to another function in the company.

Anita continues. "However, this is nothing new. Purchasing has never really had the time to negotiate with suppliers for the best price and service. For as long as I can remember, we simply expedite day in and day out."

Like Jim, Anita suggests some solutions. "If you want to improve things, from my view, sales has to improve its forecasts. With a better view of what's coming down the pike, we could do a much better job of purchasing. Unless we improve our forecasts, the situation is going to get even worse with the decision to do more outsourcing. Our suppliers will not jump through the hoops we seem to be able to jump through here to satisfy customers, at least not without higher costs being passed on to us. Actually, the costs are already higher, but it is harder to see them. They are hidden in our internal cost accounting system. When we outsource, the suppliers will document and pass on the extra costs. We won't be able to hide from our mistakes and inefficiencies," Anita concludes. She sits back in her chair and allows Mark to ponder her comments.

Mark shifts uncomfortably in his seat. The problems are complex, he decides. There are no simple solutions. "Anita, thank you for your time and insight," he says. "I'm still in information-gathering mode."

"Will you get us together to share your findings with all of us? And if so, when do you think that will be?" Anita asks.

"I am not yet sure what I will do with the findings," Mark replies. "But I certainly will communicate our next set of actions to the members of my staff."

As Anita walks out the door, Mark calls after her. "Will you let Jim Simpson know the status of the raw material for the Anderson job?"

■ ■ ■

Mark decides to meet Sam Wente, the sales director, on his turf. He walks down the hall and taps on Sam's door. Mark respects Sam. He has been with Universal Products for almost twenty years. Sam knows the products, knows the customers, and has built strong relations with key customers over the years.

Not that Sam hasn't been a thorn in Mark's side at times. Lately, Sam has become more than outspoken about the company's inability to meet its commitments to customers, especially delivery commitments. He has criticized everyone on the supply side of the business. In his latest tirade, he told Mark that the sales organization would never achieve its growth goals if on-time delivery performance did not improve.

Sam's office looks out toward the mountains. He does not hear Mark tap on the door. Sam is facing the windows and pacing back and forth as he cradles the phone on his shoulder. Mark takes a seat quietly and listens to the phone conversation.

"I'll pick you up at the airport at about eleven o'clock, Fred. That will give us a chance to grab a bite to eat and hit the golf course. We should be able to get in eighteen holes without any problem. You're bringing your sticks, right? After golf, we'll go to that steakhouse you like so well and have a great meal. See you tomorrow."

Mark feels his blood pressure go up several points. How can Sam take the afternoon off to play golf when he can't provide reasonable forecasts for the business? Is that a wise use of his time? What kind of example does that set for the rest of the organization?

Sam hangs up the phone, and Mark expresses just what he has been thinking. "Sam, I don't believe it!" Mark says, gesturing forcefully with his finger. "The company is behind plan, and I've just heard from others in our organization how you are not providing accurate forecasts. Now I find that you are going to play golf, followed by a great dinner! Where's your sense of urgency about helping the company through these tough times?"

Sam's face reddens. His blood pressure surely matches Mark's. "Why you pompous ass!" he shouts. "The truth is I don't want to play golf. That was a customer on the phone. It was Jackson Palmer of Patterson Brothers. I don't even like him. He always wants to play golf, and if I beat him, he takes it personally. Plus he always wants to bet, and you won't let me claim my losses on my expense report."

Mark starts to interrupt, but Sam is not finished. "Jackson is coming out here because we are nearly three weeks late with his most recent order. He is here to see that it ships this week, which we have promised for the last two weeks. I'm taking him golfing because manufacturing doesn't have anything to show him. I don't know what the real status of his job is. I am hoping that planning and manufacturing will have their act together by tomorrow when he comes in. And as far as the great dinner, I would much rather be at home with my wife than spend the evening with Jackson. Quite frankly, you are not paying me enough to have to put up with all this crap. Ever since you came on board, my job has become almost impossible. I'll tell you what. *You* take him to play golf and then to dinner."

Mark knows when he has mishandled a situation and readily admits it. "Sam, I apologize," he says. "I jumped on you without knowing the facts. I have no real excuse, but I have been listening to everyone complain about everyone else today, and I just blew up. I am sorry. Perhaps we should both cool down and pick up this conversation later."

Sam calms down but still has some points to score. "And just one more thing before you go," he says. "My sales force spent a lot of time a year ago developing an improved forecast, but nobody used our forecast. We would tell planning and manufacturing what customers were going to buy, and they would build something else. My whole team said to hell with it. We are not doing extra administrative work if it is going to be ignored or second-guessed by the rest of the organization."

Sam is not finished. "And another thing. You said you are meeting with all the staff to figure out why we aren't achieving our divisional goals. Mark, it does not take a genius to figure out that if you can't deliver what has already been sold, the sales force is not about to sell more. Every professional salesperson knows the only thing he or she truly has to sell is his or her own individual personal credibility. Everyone on my sales team feels like their personal credibility is gone."

Sam has more to say. "And if you could ever get Peter Newfeld in product development/engineering to complete any new products while the market demand is still there, maybe we would have a chance to grow the business. He is always late, short on product features, and over budget. When is that going to be addressed?"

Sam has one last salvo. "Yes, Mark, I think we should meet later. Give me a call when you are ready to give me some answers!"

■ ■ ■

Mark leaves Sam's office feeling like his tail is between his legs. He looks up and sees someone from sales and a customer service person gathered around Sam's administrative assistant's desk. Mark knows his conversation with Sam will be spread throughout the company by the end of the day. The company may have a communications problem, but the rumor mill works quite effectively.

Mark is worn out already from the morning's activities even though it is only a quarter of twelve. He is hungry; it is time for lunch. He doesn't feel like eating in the company cafeteria and decides to drive to Boston Chicken. It is fast food, but healthy food. It will give him time to think.

While eating roasted chicken and vegetables, Mark observes that everyone this morning told him that the problem is someone else or another department. People also are frustrated and lack any sense of fulfillment. It is obvious that everyone is working harder and enjoying it less. "We are not failing because of a lack of effort," he mutters.

A woman eating at the next table looks at him. "Don't mind me," Mark says. "I'm just talking to myself."

She laughs. "Just as long as you don't start answering yourself."

He smiles and says, "Yes, answers are what I need, but I don't have them."

"We're all searching for answers," she says and returns to her meal.

Mark starts turning over solutions in his mind. It seems like communication and cooperation are suffering. Is it a people problem? Maybe it's not a people problem at all. Maybe it's a systems or systematic problem. But the company just spent a lot of money for a computer system. It was supposed to fix these kinds of problems. That shouldn't be it. If it is not a people problem from the perspective of their capability and effort and it is not the computer system, what is it?

Mark conducts a weekly staff meeting and a monthly financial meeting. Through those meetings, he feels like he is communicating to the organization. Is Mark the problem? Sam said things got worse after he took over, and he meant it.

Am I really a pompous ass? Do the others feel the same way? Does Jack feel the same way? Am I really the problem? Mark asks himself.

Mark has been eating at the same pace his mind has been analyzing. He looks down, and his plate is empty. He glances at his watch. He is supposed to meet with Janis Novak, the controller, in half an hour. She may have a different perspective. She has a direct line to corporate through the financial channel. Maybe she will tell him candidly what she thinks and what she is telling corporate about his performance.

■ ■ ■

Janis steps into Mark's office. "Are you ready for me?" she asks.

Mark always enjoys Janis. She is fresh faced, only in her early thirties. She has worked at Universal Products for one year and worked for several divisions within large companies before joining Universal Products. Her experience brings Universal Products a fresh attitude. Janis is not locked into a "that's the way we've done things in the past" attitude. Mark has always found her to be smart, articulate, and willing to listen. She tends to base her opinions more on fact than emotion. And what Mark needs now is facts.

"Janis, I really want our conversation to be open and honest today," he says as he motions for her to sit down. "I am very interested in your perspective on what is happening here. I have talked with a number of the key managers, and I have only heard the problems. I have not been able to draw any conclusions or arrive at a solution to the difficulties we have been experiencing."

Janis's expression shows concern. "Is there an area in particular you want to discuss?" she asks in a quiet voice.

"Let's start with my personal management approach," Mark replies. "I want your opinion as to whether I am contributing to or am the cause of the company's problems. I am interested in how my management approach compares to the executives at the other companies where you have worked."

"Do you think that you're the cause of the problems we are currently experiencing here?" Janis asks. "Let me set your mind at ease," she says. "You are not the problem. And as for your management approach, I think about management in a couple of different dimensions. One of those is style. I believe you attempt to be open and honest. I believe that members of your staff trust you. There is relatively little behind-the-scenes complaining about you as the general manager compared to other places I have worked. You have a tendency to openly exhibit your frustration and make some decisions perhaps too quickly without being fully informed."

Janis pauses to see how Mark is taking this news. "Keep going," he says. "I'm listening."

"Another dimension I like to analyze is management process," she continues. "I worked for a division of one company that was truly under control. This division was remarkable in my opinion because it had experienced both growth and declining sales situations and still stayed in control. In my first job as controller at a different company, everyone in the company worked much harder than they needed to for the results we achieved. That's what it is like here at Universal Products. You and others on the management team are forced to work hard, make quick decisions without full information, and still do not achieve the desired results."

"What was the difference between the company in control and the company, like us, that was out of control?" Mark asks.

"That's what I am getting at," Janis replies. "It is an issue of management process. Let me explain. At Universal Products, we have an annual planning process that results in the annual plan and budget. I have come to believe that the annual planning process as we conduct it here is an extreme waste of time. But that's an aside. Let me continue with our planning process. Once we develop the budget, it usually causes us to do things that are counter to what we really need to be doing."

Janis pauses to see if Mark comprehends what she is saying. "Think about this, Mark," she continues. "After the first month of the new budget, actually before the budget is fully approved, the different departments here make functional decisions to optimize their functional performance, but these decisions are usually at the expense of other departments. This causes internal friction. We quickly get out of sync with each other."

Mark doesn't fully understand what Janis means, but allows her to keep talking. He wants to hear her complete analysis before asking questions.

"Our financial review every month looks at how we performed compared to budget," Janis explains. "Most of the meeting time is spent analyzing the variances to the budget. We do not spend even 10 percent of the meeting time talking about the future. In essence, we do not do forward planning. Our so-called 'forward' plans were developed when we developed the budget months ago. Yet we all know that conditions change daily, weekly, and monthly. In my opinion, we should be talking about the future, updating our future plans, and discussing changes that have occurred that impact our future plans."

Janis stops to catch her breath and take a reading from Mark's face to determine whether he is following her analysis. His expression is a blend of intensity and curiosity. "Keep going," he says. "Tell me more about forward planning."

"Let's think about change and forward planning," Janis responds. "Think about the many things that have changed at Universal Products since you came here that had nothing to do with us directly. Customers have started requesting shorter lead times. They have also begun insisting on 98 percent or greater on-time delivery. We have not adequately addressed these changes in customer expectations."

"Think of other changes generated by customers," Janis continues. "Some of our customers have begun to manage their business globally. They are thinking in terms of global demand and global supply. What's good about this change is that these customers are trying to give us better visibility of their total demands, but we still treat them as if they made their purchasing decisions locally."

"Think about this, Mark," Janis says. "Competition is stronger than it has ever been. The pressure on price and therefore costs is immense. The external factors that affect our business are changing more dramatically and more frequently than they used to. But as a management team, we don't monitor and talk about these kinds of changes and the basic factors behind the changes. We meet to discuss how we are performing to a budget that was developed months ago. We use the financial review meeting to look backward and spend valuable time discussing who is to blame for the variances. Honestly, it feels like a 'who shot John' session. What we really ought to be doing is continually looking forward and discussing what we need to do and what we need to change to succeed in the future."

Mark looks at Janis and smiles. "That is a succinct analysis, and to be honest with you, it is a breath of fresh air. You are the only person I have talked to who hasn't attacked a particular department or person. But I am wondering why you haven't shared your perspective on management processes with me before."

"To be honest with you," Janis replies, "I have been trying to figure out what was happening. Also, your invitation to meet was a catalyst to capture my thoughts. You know that I have to give an updated financial forecast to corporate every month. You and I review the numbers, and we sometimes have our disagreements about what I submit. You want to keep communicating the same budget numbers, and I disagree. This is mostly because I believe that many things have changed since the budget was set, and therefore the budget does not reflect reality. My credibility with the finance organization is hurt if I don't communicate what I believe will really happen."

"You are saying that our financial review process is flawed," Mark observes. "What was the financial review process like at the company that was 'in control,' as you put it?"

"Before I answer your question, let me make an observation about your weekly staff meeting," Janis replies. "Those sessions are valuable and probably needed today given all of our problems. But the company that was in control didn't need weekly staff meetings. They weren't needed because of the structured management process. Actually, what we had was a series of integrated management processes that enabled middle managers to do their jobs without weekly review and interference by the senior managers. These were formalized processes that enabled and empowered the middle management team to work week in and week out without extra senior management supervision. Senior managers and middle managers managed day to day by exception. The term senior management supervision was a non sequitur."

"What do you mean by weekly interference?" Mark asks.

"Some of the middle managers here perceive the executive team as a group of micromanagers," Janis says. "This is primarily because of the level of detail we all get into at least weekly before staff meetings. If we had an integrated management process here at Universal Products, you wouldn't need to manage at that level of detail."

"Janis, I thought we installed a software system that was an integrated system. Weren't we told that the enterprise resource planning system we bought included information for all departments and all functions throughout the enterprise?"

"That's a common misperception," Janis replies. "It may be an integrated software system, but let me explain it like the general manager of my previous division explained it. Do you mind if I use your white board?"

She erases a section of the board without waiting for a reply. Mark is amused as Janis stands high on her tiptoes to reach the top. She is barely five feet tall.

Janis draws three intersecting circles (Figure 1) and then points to the board. "It takes all three circles working together to operate in an excellent manner," she explains. "A computer system alone does not give you an integrated management process."

Figure 1   Business Excellence Elements (Copyright Oliver Wight International. Reproduced with permission.)

"Are you saying we lack the business process circle?" Mark asks.

"Not exactly," Janis replies. "We have many business processes, but they do not overlap. By that, I mean they are not integrated, and it takes integrated processes to enable the different functional organizations within a company to operate most effectively."

Janis picks up the felt marker and begins drawing on the board again. "This is how we operate today," she says, pointing to the new drawing (Figure 2). "At Universal Products, our business processes are structured like a group of islands with barriers between each function. There is very little if any overlap or integration of business processes. We have the technology and tools, but they are not properly applied. We have a solid group of hardworking people, but don't communicate well and don't work together." Janis looks at Mark to see if he is following her. He is studying both drawings.

"The point I am trying to make," she explains, "is that we are experiencing change that is largely driven by external factors — our customers and our compe-

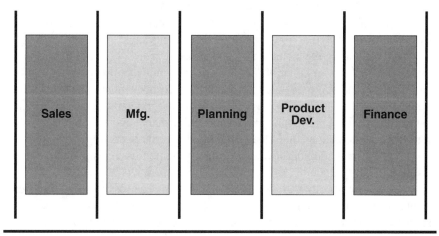

Figure 2   Island Management Approach

tition. The island approach to management may have worked thirty years ago, but it doesn't now. Change is too rapid. And if companies don't respond to change, they are mediocre at best or out of business at worst."

"Have you shared this analysis with corporate?" Mark asks.

"This is the first time I have articulated anything on this issue. Anyway, you are privy to everything I send to corporate," Janis responds.

"What does it take to develop an integrated process? How did your company under control do it?" Mark asks.

"Our general manager was cautious at first," Janis replies. "You have to understand that at the beginning, our management behavior was just like the managers here. Everyone was caught up in the confusion and blame game. No one had the perspective to change."

"So how did the general manager get people to change?" Mark asks.

"He hired a consulting firm. The consultants performed an assessment to evaluate our situation. They provided some education, and then they provided support in helping us to integrate our business processes," Janis replies.

Mark frowns. "A consulting firm? You know my feeling about consultants. We pay them to increase their education at our firm's expense. It usually is expensive and does not create lasting results."

"In our case, this firm was very useful," Janis replies. "The consultants helped us for more than a year to integrate our business processes. But there was one process that they helped us to implement very quickly, within a few months. I personally believe this process brought us measurable results very quickly. And ironically, it was the senior management business process. You'll laugh at the name of the process."

"What is it called?" Mark asks.

"Sales and operations planning."

"We do sales and operations planning now," Mark replies.

"If we were to truly do sales and operations planning like my previous company, you would laugh at how we do it today," Janis says.

"Are you issuing me a challenge?" Mark asks.

"Sort of," Janis says, smiling. "We do sales and operations planning, but within our islands. We do sales planning. We do operations planning. We do financial planning. But we do not do them in an integrated process. The sales and operations planning process improved our senior managers' communication and strengthened the management team. It helped the managers to get the company in sync at the management level. It definitely helped us manage change in the business."

Janis taps on the table with the felt marker. "This process causes a significant change in the way senior management thinks about the business and manages the business. It was not expensive to implement. It can be difficult to start at first, but we saw results within months. The hard part is the change that senior managers must make."

"What do you recommend that we do?" Mark asks.

Janis has several recommendations. "You should visit with someone from the consulting firm. I will get you a name and phone number. You should also visit with the general manager and chief financial officer of the company where I used to work. I was a controller in one of the company's divisions. The CFO was actively involved in the implementation. He is more expert on this process than I am. I was mostly a participant in the process once it was almost completely established and saw the results of implementing the process."

"Okay, get me all of their phone numbers. I will call them this week," Mark says.

As Janis leaves the office, Mark has a sudden urge to shout, "Eureka!" Finally, he has had a conversation that was rational and constructive. Janis did not point fingers and blame others. She has seen other ways of effectively managing a business.

Mark has to admit to himself that he did not completely understand her description of the circles and sales and operations planning. However, when she drew the islands on the board, he completely understood why he has been frustrated by his efforts to improve Universal Products' performance.

It is the end of the day, and Mark begins to place paperwork in his briefcase to review at home tonight. After snapping his briefcase shut, he picks up the phone and dials Janis's extension. She probably has gone home already, but he wants to leave a message.

"Janis, I want to thank you for the time you spent with me today," he says. "I felt it was very productive and insightful. Can you have those phone numbers for me sometime tomorrow morning? Thanks again."

■ ■ ■

The evenings are lonely without Cheryl. Mark calls her every night, no matter the hour.

It is nine o'clock, and the two-hour time difference between the Rocky Mountains and East Coast will make the hour late for his Cheryl, but Mark knows that she will be tolerant. He dials the phone. Cheryl answers on the third ring. "Did I wake you?" he asks.

Despite sleepiness, Cheryl exhibits her dry humor. "No, honey. I had to get up to answer the phone anyway."

Mark chuckles. "I'm sorry. I didn't get home until just a little while ago. But I did want to talk with you. How did your day go?"

"Busy," Cheryl replies. "I had to run a bunch of errands for your son."

"*My* son? I thought he was *our* son."

"Well, when he is so demanding, he is your son," Cheryl jokes. "It was not really that bad. I just had too many things going on at the same time. How was your day?"

"It started out poorly, but the day ended well," Mark replies, kicking off his shoes and stretching his long legs across the bed.

"What happened?" Cheryl asks.

"It's too long to go over with you at this time of night, but I'll give you the short version," Mark replies. He tells Cheryl about his effort to listen to his senior staff. He tells her it was an exercise in listening to everyone complain about someone else. He also tells her how some of those complaints were directed at him.

"Janis Novak was the only person who was constructive," Mark says. He proceeds to tell Cheryl about Janis's comparison of Universal Products' management processes with the other companies where she has worked. "She said the difference was something called sales and operations planning. I need to learn more about it, but it just might help us turn the business around," Mark explains.

Cheryl, who is business savvy herself, is quick to ask, "Don't you already do sales planning and operations planning?"

Mark laughs. "I asked Janis the same question. The difference, as Janis explained it to me, is that sales and operations do not operate in a vacuum. There should less independence and more collaboration. But that's about all I know about it at this point."

"So, are you going to go to a seminar or something to learn more about it?" Cheryl asks.

"We need help faster than that. I am thinking about bringing in some help, some experts in the process." Mark braces himself for Cheryl's reply. They have frequently debated the pros and cons of consultants. Cheryl tends to like them, and he tends to dislike them.

"Experts? You mean consultants?" she replies. "What did you say the last time we argued about consultants? Something like, 'They charge you to learn on your nickel, and when they leave, everything is the same as it was before they arrived.'"

"I knew you would remind me of that," Mark laughs. "But there's a difference with what Janis is recommending. She says we should hire people experienced in using the process. Based on her experience with these consultants, she thinks we can show some results in a few months."

"Good," Cheryl replies. "That means that by the time Chad and I move out there, you'll have the situation under control and we can enjoy being a family again. We're not going to want you working until nine o'clock every night."

"That's the plan," Mark replies. He wonders if that is really possible but does not voice his doubt to Cheryl.

They wish each other good night, and Mark hangs up the phone. Still stretched out on the bed, he reviews today's events in his mind. He is startled to realize that he has not yet scheduled an interview with Peter Newfeld, the product development/engineering director.

The irony of overlooking Peter is not lost on Mark. Universal Products is looking for growth. A classic way to achieve growth is through product development, yet Mark has barely paid any attention to that area. He recalls an expression that fits his situation: "When you are up to your ass in alligators, it is hard to remember that the objective is to drain the swamp."

Mark wonders what Peter must be thinking. Will he think Mark's lack of attention means that Peter and product development are of lesser importance? Or will he think that it means his department is obviously doing okay and Mark has bigger problems to handle?

Sleepy now, Mark forces himself off the bed. Can't sleep in my clothes, he says to himself while making a mental note to talk with Peter first thing tomorrow morning.

■ ■ ■

Mark arrives at work before seven the next morning. The parking lot is a quarter full. Ray Guy, the final assembly manager, and Jim Simpson, the manufacturing director, have their people starting early and finishing late trying to push orders out the door. Mark notes that Anita Cooper and her purchasing group are in early as well.

Despite the frustrated accusations to the contrary yesterday, Mark observes that the Universal Products staff is hard working and dedicated. The people are not the problem, Mark says to himself. Maybe Janis is right. It's a management process problem.

Before going to the cafeteria for a cup of coffee, Mark leaves both e-mail and voice-mail messages for Peter Newfeld, the product development/engineering director, to meet with him as soon as he comes in if at all possible. Within minutes after returning from the cafeteria, Peter pokes his head through Mark's doorway.

Mark is always pleased to see Peter. He is a vibrant, high-energy guy. Peter is over six feet tall and a lean 170 pounds. It is a daily ritual for Peter and other company engineers to run during lunch. Life-style is important to Peter, who also skis and goes mountain climbing. It is one reason, Mark knows, that Peter has spent most of his professional career with Universal Products, working his way up through the engineering organization. Mark also knows that Universal Products is fortunate to have someone with Peter's skills. Peter is well respected for his product knowledge and his technical capability.

Mark gestures for Peter to take a seat at the round table. "Peter, thanks for coming on such short notice," he says. "As you probably know, I am having chats with all the members of the executive team. I need your frank and candid perspective on why Universal Products is not as successful as you know it could be."

Peter, a natty dresser, smoothes the crease in his trousers. "I've heard about some of your other sessions. I understand that people are unloading on you about all that is wrong or needs your attention."

"That's true," Mark replies.

"Well, Mark, I'm not going to be an exception," Peter says, looking Mark straight in the eye. He proceeds to tell Mark that in order to grow the business, the company needs to develop either new products or new markets. "Since this company is short on marketing talent, that leaves new products as our only option," he observes.

"Why do you say we are short on marketing talent?" Mark asks.

"Look at our organization," Peter replies. "The staff is dominated by people with engineering and technology backgrounds. Even the marketing people have engineering degrees, and they do little more than provide marketing services, like advertising, promotions, and communications."

"Most of our growth has been simple extensions of our original product lines," Peter observes. "If we have a product or marketing strategy beyond extending our original product lines, it is not visible to me. And as the person in charge of product development, I think I should know where we are trying to go."

Mark interrupts Peter to disagree. "The whole management team met together and developed a strategy just eight months ago. You participated in the process. I do not understand why you are questioning the strategy now."

"It is very simple," Peter replies. "We are not doing what we agreed to do. We all had good intentions, I'm sure, but what has really happened? Nothing has changed. Think about it. Tell me what we have accomplished. I was supposed to have done a number of things that I started, but I have not completed 10 percent of what I agreed to do. And no one else has either."

"Well, why not?" Mark asks.

"Resources and priorities," Peter is quick to respond. "I asked for more engineers, and you did not approve them. On top of that, you did not reduce the list of projects or change when I was supposed to get them done. I am overloaded. That would be bad enough, except that the priorities keep changing. We seem to get something started only to be asked to work on something else. We have a little of everything done, but have completed nothing."

Peter goes on to explain that most of the engineers' time is consumed by support activities, rather than developing new products. It is a daily occurrence to be asked by the field service organization to solve problems with existing products. Manufacturing also asks daily for engineers to help figure out how to build what sales actually sold. "Why is it that the people in sales always seem to sell products that are standard, *except* for a few major and minor details?" he asks.

Peter expresses his concern that the engineering staff is demoralized. There is very little sense of accomplishment, and Peter does not control the product development environment. "As long as the emphasis is on responding to the problems the field and manufacturing organizations have with existing products," he concludes, "we will never meet any of the objectives from the strategic planning session."

"So, what do you recommend?" Mark asks.

Peter is ready for this question. He tells Mark to either add more resources to support product development or make tough choices on what the company is *not* going to do. Product requirements need to be defined based upon customer needs and market opportunities.

"If marketing won't use its resources to do it, then product development should do it, but I will need additional resources. The point I'm making is if we are going to have new products, we need to dedicate resources to the task," he says.

Peter also suggests that Mark establish a product policy on the mix of standard product design and special variations — and then enforce the policy. Today, sales is taking it upon itself to set the policy — one order at a time. "That is like giving kids the keys to the candy store," he comments.

"Anything else?" Mark asks.

"No," says Peter. "You may not agree with me, but that is how I see it."

"The point for today is not whether I agree or not, but what you think," Mark responds. "I'm pleased you were not bashful with your input. I hope you feel you have succeeded in unloading on me."

"Who else do you have to interview?" Peter asks.

"You're the last," Mark replies.

"What happens next?" Peter asks, pushing himself up from the chair.

"I'll be digesting all that I have heard, plus doing a bit of research on a recommendation Janis has made. Thanks for your time, Peter. Don't worry, I'll be getting back to you and the rest of the management team," Mark says.

"How soon will that be?" Peter asks.

"Soon, measured in days not weeks," Mark replies as he ushers Peter out the door.

2

A NEW BEGINNING

It is one week later, and Mark waits in his office for Ross Peterson, lead consultant for Effective Management, Inc. He has read EMI's brochure and wonders if what the brochure says about the firm is hype. Mark can't help being skeptical after more than twenty years of experience with consultants.

What interests Mark is EMI's claim to only hire people who have worked in industry and have implemented business process improvements. He glances at the passage that states, "No recent college graduates or theoretical professor types," and again wonders whether it is truth or fiction.

In the week since finishing his interviews with the management team at Universal Products, Mark has held his weekly staff meeting. During the meeting, he asked Janis Novak to share with the team what she told Mark during their interview. Mark chose not to dwell upon the findings from the other individual interviews during the staff meeting. He simply told the staff that there is a better way to manage the business. He was careful, however, not to create unrealistic expectations of an overnight turnaround.

Interestingly enough, Sam Wente, the sales director, mentioned that some of his customers had implemented or were implementing processes similar to what Janis described. He seemed supportive, but expressed concern about any pressure to resurrect his forecasting process.

Anita Cooper, the purchasing manager, commented that suppliers are asking for more detailed and more frequently updated purchasing schedules and forecasts. She recently asked two suppliers why this information was needed. They said it was needed for the more formalized planning and control processes they had implemented.

Mark also recalls his conversation with Jack Baxter at corporate when he told Jack what he was going to do. At first, Jack was a little skeptical. He, too, is wary of consultants. Mark asked Jack to talk to Janis. Their conversation spurred Jack's curiosity about the process.

A light tap on the door brings Mark back to the present. His administrative assistant, Sheri Waterman, announces that Ross Peterson has arrived. Mark walks into the lobby to welcome him.

Ross Peterson is about six feet tall and 190 pounds. He is in reasonably good shape and looks to be in his late forties or early fifties. He is stylishly but not overly dressed, and his shoes are shined. Ross appears confident as he shakes Mark's hand.

Mark ushers Ross into his office and points to a chair at the conference table. After exchanging pleasantries about plane flights and the weather, Mark says, "I'm not sure how much Janis has told you about our situation, but let me review the situation from my perspective, and perhaps you can tell me how your company can be of assistance to us."

For the next hour, Mark tells Ross the history of Universal Products and its products, markets, current objectives, and current difficulties. He is frank in expressing his concerns about being able to correct the situation. He stresses that the situation must be corrected in a short period of time.

Ross is a good listener. He asks a number of questions, but does not comment on Mark's responses. He wants to know about Universal Products' competition, position in the market, changing customer expectations, and core competencies. He asks why customers buy from Universal Products and why Mark believes companies buy from the competition. He asks about delivery performance to customers, inventory policies, and Universal Products' financial situation. He also asks a number of questions about the current management processes. He wants to know whether there is a strategic planning process and an annual business planning process. He asks how the business is managed day to day, week to week, and month to month. Ross is also interested in people and relationship problems within the organization. He wants to know about pressures from corporate.

After an hour of answering questions, Mark is ready to ask Ross a few questions of his own. "Ross, I think you have a reasonable picture of the company's situation. Tell me how the process, this sales and operations planning that Janis told me about, would help our company."

"You can't just grasp at 'alphabet soup' initiatives," Ross responds. "That's what we call the various solutions marketed by firms like ours. I asked you all those questions about Universal Products to get a better understanding of what you are facing. What I would like to do is describe the process that Janis told you about and then explore with you whether you believe it would be of help to you and your management team. I need to give you the big picture of how we work with clients in implementing any type of business process and then talk specifically about sales and operations planning."

Mark nods his head in assent as Ross hands him a diagram. "This may help you picture what I am going to talk about," Ross says.

For the next fifteen minutes, he tells Mark about what he calls the proven path. "We call it the proven path because it works," Ross states. He asks Mark to follow the diagram (Figure 3) as he explains the proven path implementation methodology.

Ross tells Mark that EMI uses a simple but disciplined set of steps in working with companies. The first two steps are an assessment and education. "We call it first-cut education because there will be more detailed education to come," Ross comments.

After these two steps are completed, EMI will help the management team to develop a high-level design, which some companies call a *vision of operations.* "This is not a lofty company vision, but a picture of how you will operate when you have implemented sales and operations planning," Ross notes.

Ross goes on to explain that the purpose of the assessment is to get a better understanding of what Universal Products is currently doing well and what areas may need improvement. With education, the management team gets a common understanding of industry best practices and has a conceptual basis for developing a high-level design. "Then we assist you and your management team in developing the high-level design, the vision of operations," Ross says.

Mark holds up a hand to signal Ross to stop. "This sounds like it will take a long time, a lot of work, and a lot of expense," Mark says. "We don't have much time, and we are all already working long hours. What I have heard from Janis and others about sales and operations planning makes sense to me. We need something like it. I do not need a lengthy assessment and education program to know I need something like a sales and operations planning process."

"I agree," Ross replies, "but you need an assessment and education to ensure that you are not like so many companies that fail at implementing improvements." He explains that the assessment is used to determine the management processes that are currently in place. This information is used to tailor the education session.

"You have shared with me how most members of your management team believe that someone or something else is at fault and how that is currently contributing to Universal Products' performance difficulties. Unless you can move your team to consensus on the solution, you will not be successful," Ross tells Mark. "You need consensus on the vision of operations and how your team will utilize sales and operations planning. We will guide your team in designing that vision, and we will provide coaching during the first few process cycles to get the process up and running quickly."

"We've been talking about process implementation, but not the process itself," Mark interrupts. "What is your definition of sales and operations planning?"

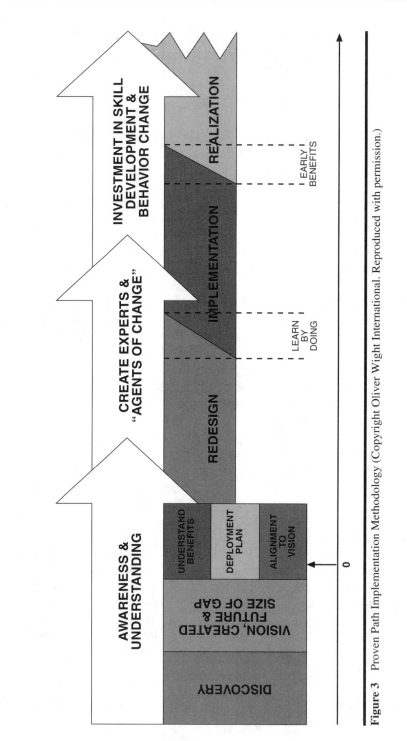

Figure 3 Proven Path Implementation Methodology (Copyright Oliver Wight International. Reproduced with permission.)

Ross pulls out another sheet of paper. It is a page copied from the ninth edition of the *APICS Dictionary* published by the American Production and Inventory Control Society. He pauses to give Mark time to read the definition.

> A process that provides management the ability to strategically direct its businesses to achieve competitive advantage on a continuous basis by integrating customer-focused marketing plans for new and existing products with the management of the supply chain. The process brings together all the plans for the business (sales, marketing, development, manufacturing, sourcing, and financial) into one integrated set of plans. It is performed at least once a month and is reviewed by the management team at an aggregate (product family) level. The process must reconcile all supply, demand, and new product plans at both the detail and aggregate level and tie to the business plan. It is the definitive statement of the company's plans for the near to intermediate term covering a horizon sufficient to plan for resources and to support the annual business planning process. Executed properly, the sales and operations planning process links the strategic plans for the business with its execution and reviews performance measures for continuous improvement.

Mark now knows why Ross was asking so many questions about the annual business planning and strategic planning processes. He also feels a bit of discomfort in his stomach because he does not understand the terms detail and aggregate level. Thinking about the disagreement among his management team during his interviews about the various departments' plans, he wonders if it would ever be possible to reconcile all supply, demand, and new product plans. He keeps these thoughts to himself as he looks up from the paper.

"Sales and operations planning is a simple concept, but it is not so easily described in a few words," Ross says. He explains that one of the key concepts is *a focused, aligned, and engaged enterprise.*

"I was just thinking about that," Mark comments ruefully.

From his years of working with executives, Ross knows what Mark is thinking. How can Mark ever get his management team to align on a single plan, especially when the only time his managers are engaged is when they are disagreeing with each other?

"Where management and planning processes go awry," Ross explains, "is in assuming that nothing will happen to cause plans to change. Therefore, managers are extremely uncomfortable when change occurs and frequently refuse to alter the plans to accommodate change."

"The key about sales and operations planning," Ross tells Mark, "is that it provides a mechanism to deal with continuous change. It provides a methodology for the management team to collectively decide the priorities of the enterprise. And you don't have to have a bloodbath in managing change and setting priorities."

"I was just thinking about that," Mark says.

"Think about this," Ross says. "To deal with continuous change, you actually need a *replanning* process. This is a key concept that you and your management team need to understand. You cannot set plans in stone. If you do, you will fail as a company. You must create an environment where change is not just okay, but is expected. To create this environment requires developing the skills and discipline to *replan*. That's what sales and operations planning will give you."

Ross goes on to explain some other key concepts:

- Sales and operations planning includes all the management functions of the company.
- When sales and operations planning is correctly implemented, it is a demand- and strategy-driven process.

"Sam Wente, our sales director, will like being demand driven, but I don't know about the operations folks," Mark comments.

"They will like it when they realize that sales and operations planning addresses the resources required to support customer demands and expectations — and that the sales and supply plans are expected to be balanced," Ross replies.

"The previous definition is a bit long-winded, but this is really a simple and powerful process. In the companies that do it well, I would describe it as sophisticated simplicity," Ross says.

"Well, you've convinced me that we are going to need education on the process. It doesn't seem too simple to me now," Mark replies.

Ross explains that this initial reaction is normal, but the process has been used in industry for more than twenty years. During that time, best practices have emerged that make the process not only effective but also efficient to operate. These best practices are taught in the education session.

"There's one more thing I want you to think about," Ross adds. "I tell my clients that the general manager of the enterprise should be fully in control of the enterprise and should spend less than four hours per month on this process. The general manager can spend the rest of his or her time where it is best leveraged for the company. The company should just keep on running and running and running."

Mark wonders to himself whether this is hype or truth. But even if he spends twenty hours per month on the process, if the process is effective, he and his team would be in a better position than they are today. He would also have more time than he has now to plan for the future.

Mark decides to get straight to the point. "How much money and time are we talking to get sales and operations planning up and running?" he asks.

Ross responds that the sales and operations planning assessment will take two to four days for a medium-size division like Universal Products. The education session for the senior executive team takes one to two days.

There should be additional education for the people who will participate in the sales and operations planning process. That will take two to four days, depending on the number of people who need to be educated. A separate session designed specifically for the sales organization will be needed, which usually takes one to two days. The high-level design, or vision of operations, can be completed in two to four days in a division the size of Universal Products.

Hands-on coaching is usually needed for a number of days each month for the first few months of the sales and operations planning process. This coaching helps put the details together to begin the process. The amount of coaching support depends upon what is found in the assessment, but after the first six months of the process, less coaching support is needed. After the first six months, an occasional process review is needed for the next year or so to ensure that the process continues to improve.

"This is not a massive consulting engagement," Ross says. "It is nothing like the consulting support required for installing an enterprise resource planning system. That usually entails an army of people over a period of time that seems like forever. With sales and operations planning, you should expect to start the process within two to three months."

Ross does not want Mark to think that implementation is as simple as attending a few education sessions and telling his team to "go get 'em." He wants to paint a realistic picture and points out that, depending on what is found during the assessment, it is likely that Universal Products will need additional support in the area of demand planning, specifically forecasting, and supply planning, specifically rough-cut capacity planning. Typically, at other companies Ross has guided, those involved in forecasting and rough-cut capacity planning require additional education and consulting support.

"Again, I'm not talking a huge consulting engagement," Ross explains. "Our objective is to get you up and running as quickly as is practical and provide coaching for your people so you can continue to achieve sustained, lasting results when we are gone. One of the keys to success is to implement as quickly as you practically can. Our method is designed to shorten the time to results. Bigger benefits are achieved sooner when you shorten the implementation time."

Mark has heard this spiel before from other consultants and decides to hold his tongue. He is curious about whether Ross is telling him that he has to hire additional people to support this new process.

Ross cannot answer the question definitively. He does not know Universal

Products' organization well enough. He shares his experience with other companies. They typically don't increase head count, and the ongoing expenses of the sales and operations planning process are minimal.

"Sales and operations planning is about managing the company. In theory, you are already paying people to do this," Ross says. "When sales and operations planning is properly implemented, the senior management team often realizes a significant time savings. It increases the amount of time available for the management team to do truly constructive work. One of the biggest benefits of sales and operations planning is it frees up your time and your management team's time to work on opportunities rather than problems."

Ross points to some literature he has brought Mark. The literature details the operational benefits of sales and operations planning, including improved on-time delivery, lower inventories, and lower manufacturing cost.

Ross offers another view of the benefits, based on his experience. In practice, the greatest benefits come from strengthening the management team, helping to enable those in management to operate as a team, and making them more effective. When this happens, companies realize increased market share and increased profits.

"In a division the size of Universal Products, you should begin to see results within three months after you have completed the design, or vision of operations. The president of a client company shared with me just last week that his organization increased sales 40 percent — that's right, 40 percent — just twelve months after beginning implementation."

Mark whistles softly and then says, "That's one big fat claim."

"It's not a claim, it's the truth," Ross responds. "Let me tell you about the company." He explains that the company struggled to deliver product to its customers. The sales force finally gave up trying to sell what it knew could not be delivered, and sales revenues further deteriorated. Once the sales and operations planning process was up and running, the company was able to identify and correct the major constraints that prevented it from being a reliable supplier. Product design and quality were no longer issues, and the market wanted to buy its product. When the operational constraints were fixed, the sales force began selling again, and the customers started ordering again. And the company was able to deliver those orders on time. "Voila! Increased sales!" Ross concludes.

"You've just described a company like ours. I hope we can get the same or better results," Mark comments and then switches gears. "What is the primary obstacle to getting the sales and operations planning design completed and the process started?"

"The primary constraint on the design and starting the process is *you*," Ross answers. "We find it usually takes longer for the client to make a decision and to schedule the management team than it does to complete the design. I can have a proposal to you by the end of the week. From that point on, how long it takes to start the process is up to you."

Mark, who has been a salesperson himself, bristles. "Are you trying to give me the old hard sell?"

Ross is equally assertive in response. He explains that he has helped companies implement sales and operations planning for more than fifteen years. The single largest cause of delay in achieving results is lack of decision making by the executive team.

"Companies have a tendency to study things to death," Ross says. "By the time they get around to doing something, often some of the management team is no longer there. They have to start the education process over again, which delays the implementation and improvement of the process."

Mark is reassured. "I appreciate your comments and your frankness," he says.

Ross pushes himself away from the table and stands to leave. They agree that Ross will e-mail the proposal to Mark by the end of the week, and Mark will contact Ross after he reviews it.

Mark walks Ross to the reception area and watches as Ross makes his way into the parking area.

■ ■ ■

As Mark walks down the hall to return to his office and Ross pulls out of the parking lot to drive to the airport, both men are thinking about risk.

Mark thinks about risk in terms of cost, time, probability of success, and consequences if he chooses to do nothing. The cost sounds minimal. He values Janis Novak's advice, and she has seen this process work elsewhere. The other executives Janis recommended he talk to were quite positive about the process.

The biggest risk is time. Mark knows he does not have much time to turn around Universal Products. Should he spend valuable management time on sales and operations planning or some other solution? Come to think of it, he doesn't have another solution.

He decides to call Jack Baxter at corporate. He will want to know what Mark has learned, and Mark wants to make sure Jack will support the effort if he decides it is the right thing to do.

Meanwhile, Ross negotiates his way through stop-and-go traffic. He decides that at this time of the afternoon, city streets will be faster than the freeway. His plane reservation is not until six o'clock, but if he gets to the airport early, he may be able to catch the four o'clock flight.

The earlier flight is a powerful incentive. Ross could arrive for his next client visit a few hours early, hopefully in time to have dinner somewhere other than on the airplane.

Ross has driven this route many times before, and he lets his mind roam. As an educator and consultant for more than fifteen years, he has seen literally hundreds of companies in different industries in various business situations. Over time, he has developed the ability to listen well to clients and to quickly make a high-level assessment of the situation.

Most of the time when he is called into a company, it is because there are "problems." Almost always, he finds a management process that does not effectively cope with the changes occurring in the industry.

Most often, symptoms of the lack of process are viewed as problems by the members of the management team. The symptoms typically include missed deliveries, long customer delivery lead times or poor availability of product, higher costs both in the supply operations and in administration, high inventories, poor new product development performance, and poor financial performance. The persistence of these symptoms results in what Ross calls organizational frustration.

Most companies that ask for Ross's help have a history of business success, but something has occurred to cause a significant change that erodes their success. What usually has changed are customers' expectations, stronger competition, more demanding shareholder expectations, and technological and market developments. Most striking to Ross is not just the number of changes, but the rapid increase in the rate of change.

Almost always, Ross finds that the management processes are insufficient to deal with the rate of change. Companies continue to use old management processes that simply are inadequate to ensure success in a business within an environment of continuous change.

Based on Mark's description of the current situation at Universal Products, Ross believes that the division does not have the management processes to adapt to frequent change. Ross is confident of his skills, and as he pulls into the rental car parking lot, he thinks that Universal Products should be able to make significant improvements quickly if only Mark will let EMI help.

On the crowded shuttle bus ride from the rental car return to the airport terminal, Ross is reminded why he is finding it more and more difficult to travel. He likes his work and the clients, but airplanes feel like crowded buses even in first-class seating. Highways are congested, even when it isn't rush hour. All hotels look and feel the same. Ross has been thinking about slowing down, working less, and maybe retiring early, but it will be a few more years before he has the financial security to retire.

Ross uses his frequent-flyer miles to upgrade to first-class seating and boards the plane when first-class passengers are called. As he takes his seat and orders a cup of coffee and a glass of water, he reviews his conversation with Mark Ryan. He is concerned that he did not connect as well as he should have with Mark. He thinks he may have come on too strong. He wasn't really being forceful as much as he was being impatient.

After fifteen years of working in this field, Ross knows that the main reason companies do not implement sales and operations planning is that they have inadvertently chosen not to do so. Sometimes it is a conscious decision, but most often it is an unconscious choice. Most companies do not know that sales and operations planning exists as a best business practice.

Ross recalls a joke he once heard and has modified for his own use when teaching about sales and operations planning: A couple of senior executives are overheard in a conversation. The first executive says, "With what we now know about sales and operations planning, why don't more companies do it? Is it ignorance or is it apathy?" The second executive replies, "Well, I don't really know — but that's okay because I don't really care."

Ross knows that senior executives like Mark have a lot on their minds. He knows that, like other companies he has served, sales and operations planning is not the only improvement Universal Products needs.

Sales and operations planning gives executives the ability to identify and prioritize real company needs. How can Mark possibly filter all the blaming and complaining he heard from his staff? He needs a process like sales and operations planning to determine which complaints are valid and in what priority changes should be made.

Time and again, Ross has seen companies implement major initiatives to fix a "problem" only to find that they were fixing a symptom of the wrong problem in the wrong priority. The end result: minimal long-term results and the learning gained from the initiatives tends to atrophy. Eventually, the benefits fade away.

Ross decides that he will work on the proposal early in the morning. He will e-mail it to Mark before calling on his next client, and he will call Mark late tomorrow. Maybe his responsiveness will overcome any negative feelings Mark may have had about him.

He would like to get this engagement. He thinks he can help Universal Products in a short period of time.

■ ■ ■

The alarm startles Mark when it rings at 4:30 a.m. It takes him a moment to remember why he set it for so early. Corporate headquarters is in the eastern time zone, two hours ahead of Colorado, and Mark wants to catch Jack Baxter at the start of his day. Anxious to discuss what he learned about sales and operations planning, Mark doesn't want to play phone tag all day, and he does not want to have to resort to e-mail to communicate the pros, cons, and risks.

Mark has just enough time to shower, shave, and drink half a cup of coffee before making the call. He is relieved to hear Jack personally answer the phone.

"You are certainly up early, Mark. What's on your mind?" Jack says.

"I want to tell you what I learned about sales and operations planning yesterday, and I need your candid input on it. Before I start the effort, I want your opinion as to whether you think it is the proper thing to do. Do you have any misgivings or concerns? Do you think I should be doing something else?"

Jack tells Mark that after their last conversation, he began his own investigation into sales and operations planning. He received positive comments from a number of people. He learned that sales and operations planning is considered a best practice in many different industries and is used by a significant number of companies. He called some people he met in the Young Presidents Club a couple of years ago, and they were quite familiar with the process.

"I am not as close to the issues at Universal Products as you are, so I cannot really tell you whether or not it is the right thing to do," Jack says. "I do know that you have tried a number of other things to improve the division's performance without significant results. You replaced some key individuals. You have made some marketing moves on products and price. You tell me. Do you think it is the right thing to do?"

"I am becoming more convinced by the day," Mark answers. "Some of the things the consultant told me were right on target. I believe we have found the right consulting resource to help us. Ross Peterson is the consultant from Effective Management, Inc., and he clearly knows his stuff. Not only that, he does not hesitate to tell it like it is. He put the responsibility to make this happen squarely on my shoulders."

"So what's it going to cost?" Jack asks.

"I don't know yet," Mark replies. "I'm waiting for a proposal. But the good news is this is not one of those huge consulting contracts. Ross Peterson was talking in terms of extensive consulting time for about six months and then periodic visits for another six months. Based upon what he said, the cost should be quite reasonable."

Mark tells Jack that first EMI will do an assessment and then conduct some classes to get the management team on the same level of understanding. The consultants will also provide one-on-one coaching throughout the implementation.

"I would like to attend one of the classes, if you don't mind," Jacks says. "You've piqued my interest about sales and operations planning. I hope my attendance will not put a damper on the communication among your group."

"Not at all!" Mark says. He is pleasantly surprised. Jack's attendance at the class will send a message to the management team that this effort is important and has the eye of corporate. "I should ask Ross, though," Mark adds, "to make sure he agrees."

Mark leaves the office around six o'clock. It has been a good day. The staff meeting went well. It still lasted four hours, but something was different. Mark tried very hard to direct the discussions so that more time was spent talking about what is needed to correct the *business,* rather than specific problems. There was very little discussion about detailed plant schedules and specific customer priorities.

While driving home, Mark decides to spend the weekend in Vail. He will quickly pack a change of clothes and stop for dinner at a newly opened restaurant on Highway 70 in the foothills.

He is alone this weekend. Cheryl and Chad decided to visit her parents in New Hampshire, and two days is not enough time for Mark to get there, visit, and return. To pass the solitude, he will hike in the mountains tomorrow.

While driving up Highway 70, Mark thinks about the plans he reviewed today for implementing sales and operations planning. Ross Peterson was very prompt in sending the proposal, and there were no surprises. The effort will start with an executive-level assessment that should take two to three days to conduct. Ross and another associate will interview all the key managers and review the various reports and information currently used to run the business.

At the staff meeting, Mark used one of the charts Ross left to present the concept of sales and operations planning. He told his managers to expect to spend one to two hours with Ross or his associate. He emphasized the need to be candid and not to be hesitant to air Universal Products' dirty laundry. If the consultants do not hear the problems that Universal Products is experiencing, they will not be able to offer the proper solutions.

Mark also reviewed the schedule for the education sessions. He emphasized that attendance is mandatory, not an option.

What pleased Mark the most today was the attitude exhibited by his staff. Sam, Ray, Jim, and Anita were supportive of sales and operations planning.

Mark called Ross after the staff meeting to coordinate some final details. Ross was a bit surprised by the support from Sam. He said it is common for the sales team to be one of the last functional areas to truly get on board with sales and operations planning.

Ross mentioned, however, that he has observed sales and marketing managers more and more frequently leading the effort to implement sales and operations planning. Ross recommended a book to read, *The Marketing Edge: The New Leadership Role of Sales and Marketing in Manufacturing.*

In thinking about the staff meeting, Mark was a little surprised by Susan Callahan's and Janis Novak's behavior. They both seemed a bit quiet. He wonders if they are concerned about how this process will change their jobs.

As the head of planning, Susan is at the center of all demand, supply, and scheduling activities. Perhaps she feels she will have some loss of control or power. Mark makes a mental note to talk with her on Monday.

As for Janis, Mark fears she is concerned about the credibility of her financial forecasts. She bristled a bit when he told the staff that the output of the sales and operations planning process is one set of numbers; the operational numbers and the financial numbers will be the same. Mark knows Janis has no confidence in the sales forecast, and she has little confidence in the shipping forecast. Ross downplayed Mark's concern when he told him about it. He said it is to be expected.

Until the sales and operations planning process is working completely and credibility is established in the output of the process, the business must go on. Janis still has to provide her financial projections to corporate.

Ross said that every member of the senior management team will become concerned at some point in the implementation, but the staff members will learn to trust the process. Mark will be able to use the process to identify and resolve their individual issues.

Mark spots the restaurant up ahead. He is hungry, and he is ready to think about something other than work.

He is looking forward to tomorrow and hiking in Vail. The snow has melted in the town of Vail and in the valleys, but he knows there is too much snow to hike in the highlands yet. Still, early spring in the canyons is beautiful. He just wishes that Cheryl and Chad were there to enjoy it with him.

3

FACING REALITY

For two days, Ross Peterson and Nolan Drake, a colleague at Effective Management, Inc., conduct interviews throughout Universal Products. The broad subject of the interviews is planning and control.

They talk to the general manager, senior management team, middle managers, and individuals on the shop floor. Every function within the company is covered: sales, marketing, planning, manufacturing, finance, engineering, project management, customer service, purchasing, order entry, and master scheduling.

Ross and Nolan frequently team together to work with clients. They have complementary experience and personalities. Before joining EMI three years ago, Nolan held supply management positions at two different companies, both of which implemented integrated enterprise management processes.

Nolan and Ross frequently joke about how the names of these processes change as marketers attempt to gain name recognition. In the 1980s, the term was manufacturing resource planning, or MRP II. In the 1990s, the buzzword was enterprise resource planning, or ERP. But to Nolan and Ross, it really is organized common sense.

Ross has spent more than fifteen years working with the executive teams of companies to implement organized common sense, and he likes to joke that he has the gray hair to show for it. Nolan, in his early thirties, has jet black hair with no traces of gray. Ross tells him that is because he has only been at this organized common sense business for eight years, five years as a practitioner and three years as a consultant.

Ross and Nolan work well in tandem. Ross interviews the senior executive staff and the sales, marketing, and product development managers and key people. Ross spent fifteen years as a sales and marketing executive for instrumentation manufacturers before becoming a consultant. He understands what it is like to steer a company and to develop new markets and products and market those products. He knows the challenges and frustrations of developing client relationships and selling product when there is not a lot of confidence that the factory will deliver.

Nolan interviews the supply-side managers and people. He has held management positions in purchasing, supply chain, and production. He easily relates to the problems and challenges of getting quality product shipped on time.

Ross and Nolan are in listening mode during the assessment. They ask pointed questions and gather data, but express little in the way of judgment and opinions.

During the assessment presentation, education seminars, and one-on-one coaching, they will listen less and talk more. That is when Ross usually ruffles feathers, and Nolan helps smooth those ruffled feathers.

In dealing with company leaders, Ross has learned that the most effective approach is to not mince words. The higher up people are in an organization, the more isolated they become from the realities of the day-to-day problems of the business. They do not want to hear bad news.

Ross sees his role as delivering a wake-up call. Many senior executives do not like to hear the message Ross delivers. Ross knows, however, that if he were less than honest and direct, many of his clients would still be floundering or, worse yet, their companies would have been merged, downsized, or out of business.

So he does not hold back, and he will not allow a single key member of an executive team to keep the rest of the team from implementing changes. An aspect of his role in coaching companies is to ensure that each of the senior executives knows and fulfills his or her role in the management process.

Nolan frequently finds himself smoothing feathers that Ross has ruffled. Once a manager receives a wake-up call from Ross, Nolan uses logic and reasoning to demonstrate the need for change. He uses his experience to help show how change can be implemented, what steps the executive should take, and how he or she should manage the changes throughout the organization.

Nolan has enjoyed working with Susan Callahan, the planning manager. Mark assigned Susan to coordinate the visit. He shared with Ross and Nolan his concerns about Susan.

Nolan, a former planning manager himself, understands why she might feel that a loss of control could result from any proposed changes. He has undertaken a subtle education process while working with Susan to schedule the interviews.

The interviews were completed during the first two days. Now, on the third morning, Ross and Nolan assemble their findings and observations. Presentation of a preliminary report to Mark and his executive team is scheduled for this afternoon.

Ross and Nolan are sequestered in a conference room. Stacks of notes, reports, and data litter the mahogany table. Through their years of working together, they have come up with an efficient approach to developing their reports. They take turns asking one another questions.

"Any surprises?" Ross asks.

"None in the production and inventory control areas," Nolan replies. He pulls out a model of an enterprise resource planning process that they will use in their presentation this afternoon. He modifies the model to show what he found at Universal Products (Figure 4).

Nolan and Mark know that two-way arrows should connect all elements in the model. Nolan tells Ross that there is no real master scheduling. Demand and supply are not decoupled, except in a few minor exceptions, and where they have been decoupled it has not necessarily been for the right reasons. They certainly have not been decoupled with visibility of the consequences of the choice to decouple.

Nolan observes that there is far too much inventory, yet inventory has not enabled better customer delivery. That is because inventory records are inaccurate and are not perpetually updated and maintained. Cycle counting is not done at all.

"How about the customer commitments? Do they keep internal dates valid on customer orders in the backlog?" Ross asks.

"The dates in the system do not reflect reality," Nolan says. "Therefore, they can't use the dates in the system to communicate priorities."

Ross knows what this news means. Many people end up spending their valuable time expediting individual orders. Generally, either the squeaky wheel or the last one to holler becomes the priority.

"I didn't find anything unusual or out of the norm. It is what we would expect to find in a company that lacks integration of its planning processes," Nolan concludes. "What did you find in sales and marketing?" he asks.

"Mostly pleasant surprises," Ross replies. He explains that he found it heartening to see the level of planning and communication that presently exists within sales and marketing. The planning information is not visible to operations or to finance, however. Finance develops its own forecast independent of the sales and marketing planning, as well as independent of the supply planning activities.

Nolan knows what this news means. There are many sets of planning numbers that supposedly define what the division is going to do and when. Even though Universal Products spent a huge sum of money on an integrated planning software system, the company is being run with multiple disconnected spreadsheets.

"What about product development? Any chance that process is under control?" Nolan asks.

"Nope," Ross replies. He tells Nolan that he estimates the development re-

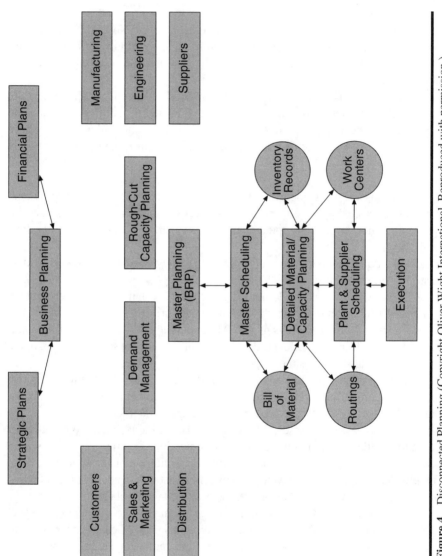

Figure 4 Disconnected Planning (Copyright Oliver Wight International. Reproduced with permission.)

sources are overloaded by 80 to 100 percent. Not surprisingly, new products are rarely completed on time without sacrificing some functionality.

Sam Wente, the sales director, is particularly concerned with this situation. He tends to blame the engineering group and does not have very much positive to say about the competency of that department. But the fact of the matter is that there is not an appropriate process to capture, prioritize, resource, and monitor product development opportunities and projects. The sales force continues to sell products that simply do not yet exist based upon schedules that can't possibly be met.

"What about an integrated sales and operations planning process? Is there any semblance of one in existence?" Nolan asks.

"If you mean do they have a monthly management meeting, the answer is yes. However, I can't say it resembles a properly designed and operating sales and operations planning process," Ross replies.

He further observes that it is a shame to see all that talent wasted in weekly meetings. They ought to be using their time for more productive things. The weekly meetings mostly involve expediting, complaining about problems, assigning actions that generally do not get completed in a timely manner, and deciding what numbers they are going to tell corporate regarding past and anticipated division performance.

"It appears to be one of the classic situations we regularly find," Ross sums up. "There is no integrated aggregate planning process. Each department decides what it is going to do independent or semi-independent of the other departments. There is either no master schedule or an ineffective master schedule. Dates are not kept valid and therefore cannot be used for prioritization, and basic data, like inventory accuracy, are poor."

Nolan nods his head in agreement. He focuses on the one positive — sales and marketing planning. "Does it have all the elements we look for in a best practice?" he asks.

"No," Ross replies, "but at least they will not be starting from ground zero."

Nolan knows what ground zero means. He and Ross are working with another client that has virtually no marketing and sales planning. The client has one hot product, and its sales team buries the company with orders without providing visibility or advance notice that the demand is coming.

"Universal Products has a marketing function and a sales department that report to a single executive, and there appears to be a close working relationship between sales and marketing," Ross says.

He further explains that there is no formalized product management or market management other than through the sales planning efforts. As a consequence, the marketing effort is mostly reactive rather than proactive. But the field communication is good. The communication process is both qualitative and quantitative, which is a start.

Universal Products will need to build greater detail into the planning process and expand its planning horizon if the information is to be used effectively by the supply side of the business. The company will also need to develop a demand manager. Currently, the sales administration function helps coordinate the quantitative communication.

"The variety of marketing channels will present a challenge in developing a planning process, but it is certainly not insurmountable," Ross observes. He learned that Universal Products uses a direct sales force to sell some of its products. The division uses independent manufacturers' representatives in some geographic areas and sells one of its products through dealers. An e-business channel is being tested as well. A push–pull marketing approach is used in some markets, which makes marketing in those areas a critical key variable. There are also sales to original equipment manufacturers and end users. About 45 percent of the demand is from outside the United States.

"Generally speaking, there is a little bit of everything present on the demand side of the business," Ross says. He then switches gears. "What did you find in the area of rough-cut capacity planning?" he asks Nolan.

"It really doesn't exit," Nolan replies. He tells Ross that some rough-cut planning is attempted, but it is not particularly useful since there is little visibility of demand. The planning organization knows about the concept of rough-cut capacity planning and can talk a good game, but the planners do not practice what they preach. When Nolan reviewed what the planners are actually doing, he found that they are really order launching and expediting. Their typical planning horizon is really just the current week.

"I believe Susan Callahan has a vision of how it should be done, but I am not sure she really has worked in an environment that properly utilized planning and control," Nolan says. "She is APICS certified, but as you and I both know, that does not mean that you have direct experience in a well-functioning planning and control environment."

Nolan is not discouraged, however. "The good news is that the supply processes are pretty straightforward. There are only a handful of critical resources, which means rough-cut capacity planning can be up and running quickly."

Ross glances at his watch. It is eleven o'clock. Time to sum up before the presentation this afternoon. "If I have understood what we have learned," he says, "this is a classic case. Quite frankly, that is the good news. We have seen this situation hundreds of times before, and the corrective action plan is pretty straightforward. Sales and operations planning clearly needs to be an immediate priority in order to gain control of the company. This is not all they need to do, but based upon the business scenario painted by Mark, they should start sales and operations planning as quickly as is practical."

Nolan nods his head in agreement. They are in sync. They discuss who will present what during the presentation. Ross will take the lead role, and he will brief Mark Ryan, the general manager, before the presentation.

"By the way, that brings to mind Jack Baxter, the corporate president. He wants to attend the education session," Ross says. Ross is against this idea. He fears that by virtue of Jack's position, people will be afraid to speak out during the class. Mark is hesitant to tell that to Jack, however, so he probably will attend.

Ross also recognizes a risk. Based on what Mark has told him about Jack, Jack will become enamored with rough-cut capacity planning. He will want the parent company to have that kind of visibility on a global basis. Implementation at that level, however, will not be as simple and straightforward as it will be at a single division like Universal Products. "We need to be sure," Ross points out, "not to lead the group into believing that rough-cut capacity planning and sales and operations planning will be implemented in three to six months time on a global basis."

"So noted," Nolan says. He pulls up his calendar on his computer. "While we're coordinating, when do you expect the education sessions to be delivered?"

Ross looks over Nolan's shoulder and laughs. "Your calendar is as booked as mine," Ross says as he opens his laptop computer. They spend the next fifteen minutes juggling their schedules so that they are both available on the same dates for the education sessions.

■ ■ ■

Ross Peterson and Mark Ryan walk down the hall together toward the conference room. Both are quiet.

Ross is preparing his final thoughts for the assessment presentation. Mark is thinking about his one-on-one meeting with Ross that just concluded. Based on what Ross told him, Mark wonders what he should say to his executive team during the presentation.

Mark appreciated the advance preview of the assessment findings. He also appreciated Ross's sensitivity toward him. Since the findings were not particularly favorable, Ross wanted to make sure that Mark didn't take the report as personal criticism, which he did not.

Ross was pleased with Mark's response. "Tell it like it is, and let's get on with it," Mark told him. With this green light, Ross is prepared to be open, honest, and direct.

Ross and Nolan start the presentation by passing out a reference book, *The Oliver Wight ABCD Checklist for Operational Excellence*. Ross explains that the book contains a set of criteria for defining operational excellence. It is divided into sections on strategic planning, people and teams, total quality and continuous improvement, new product development, and planning and control.

He tells the group that the criteria defined in the book are an industry standard benchmark that has evolved over almost three decades. They are used as a basis for evaluating key operational management processes. The checklist can be applied to other industries, but it is written in the language of manufacturing, engineering, and distribution companies.

Many companies use the criteria as a basis for developing company best practices. They are also useful when companies have multiple divisions or facilities that are located throughout the world. The criteria help to ensure that common practices and standards are used.

Ross segues into the assessment. The focus of the assessment was on only one section of the checklist, planning and control. He asks that each person read this section at his or her convenience and notes that the written report will refer to planning and control benchmarks.

He also notes that eventually the team members will be asked to assess their areas of responsibility against the checklist. He points out that the criteria for sales and operations planning, demand management, and supply management are in the section on planning and control.

Ross is careful to pace himself. He wants to allow adequate time for questions and answers. He tries to be candid, but tactful, in his presentation. He does not want to ruffle too many feathers at this point.

He and Nolan present their findings. The executives frequently nod their heads in agreement as deficiencies are pointed out. From the nods, Ross and Nolan understand that there are not many surprises in their findings.

Ross strives to give the team a perspective on the findings. He says that the success of any company is determined by a complex matrix of many things. The negative evaluation of Universal Products' current planning and control processes does not imply that the company does not have good products. It does not imply that the company does not treat its employees well. It does not imply that the company is not profitable. It does not imply that the company does not have solid, motivated, capable people.

The negative evaluation *does* indicate that there are opportunities to significantly improve the company's position with customers. It suggests there are significant opportunities to improve operational and financial results.

An integrated planning and control process is primarily an enabler, or part of the infrastructure that enables a company to do the things that really matter to customers and other stakeholders. It enables a company's management to *regularly and routinely* focus, align, and engage the company to profitably meet or exceed customer expectations.

Ross observes that companies experiencing poor customer service often also *simultaneously* experience high inventories, high manufacturing costs, higher purchasing costs, significant expediting, poor financial forecasts, and departmental

- Missed customer deliveries
- Loss of credibility with customers
- Lost customers
- Expediting
- Higher manufacturing costs
- Excess overtime
- Premium costs and freight
- Reduced flexibility and responsiveness
- Higher working capital in inventories
- Late new product introductions
- Reduced operational performance
- Reduced financial performance

Figure 5   Symptoms of Inadequate Planning and Control

infighting. He points to the visual projected on the screen at the front of the room (Figure 5).

"Why do these problems occur simultaneously?" Susan Callahan, the planning manager, asks. "I always thought that there are specific defined relationships between such things as inventory and customer service. The more inventory, the better the customer service. Why is this not really true?"

"Good question," Ross responds. "People tend to draw wrong conclusions from partial truths. Let me give you the bad news and the good news." The bad news, he explains, is that if the planning and control system has not been properly implemented, it does not work properly. That results in all or most of the symptoms he mentioned. The good news is that if the deficiencies in the planning and control system are fixed, simultaneous improvements in all those areas are realized.

"More importantly," Ross says, "you will build an effective infrastructure that frees up management's time to work on real business issues, hopefully opportunities. When companies operate with best practices in planning and control, or what we refer to as a Class A level of performance, they gain market position, market share, and improved financial performance. Why? Because the people in the organization are able to operate more effectively."

Ross points out that there is a difference between effective and efficient. "Effectiveness is a social concept; it applies to groups. Efficiency is an individual concept; it applies to isolated acts," he says.

He quotes Paul Strassman, who wrote in *Information Payoff* that departments can operate *efficiently* independent of other departments, but for companies to operate *effectively,* all the departments, functions, and processes must operate synchronized with one another.

"I will take an inefficient, effective company over an ineffective, efficient company every time," Ross says. "The effective company will win. Why do I make this point? Sales and operations planning is all about making a company effective. Once a company has the infrastructure to make it effective, it can more effectively become efficient. In fact, sales and operations planning implemented well helps a company to prioritize where it should spend its efforts in becoming more efficient."

"I don't know if I entirely agree with you," says Peter Newfeld, the product development/engineering director. "But then I don't fully understand sales and operations planning. How does it work?"

"I will give you an abbreviated answer," Ross says. "In the education session that will be scheduled in a couple of weeks, we will review sales and operations planning in great detail."

Ross explains that a properly integrated planning and control process continuously establishes anticipated results in demand, supply, finance, strategic initiatives, new products, and key processes. It continuously monitors performance. It enables company management to take actions and make changes to keep resources in balance with the work required to achieve the anticipated results. It enables the people in the company to keep the resources in sync with the work requirements and with the timing and required schedules.

"This process is actually an ongoing *replanning* process," Ross says. He explains that the work, time, and resources are replanned as changes occur. A fundamental principle is that the output of the process is a valid plan. A valid plan is one that represents the needs of the company; otherwise people will not follow the plan.

A valid plan also must be attainable. If there are not adequate resources to support the plan, the plan is nothing more than a wish list. With a valid plan come commitment and accountability to make the plan happen. Plans and execution are directly connected.

"During the education session, I will emphasize and reemphasize a number of fundamentals that underlie effective planning and control," Ross says. He advances the computer to show a new diagram (Figure 6).

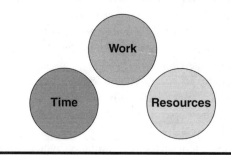

Figure 6   Three Control Variables

Ross explains that the diagram illustrates a basic management fundamental. Management has the responsibility to control three knobs that are tied to three key variables: work, time, and resources. These three variables must be kept in balance, or in sync. Once they are in balance, a change in one of the variables requires a change in at least one of the other two.

"Let me say that again," Ross says. "Once *work, time, and resources* are in balance, any change in one requires a change in at least one of the other two." He explains why he emphasizes this fundamental. Again and again, he finds that companies do not have the ability to recognize that something has changed. Even if they do recognize change, the management team does not have a *regular and routine* process to effectively deal with the change.

As a result, the company operates out of sync: (1) it is out of sync with the market or customer demand, which is the required work; (2) it is out of sync with the time, or schedules and due dates, required to meet the demand; or (3) it is out of sync with the resources (people, machines, materials, suppliers, cash, etc.) required to complete the work on schedule.

When a company is out of sync, performance in all areas deteriorates. Customer service is down, inventories are up, ineffective and inefficient expediting causes higher manufacturing and engineering costs, and financial plans are not met. Often, the company feels like it is operating out of control. "Coming to work feels like walking into chaos," Ross says. He sees heads nodding in agreement.

"But this is not the worst of it," he continues. "What makes the situation worse is that good, capable people are individually trying their best to perform. Often, the harder they work, the worse it gets. That is because when one area of the company is working harder or faster than another, the out-of-balance situation becomes worse. In fact, it looks and feels like a negative spiral."

Mark interrupts Ross. "Let me see if I understand. It is the individual departments, or functions, or processes operating out of sync that causes poor performance in multiple areas simultaneously. The demand, or work, must be synchronized in quantity and time across all areas of the company. This drives the resources required. If the work (demand), the time (schedules), or the resources (supply) are not kept in balance, chaos may result. If changes to demand (work), supply (resources), or time (schedules) are not effectively identified and managed or synchronized, chaos will ultimately result."

Ross smiles. "By Jove, I think he has got it."

By the look on his face, it is obvious that Sam Wente, the sales director, does not yet understand. He raises his hand. "Mark may get it, but I don't," he says. "I don't see how being out of sync causes all the problems you mentioned simultaneously."

"Let me use an analogy," Ross says. "Picture an orchestra warming up. For those of you who have been to a live performance of an orchestra, the warm-up period sounds like what?"

"Noise," says Anita Cooper, the purchasing manager.

"Exactly," Ross says. "When the orchestra is warming up, it is a group of individually talented people all playing independently, out of sync. What they produce is noise."

"Now think about the performance itself," Ross continues. "When the conductor leads the orchestra and every talented individual plays in harmony with others, what we hear is music, beautiful music."

"Let me try another analogy," he says. "What happens when the timing of your car's engine needs to be adjusted, or when the timing of the combustion cycle in the cylinders is not proper?"

"The engine runs rough, if it runs at all," answers Ray Guy, the final assembly manager.

"That's right, and what else happens?" Ross asks.

"What do you mean?" Ray replies.

"I mean," Ross says, "what other things happen as a consequence of the timing being off? You gave us one consequence: the engine runs rough."

"Well, if the engine is running rough, it will need more fuel for the car to travel the same distance. This will cause the owner to spend more money for gasoline. Some of the engine components will wear more quickly, causing other problems to occur," Ray says and then pauses.

"Ross," he continues, "I think I see what you are trying to show us. In this case, the timing of the engine is the root cause of potentially a lot of different problems or, more correctly, symptoms, which occur simultaneously."

"That's right," Ross says. "Now let me be more specific to a manufacturing company. Let's say that demand is coming in faster than manufacturing and engineering expected. What is the result?"

Peter Newfeld, the product development/engineering director, thrusts his hand in the air. "Lead times increase, since we would not have enough engineers to handle the work in the standard lead time."

Jim Simpson, the manufacturing director, interrupts. "The lead time may increase in reality, but the company does not acknowledge it. We don't tell customers. We don't even tell ourselves until we are truly in trouble. I have my people working overtime trying to ship to the standard lead times, but we find that to do so, we have to expedite materials and engineering. As if expediting engineering is possible!"

Peter bristles at Jim's last comment. "Wait a minute. My engineers are working overtime as well. And we respond as best we can to all the demands. In fact, we respond to the point where we cannot work on new products. So new products miss their due dates. If we had better visibility, we would have time to get more engineers. Better yet, I could get Mark to authorize more engineers."

"Let me finish, Peter," Jim says. "We complete as much of the work as we can and then work on something else while waiting for materials or engineering or whatever else is missing to show up. But that's not all. The sales organization is constantly changing priorities because we have made unrealistic promises to customers. We end up with lots of partially completed orders. Work in process stacks up, and shipment targets are missed."

Now Sam Wente, the sales director, is bristling. "We wouldn't be changing priorities if you had met the original promised ship dates."

Janis Novak, the controller, chimes in. "What I see are revenue targets that are missed because of lack of shipments. Inventories go up because of the increase in work in process. Cash flow is at risk because we have to pay suppliers and employees, and both manufacturing and engineering costs go up. This all seems strange because the problem started with increased orders from customers. The orders are coming in and customer backlog is up, but shipments are just not going out."

Anita Cooper, the purchasing manager, interrupts. "Don't forget increased cost of purchased materials because I am ordering inside our suppliers' lead times and paying expediting fees and increased transportation costs."

"Whoa!" Mark interrupts. "I think we get the point. Ross, how long were you going to let this go on?"

"Until Sam says he understands," Ross says, smiling.

By the frown on Sam's face, he obviously has concerns. "I think I get the picture," he says, "but in your example, it sounds like we're blaming the problems on the forecast and the customers. The customers bought more than we anticipated. That is going to happen. We are not going to have 100 percent accurate forecasts."

"Sam, of course that is going to happen," Ross replies. "It's going to happen the other way as well. Customers may not be buying what you thought they were going to buy. That is why it is necessary to have a *regular and routine* management process in place to deal with change. We could just as easily gone through a similar discussion starting with the supply side of the business. For example, what happens when manufacturing in one area doesn't perform for whatever reason?"

Janis is quick to respond. "Similar things occur in the different areas of the company when there isn't a process to identify and communicate the situation in order to keep everything synchronized, in balance and alignment."

Ross smiles his approval. "I really like the word *alignment*. This is what we must do to operate most effectively. We must keep the elements of the organization in alignment to operate most effectively."

Mark begins to play the role of facilitator. "Ross, I think this has been helpful, but in the interest of time perhaps you can talk about the next steps."

"Sure," Ross says. "It should come as no surprise that Nolan and I found that although you are doing many things well, your integrated planning and control process is broken."

Ross relates Mark's concern that any corrective actions taken need to deliver results very quickly. "It is our recommendation that you implement a formalized sales and operations planning process as quickly as is practical," he says. "You need more than sales and operations planning to truly achieve the benchmarks in the checklist criteria. However, you can get benefits from sales and operations planning quickly."

"What about the other things we need to do?" Susan Callahan, the planning manager, asks. "Are you recommending that we also do them? And if so, when?"

"We are recommending that you do a number of other things," Ross replies. He cites the need to improve the fundamental planning data, such as inventory records. Numerous improvements are also needed in the detailed planning and control processes.

"At this point, we haven't recommended specific timing for those improvements," Ross says. "One of the things we have observed is that the additional areas where improvement is needed will surface if you do sales and operations planning well, and the process will help to prioritize which improvements should be worked on first."

Mark interrupts Ross to assert his leadership. He stands up and addresses his team. "Ross has provided me with his recommendations for what needs to be done to achieve what he calls a Class A level of performance. I have decided to focus first on sales and operations planning. This will include demand planning, rough-cut capacity planning, and connection to master scheduling. One of the interesting things Ross pointed out to me is that the word 'focus' can best be described as deciding what we are *not* going to do. We are going to focus on sales and operations planning for now. That means we are not going to do some other things. Susan, let's get that working and then come back and ask the question again."

Jim Simpson, the manufacturing director, lifts his copy of *The Oliver Wight ABCD Checklist for Operational Excellence* in the air. "I have been thumbing through these benchmarks. There are ratings of A, B, C, and D. How did we come out in the assessment?" he asks.

"The results of the assessment showed you to be a Class D in sales and operations planning," Ross replies. "But don't be discouraged. When companies ask us to perform an assessment, we rarely find performance higher than a Class C. After all, that is why we were hired."

Mark intervenes. "From my perspective, the D rating is good news," he says. "If we were already Class A and still had our current problems, I would not know where to turn for improvement. Ross, tell us your recommendations for implementing sales and operations planning."

Ross explains that the most effective implementation is one that gets the process up and running quickly. Therefore, a lot of time will not be spent on planning the implementation.

"The focus is to start using the process very quickly and to make decisions, which is also known as managing the business," he says. "We strive to have a viable process up and running inside a division in three cycles. Each cycle is one month. We expect a strong but still improving process within six cycles. How we do this will be the subject of the education sessions."

Ross explains that the education sessions will be closely followed by process design, immediately followed by implementation of the process. Implementing the process includes developing whatever tools are chosen to support the process.

"What level of help or support is provided to help us get going?" Sam asks. "I'm concerned that this just adds one more thing to our already overflowing plate of things to do."

"We have found that you cannot have the process up and running in three months without some support and coaching," Ross replies. "Our proposal to Mark includes education, assisting in the process design, and providing hands-on support and coaching as you implement."

Ross provides some details about the education. The purpose of the education is for the senior executive team and middle management to gain a common understanding of what sales and operations planning is, what it is not, how it works, and the individual roles and responsibilities in making the process work effectively.

Education helps to develop an understanding of industry best practices for sales and operations planning. The education sessions also provide an opportunity to ask and answer whatever questions arise.

Ross explains that the design step is completed immediately after the education. The design should not take more than a few days. The first official cycle of the sales and operations planning process will occur immediately after the design is completed.

"Do we have dates for the education?" Peter asks.

Mark instructs his team to check their calendars and give his assistant, Sheri Waterman, the dates when they are available. "Some of you may have to change your schedules," he says. "I want all of you to attend the education session."

"So attendance is not optional?" Sam asks.

"No, Sam, it is not," Mark responds.

"I knew that, but just thought I'd check," Sam replies, and everyone in the room laughs.

"Always testing, aren't you, Sam," Peter says.

"I just wanted to see how committed Mark is to this," Sam replies.

Mark welcomes the opportunity that Sam just offered. "Don't underestimate my commitment," he says.

Mark watches his staff file out of the room. He is pleased and surprised to see almost everyone individually thank Ross and Nolan. He senses palpable relief that there may be an answer to Universal Products' problems.

Watching his staff interact with Ross and Nolan, Mark thinks of his team. He is reminded of the definition of a team in the book *The Wisdom of Teams*:

> A team is a small number of people with complementary skills who are committed to a common purpose, performance goals, and approach for which they hold themselves mutually accountable.

Mark knows he does not yet have a team by this definition, but it is apparent to him that if the people on his staff do sales and operations planning properly, they can develop into a team. He thinks he should establish Class A best practices as a common goal for his team.

Mark thanks Ross and Nolan himself. Ross promises to be in touch next week to discuss some details of the education session.

Janis offers to usher Ross and Nolan out of the building. Mark is grateful. He needs to check his phone messages and e-mail, and it is already five o'clock.

Mark's attempts to return phone calls are interrupted three times. First Ray, then Jim, and finally Sam drop by his office to discuss the assessment. Each has suggestions on ways to improve.

Mark knows the purpose of their visits goes beyond making suggestions. Each is feeling out his level of commitment.

Sam is the most forthright. "Were you serious when you said you're committed to this process?" he asks.

"It makes sense, and it appears that we can do this quickly," Mark replies. "Yes, I'm committed, Sam. Spread the word."

Mark pushes away from his desk and reaches for his briefcase. He places the assessment report inside to review over the weekend. Just as he is about to snap the briefcase shut, Mark realizes with a stab of guilt that Cheryl and Chad will be arriving tonight for the weekend. He mentally chastises himself for being so preoccupied with business that he has ignored his personal life.

Bottom line: The bed is not made. There is no food in the house except junk food, soft drinks, beer, wine, and a couple of apples. He is in big trouble unless he can get to the grocery store and clean up the house in the next two hours. No problem, he tells himself.

Mark heads for the grocery store. While waiting in traffic, he ponders the weekend. Cheryl and Chad are only able to stay until Monday morning. Mark has promised that they will spend Saturday and Sunday in Vail. Chad wants to take advantage of what is left of spring skiing, and Cheryl wants be in the mountains once again. Mark just wants to get away from the business and be with his family.

Mark hustles through the aisles at the grocery store. He looks for the essentials as well as Chad and Cheryl's favorite foods. While pondering the many, too many, choices of orange juice — pulp or no pulp, calcium or no calcium, he hears a familiar voice behind him.

"So, Mark, we *all* have to do domestic tasks once in a while." He turns and sees Janis Novak smiling at him.

Mark is unabashed. "Cheryl and Chad are coming for the weekend. I thought I had better put something in the cupboard other than beer and peanuts."

Mark and Janis chat for a few minutes. He tells her about going to Vail for the weekend.

"I was there last weekend, and the snow is disappearing from the slopes fast," Janis says. "It has been so warm recently. I hope you have at least fair skiing this weekend."

"That's bad news and good news," Mark says. "Bad for Chad, who is anxious to ski. Good for Cheryl and me. We want to take some side trips into the mountains and stay away from the crowds."

They chat about the weather in Vail, things to see, and places to go. As the conversation winds down, Janis turns to business.

"I just wanted to say that I'm impressed and excited by what is beginning to happen at the company. The other staff members seem to be as well. If you will permit me to offer some advice," Janis says.

"Certainly, Janis. What is it?"

"Follow through with the sales and operations planning effort. Do not let it falter. The management group sees the need; we feel your leadership. Do not let this drag on. It is important that we get started and get it done. If it drags on, it will look and feel just like all the other company initiatives. Lots of rhetoric from management, but little real action and support. We need a winner, and sales and operations planning can be it."

"I hear you, and I agree," Mark says. "I appreciate your input and would like you to continue to help me in this project. Let me know your observations and your feelings as we implement."

"Sounds good," Janis replies. She looks at her watch. "Oh, oh. I'm late. Have a great weekend. I will see you Monday!"

Mark watches her head for the checkout counter. He looks at his watch. He is going to be late, too. Better decide on this orange juice and get going!

■ ■ ■

At 5:10 a.m. the next day, Mark is wide awake. It was a late night. The plane was delayed, and Cheryl and Chad are still asleep. The two-hour time difference made it a long day for them.

Mark decides to get up and make coffee. His mind is turning over thoughts and ideas for implementing sales and operations planning. He knows he will not go back to sleep.

As he puts on his robe, Mark looks at Cheryl sleeping. She is such a wonderful woman. He knows he is lucky to have her as his wife. She is intelligent, articulate, witty, and very attractive. As they get older, Mark is the one who is gaining the weight and looking his fifty-three years of age. Not Cheryl. She is slim and trim and very health conscious. Mark misses her when they are apart and is anxious for her to move to Colorado so that they don't have to maintain a long-distance relationship.

Padding down the hall, Mark peeks in on Chad. It looks like he must have tossed and turned all night. The covers are a mess. Hopefully, he will have gotten sufficient rest to have a good day on the slopes.

Mark drinks coffee while waiting for Cheryl and Chad to wake up. His mind continues to ponder sales and operations planning. He thinks of the words that Ross Peterson used — organized common sense. That's what Universal Products needs. It seems that the effort to solve the many problems has only created more problems and more complexity. If they could identify supply and demand problems earlier on, maybe they could eliminate the complexity. What Ross described seems simple and straightforward.

Mark thinks about Janis Novak's parting comment last night. Ross Peterson offered similar advice. The sooner sales and operations planning can be implemented, the sooner the results. The quicker the results, the better the morale. Ross's emphasis on time to results makes sense.

Mark's musings are interrupted by the sound of the shower. His household is waking up, probably aided by the smell of freshly brewed coffee.

Mark is relieved. He doesn't want to think about business. He wants to enjoy his family for the next two days.

SALES AND OPERATIONS PLANNING FUNDAMENTALS

Two weeks later, Mark Ryan arrives at the office early. Today is the one-day education session on sales and operations planning for the senior management team. He wants to make a few phone calls and review the latest financial report from Janis Novak before heading to the hotel in the foothills where the session will be held.

While walking to the cafeteria for a cup of coffee, Mark thinks about the events of the past two weeks. The weekend in Vail seems a long time ago. The problems at Universal Products have consumed Mark these past two weeks.

The performance of Universal Products has not improved; in fact, it may be worse. Deliveries continue to be late. Manufacturing is fighting with engineering, and sales is fighting with manufacturing.

In trying to deal with these problems, Mark found that the context of his thinking has changed. The assessment presentation by the Effective Management, Inc. consultants sensitized Mark to certain conditions and behaviors, which were presented as being classical in a manufacturing environment.

When manufacturing was blaming engineering for the late deliveries and sales in turn was blaming manufacturing, Mark asked all three managers to bring him their plans. Each manager brought Mark a different plan. Engineering's priority was the Anderson design changes. Manufacturing's priority was producing the

Kendall order, not the Anderson order. Engineering did not even have the Kendall order in its plan. And sales was promising delivery in two weeks on four orders that were not in the engineering or manufacturing plans.

Mark recalled Ross Peterson of EMI telling the management team during his assessment presentation about the need for valid plans. Well, Mark had just discovered that his team was operating off of *three* invalid plans that did not represent what Mark thought he had clearly communicated as the priorities.

Mark's first instinct was to yell at all three managers and ask why they did not get together and share their plans. He remembered, however, Ross saying that the root cause of the problems needs to be understood. Instinctively, Mark knows that the three different plans are responses to problems each department perceives, without much thought to the impact on the other departments.

Mark also remembered Ross implying that operating the business should be simple and straightforward. Right now, Mark does not think anything is simple and straightforward.

He is anxious for the education session to begin and for the opportunity to talk with Ross. He hopes the session will help show him how to get at the root cause problems and create a simple and straightforward operation.

■ ■ ■

Mark finds Ross Peterson and Nolan Drake of EMI in the meeting room at the hotel. The room is set up with a projection screen in front of tables and chairs arranged in a u-shape.

Ross had suggested meeting off-site, and Mark thinks that was the right choice. There would be too many distractions at the Universal Products facility.

Ross had also suggested on the phone last week that Mark open the education session with some introductory remarks. Mark pulls Ross over to the side to review his remarks.

He plans to ask everyone to turn off their cell phones and pagers and to make phone calls only during breaks in the session. He also wants to make sure his management team knows that he is behind the sales and operations planning initiative and is going to expect it to be implemented quickly. "Anything else I should cover?" Mark asks.

"Make sure you emphasize that this session is not education for education's sake. It is to prepare your team to design the sales and operations planning process and to begin operating the process. It is preparation to take action," Ross responds. "Also, please thank Susan Callahan. She came over here after work last night and helped set up the room."

Mark walks to the front of the room and claps his hands to get everyone's attention. Most of the group is gathered around the coffee, fruit, and Danish pastry at the back of the room. "Let's take seats and get going," he commands his team.

After everyone is seated, Mark begins to talk. His approach is low-key, almost conversational. He thanks the team for coming to the session and being prompt. "I appreciate the fact that all of us have much to do back at the office and plant," he says, "but over the past two weeks, I have come to believe that sales and operations planning is the single most important initiative our company needs to implement at this time."

Mark explains that the purpose of the class is not just to educate. It is to stimulate action. His expectation is that the education session will prepare the team to implement sales and operations planning and to understand each individual manager's role in the process. "I expect each of us to do our individual part to enable this process to be implemented quickly," he says.

Next, Mark makes several personal comments. He thanks Susan for her help in making arrangements for the session and setting up the room. He thanks Janis Novak for recommending that he look into sales and operations planning. He also notes that Jack Baxter had planned to attend the session but was called away at the last moment.

"Before turning over the session to Ross and Nolan, I want to make one point," Mark says. "I believe that our company has quality products. We have good, hardworking people as employees. We have a clear market opportunity. The fact is, however, we have not been meeting our goals or our commitments to the corporation. I believe it is lack of integration between functions, being out of sync, that has primarily caused much of our poor performance and individual frustration. It is my belief that if we do sales and operations planning well, it will greatly improve our company performance. And it will help build a stronger management team working together to move the company forward. I will accept nothing less."

On that note, Mark gestures to Ross to take over and finds a seat next to Sam Wente, the sales director. Mark scans his team. Yes, he believes he has good players in all positions. The issue is whether they all can, all will, work together in harmony.

The fact that everyone seems to blame someone else for Universal Products' problems still bothers Mark considerably. Ross has told him that the sales and operations planning process will reduce that problem significantly. He sure hopes Ross is right.

Ross is full of energy as he stands in front of the room. "Good morning!" he says heartily.

The management team responds with a weak, "Good morning," in return.

"Let's try that again," Ross says. "Good morning!"

This time everyone responds in unison with vigor, "Good morning!"

Satisfied, Ross moves on. "I just wanted to make sure everyone is awake and ready to go," he says. "Nolan and I have met all of you before, so introductions are unnecessary this morning. Let me explain the session logistics."

He and Nolan will present sections of the material. They also will be conducting the managers' class over the following two days. He points out that the class reference book contains the visual material presented in class, so it is unnecessary to take copious notes.

Ross also points out that this is the management team's session, not his or Nolan's session. "Therefore, I would like you to stop me to ask questions at any time during my presentation," he says. "If I say things you don't understand, if I use jargon you are unfamiliar with, if you disagree with what I say, please stop me. Comment. Ask questions. As Mark said in his introduction, the purpose of this session is not just education. It is to prepare you to take action, to implement the process known as sales and operations planning. We expect you to go through your first sales and operations planning cycle next month."

Sam Wente raises his hand. "Do you really mean next month? Am I supposed to have a forecast in place by next month?"

"Yes, Sam, I do mean next month," Ross replies. "The scope of what can effectively be handled the first month will be discussed and agreed upon, but I want you to go through the process steps as quickly as is practical. Unless there are mitigating circumstances, that will be next month."

Sam's question creates an opportunity for Ross to make a point he feels is essential for the team to understand — the earlier the better. "Nolan and I are here to help you get the sales and operations planning process up and running immediately," he says, "so do ask questions. During the course of this session, Nolan and I will frequently ask whether there are any questions or concerns. If we hear no response, we will assume that silence is approval. By that, I mean your silence indicates that you heard what we said, understood what we said, and agreed with what we said. We use this approach to help ensure that as we implement, we minimize the possibility that someone will say, 'I didn't agree to that,' or 'I didn't understand that.' This is serious business, and I want to start out with a common understanding that each of us, collectively and individually, will do our part to make the process work." Ross pauses for a moment to allow his point to sink in with the team members.

Susan Callahan, the planning manager, raises her hand. "Will we complete the process design today?"

Ross explains that he and Nolan will be looking for the team to agree on some high-level process concepts and principles as well as on some high-level roles and responsibilities. The process design will not be completed until after a design workshop that will follow the managers' class. "However, as the executive team, you will have a pretty clear picture or vision of the new process by the end of today," he says.

"When will this process affect what we actually do? And how many months will it be before we see some effect of the implementation of the process?" Jim Simpson, the manufacturing director, asks.

"If you follow the implementation method which we prescribe," Ross replies, "you will certainly begin seeing the effect of the process by cycle three, which is in three months. However, most companies see some benefit starting in cycle one. That is next month."

Janis Novak, the controller, raises her hand. "How soon will I see the process affect my financial forecast?"

"That's an excellent question," Ross comments. "With your permission, I would prefer to hold my answer on that until later in the day. After I explain the implementation process, the answer will become obvious. However, let me capture that question on the flip chart to make sure I do not fail to answer it later."

After writing on the flip chart at the side of the room, Ross turns to address his audience. "Are there any other specific issues or questions I should capture before I start the presentation? I want to make sure that we get your questions answered."

Nolan, standing at the back of the room, asks a leading question. "What software support is required to accomplish the task? Do we need to get corporate involved for software support, and will that slow us down?"

Ross smiles knowingly and says, "Thanks for bringing up the software issue." He explains that minimal software support is required to get started using the methodology that will be presented today. A software template will be provided by EMI to help get things going quickly.

"At EMI, we have been working to shorten the implementation process time to help clients improve their time to results," Ross says. "We have found over time that software support is a constraint and that traditional spreadsheets, while they will work, are difficult to maintain. You may choose to use some other presentation software tool, but our template gives you a good model to follow."

Ross is pleased with the number of questions. It demonstrates the level of interest. The questions also will uncover any early resistance. The questions continue.

"Will we learn about forecasting today?" Sam asks.

"I will present forecasting, which I prefer to call demand planning, this afternoon," Ross explains. "You will get an executive overview today, but you and your sales and marketing team will need additional education and training in demand planning."

"What about purchasing?" Anita Cooper, the purchasing manager, asks. "As you know, we seem to be at the end of the whip. All the planning problems seem to end up in purchasing as expediting problems. Will we discuss that today?"

Ross observes that purchasing, like the factory floor, gets all of the expediting caused by poor visibility and poor planning. "We will talk about that conceptually, but we will not get into the level of detail I know you are looking for today," he says. "We can discuss this issue separately after we get the process design completed if you wish."

Mark feels the need to interrupt the questions. "Ross, I think we need to get started. I am sure most of these questions will surface throughout the day. I do want to encourage the questions, but let us get an understanding of the basics first. Okay?"

■ ■ ■

Ross walks into the center of the u-shaped tables and scans the faces in the room. He explains to the group that the class will start with the high-level concepts of sales and operations planning and work down to the detail.

One objective of the class is to get a common understanding of sales and operations planning when it is operated in an industry best practices manner. The second objective of the class is to gain agreement in concept as to how Universal Products will operate sales and operations planning.

Ross displays on the overhead projector a list of companies that use sales and operations planning. The list includes Caterpillar, Procter & Gamble, Lockheed Martin, Merck, Ericsson, Reilly Chemicals, ICI, Zeneca, Chevron, DuPont, Dow, Solar Turbines, Lufkin Gear, Bently Nevada Corporation, Keystone International, Heinz Canada, Delicato Vineyards, Novartis, Motorola, Kodak, Allied Signal–Honeywell, Flowserve, and EMI.

"There are companies in all industries, big and small, making all sorts of different products, that use sales and operations planning," he explains. "Please note that not all the companies mentioned use the process in all divisions, nor do all companies operate it at the same level of proficiency. Some companies call their sales and operations planning process by some other name. For example, Allied Signal calls its SIOP, with the 'I' standing for inventory."

Ross steps back and points at the list of companies on the screen. "Why do so many companies implement sales and operations planning?" he asks. "Because it is organized common sense," he answers.

He steps back toward his audience. He notes that most people relate to the phrase "common sense." However, the key word is *organized.*

The power of sales and operations planning comes from integrating multiple functions and disciplines in an organized, synchronized, and disciplined manner. Through this integration, problems and opportunities surface with sufficient visibility and in sufficient time to enable management to effectively and efficiently do something about them.

Susan Callahan, the planning manager, shifts in her chair and raises her hand. "Does the sales and operations planning process operate the same in all those different companies?" she asks.

"That is a good question," Ross replies. "Some fundamental things are the same, but each company tailors the process for its business. Later on, I will present the fundamentals and give some examples of how companies have tailored their processes differently."

Ross clicks the mouse to advance the computer to the next slide. He explains that most published materials highlight improvements in operating performance that result from implementing sales and operations planning. Those improvements are legitimate. Most companies achieve simultaneous improvements in customer service, inventory turns, manufacturing costs, and purchased materials costs.

"However, it is my observation and belief," Ross states, "that the biggest benefits from implementing sales and operations planning come from a better understanding of the customer and market opportunities coupled with an improved understanding of the company's current capabilities. This understanding and visibility enables improved, more timely tactical and strategic choices and changes. The real benefits of sales and operations planning come in gains in market position and market share as well as increased profitability and improvements in the company's capabilities."

Ray Guy, the final assembly manager, interrupts without raising his hand. "What made the companies you mentioned implement sales and operations planning? They obviously didn't always use it."

Ross answers that most companies, unfortunately, implement it when they find they have a significant performance problem. Usually, something has changed in their business that creates the problem. Sometimes the competition has figured out how to deliver quicker, more reliably, at a lower cost. Other times, shareholders have expressed a need to get a better return on invested capital. Sometimes it is triggered by a need in a particular area, like reducing inventory or improving customer service. Still other times, the obvious dysfunction in the organization causes management to take action. Sometimes it is the recognition of a glaring weakness in executing the company's strategy. Some progressive companies implement it because they know their growth will be stifled without it.

Ross refers to a book published a number of years ago, *The Discipline of Market Leaders* by Michael Treacy and Fred Wiersema. The book is the result of a study by the authors to better understand what market leaders did to sustain their market leadership position.

One of the key findings of the authors is that companies which sustain market leadership focus on one of three value disciplines: product leadership, client intimacy, or operational excellence. Through this focus, companies strive to become the best in their chosen value discipline.

This approach is similar to what Harvard Professor Michael Porter presents as three broad positioning alternatives in his book *Competitive Strategy*. He defines the positioning alternatives as product differentiator, the low-cost leader, or the nicher.

Treacy and Wiersema make another observation that is even more powerful than focusing on a value discipline. The authors found that once a company has focused on a value discipline, it must be at least competent in the other two value disciplines to sustain market leadership. Balance is essential for sustained market success.

"Let me give you an example of this concept," Ross says, "as a way to demonstrate why companies implement sales and operations planning. I have a client that clearly is focused on product leadership. I find this is often the case in business-to-business product companies, or companies that make products for sale to other companies as opposed to companies that make goods to sell to consumers.

This client has the best products and markets them at a fair price. However, some of its largest potential customers, or I should say ex-customers, have blackballed the company. It has been eliminated from the list of acceptable suppliers. Why?"

Susan Callahan, the planning manager, quickly responds. "Because the company has poor quality or delivery?"

"Exactly," Ross replies, smiling at Susan. "In this case, quality is not the issue. My client leads the industry in quality, but is unreliable in delivery. The company has had a product focus, but it has been out of balance in its operational excellence. It must change its management processes so that delivery becomes a nonissue. Or better yet, make it a competitive advantage."

"That sounds like us," says Sam Wente, the sales director. "We have the best product on the market. Our quality is better than the competition. Don't let those manufacturing types, Jim and Ray, hear me say that, or Peter in engineering either. They will get big heads. But we cannot deliver. Even though we are below our revenue budget, we cannot promise delivery or availability with any confidence that the promise will be met."

"And that's why we are here," Ross replies. "Let me ask you a question. If you could deliver on time 98 to 100 percent of the time, would that increase your sales?"

"Absolutely," Sam says. "We are missing so many opportunities. Just the improvement in my sales organization's morale would bring in more business."

"Let me tell a story about myself," Ross says. He tells the group of the time he worked for a manufacturer of industrial products. The company had the best product on the market and most of the available market share for its specialty product. Demand was great.

"We had one minor problem," Ross explains. "The orders were coming in faster than we could deliver the product. Our lead times increased. We were doing all sorts of extra things in operations to try to deliver. We had expediters expediting expediters. We were working overtime and weekends, and we subcontracted what we could. The harder we tried, the worse it seemed to get. Our costs were going up as a result of all the extra effort, and we raised our prices.

Then, for the first time, we faced some very formidable competitors. We knew we had to do something different."

Ross tells the group that the company implemented an integrated planning and control system, which was called manufacturing resource planning, or MRP II, at the time. Today, it might be called enterprise resource planning, or ERP.

"More important than what we called it, *we changed the processes by which we managed the business,*" Ross says. "One of the most important things we did was to implement sales and operations planning as part of the integrated planning and control system. In essence, we were working on becoming competent in operational excellence to complement our product leadership."

Ross goes on to explain that he was vice-president of sales and marketing for this company and was responsible for the forecast. He looks at Sam as he shares his experience.

"I didn't know anything about forecasting. My entire organization was focused on the technical aspects of our products. A wonderful thing happened. As we implemented sales and operations planning, the need to improve our forecast of demand became readily apparent.

"As we worked to improve our forecasts, we found that a better understanding of the market and our customers was required. We developed a sales and marketing communication process. The result was an improvement in marketing and sales planning and execution. We also improved our inputs for product development.

"This all resulted in growth of the business and improved market share. Using the Treacy and Wiersema model, when we began to forecast, we added some of the characteristics of customer intimacy. Ultimately, we learned that when all three value disciplines work together, the results can be fabulous."

Mark Ryan feels the need to jump in and reinforce Ross's point. "Let me summarize to see if I understand what you are saying," he says. "The market leaders pick one of the value disciplines — either product leadership, or operational excellence, or customer intimacy — and focus on that area in order to excel and beat the competition. But to focus on just one of those value disciplines without properly addressing the other two is risky and may cause problems with customers. We need to be adequate in the other two value disciplines we have not chosen as our primary area of focus."

Ross nods his head approvingly. "That's right, and I would make one other point. I believe you can excel over your competition in more than one value discipline. I expect my clients to have excellent, quality products at fair prices with confidence in product availability and delivery. Sales and operations planning generally is categorized under operational excellence, but it has a direct link to company strategy. It will bring to the surface the kinds of issues, such as marketing strategy and tactics for getting closer to the customers, that we just discussed."

Ross brings up another book, *Competing for the Future* by Gary Hamel and

C.K. Prahalad. The authors point out that many companies have spent years focused on operational excellence by using reengineering to attempt to improve quality and lower their costs. In many cases, this focus has meant the exclusion of addressing strategies for growth. Companies have ignored the other value propositions. Many of these companies have found themselves unprepared to properly meet their shareholders' expectations for growth.

"The point I am trying to make is that *management* is about balance," Ross explains. "Sales and operations planning is a process for management to achieve that balance. It is a process that stimulates strategic management and the linking of execution to agreed-upon strategic choices." He can see that the group is trying to digest his last point.

Janis Novak, the controller, places her hand on her chin and looks across the room thoughtfully. "Did I understand you to say, Ross, that a company could excel in more than one value discipline?" she asks. "Isn't that counter to the fundamental notion of focusing?"

"Yes, that's what I said, and yes, you are correct regarding focus," Ross replies. He explains that the definition of the word "focus" implies concentrating on one thing. It further implicitly implies that one should not focus on many things simultaneously. What must be considered are the resources required to implement many things simultaneously.

Ross raises himself up to his full six feet and states forcefully, "I contend that most companies do a poor job of managing their strategic initiatives because they have not made the tough management choices as to what they are *not* going to do. The key issue is priority and timing. Every company has limited resources. So the question is what to work on first. It is far better to choose what is most important for the company now. Focus on that item and get it done. What I see is many companies trying to do too many things at the same time and ending up doing none of them well."

Ross pauses, then softens his voice. "Back to your question, Janis. If a company implements completely and properly, it can be excellent at multiple value disciplines when compared to the competition. This should involve a strategic discussion that addresses customer needs, competition, technology, shareholder expectations, resources, etc."

He goes on to explain that market leaders have one of the value disciplines as the primary driver. This influences the fundamental structure and infrastructure of the company. However, the other two value disciplines should not be ignored.

"But here is the good news," Ross says. "If you implement sales and operations planning as I recommend, you will have a forum to deal with value disciplines and other strategic issues on a *regular and routine* basis."

Ross looks around the room. The managers are quiet and thoughtful. He has given them plenty to think about as a fundamental grounding. "Let's take a ten-minute break," he says.

People get up, stretch, and head out the door. Mark, however, stays behind and pulls Ross to the side. "I'm concerned we are spending too much time talking about things other than the sales and operations planning process. Are we going to have enough time to get everything done we need to do today?"

Mark's question is not uncommon at this point in the class. "We will get done what we need to get done today," Ross replies. "It is important to cover the high-level material as well the detail. With your prompting, I will get into the characteristics of the sales and operations planning process after the break. Do you have any other concerns?"

"No," Mark answers. "I just want to make sure we get to the meat of the subject today."

Ross and Mark go outside for a breath of fresh air. It is a beautiful day. The mountain air is clean and crisp. A few fluffy clouds in the distance create shadows on the lower foothills and distant plains.

Ross comments to Mark that Peter Newfeld, the product development/engineering director, has been very quiet. "Is there a reason to be concerned? Should I actively seek his participation?" Ross asks.

"I noticed that as well," Mark says. "I would not be concerned yet. Peter is the strong, silent type. We should just wait and see how it goes. If he does not begin to participate, we will need to discuss how to bring him more into the discussions."

Satisfied, Ross heads back to the meeting room. He is relieved to see that Nolan is talking with Peter. Nolan will let Ross know if Peter has any criticisms or reservations.

Ross stands in front of the computer and browses through the overheads for the next section of his presentation. There are several fundamental principles he wants to discuss in some detail before getting to the characteristics of sales and operations planning.

■ ■ ■

As people take their seats again, Ross begins to talk. He explains that before getting into the details of the sales and operations planning process, he wants to introduce a couple of additional concepts.

He clicks the mouse and advances the slide presentation. Pointing to the circles in the graphic (Figure 7), Ross explains that in his experience, he has found that people, process, and tools must all three work together to achieve effective management.

The *people* circle represents that whatever the management process, it is operated by people. They need to be knowledgeable, trained, and understand what is expected of them. They also need to operate the process in accordance with agreed-upon principles, policies, and procedures.

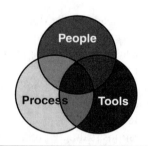

Figure 7   Business Excellence Elements (Copyright Oliver Wight International. Reproduced with permission.)

The *process* circle represents the need for a defined process. This defined process includes process steps, inputs, outputs, defined roles and responsibilities, and measurements.

The *tools* circle represents the need to provide people with the tools necessary to fulfill their part in the process. These tools may include hardware, software, manuals, communication systems, etc.

"The notion is that when these three elements work in concert, represented by the overlap of the circles, you can achieve excellent results," Ross says. He then relates sales and operations planning to the three circles. Sales and operations planning is fundamentally a management process. It is designed to help people better manage the business. It requires some limited number of tools, mostly communication tools and presentation software. For maximum results, it operates under a set of fundamental principles or behaviors.

To illustrate the next point, Ross clicks the mouse and advances to the next graphic (Figure 8). "Let me give you an example of what I'm talking about," he says. He points to the three circles and tells the class that the concept represented by the three circles was introduced by the author Thomas E. Wallace while speaking about project management many years ago.

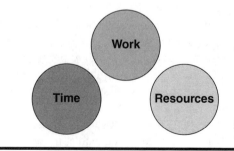

Figure 8   Three Control Variables

The circles represent knobs. When managing a company, or a project, there are three knobs to control. The first knob is the *work,* which is defined as what is to be done. It implies volume of work and the scope of work to be achieved.

The second knob is *time.* It refers to the amount of time available to do the work and is usually expressed as a schedule. This is when the work is to be performed and completed.

The third knob is *resources.* It refers to the resources available in the organization to accomplish the task. Resources may be people, machinery, materials, suppliers, cash, etc.

Ross explains that there are principles which apply to the knobs. First, the three knobs should be in balance. This means, for example, that the scope of the work should not exceed the resources available to complete the work in the defined time frame.

The second principle to remember is that to achieve excellent results, one knob cannot be changed without changing at least one of the other two knobs. This means, for example, that if the time frame to accomplish the work is to be accelerated, then either the scope of the work must be changed or additional resources must be acquired.

"I have seen so many companies where management does not recognize this fundamental principle," Ross says, pointing to the knobs on the screen. He explains that management operates with insufficient information, and management direction is often limited to statements like "work harder," "do the best you can," or "find the individual who's the problem."

"That type of management direction is futile," Ross comments. "It does not address the root issues at hand and almost never results in the work getting done on schedule."

Ross points to the three circles again. "Think about these three knobs in the context of your environment. If there is more work than time and resources, and management is not focused on balancing the work, time, and resources, what happens? The end result, no matter how hard you work, is missed shipments, unhappy customers, and poor financial results."

Ross pauses to let his point to sink in. "Before we move on, I would like each of you to agree that Universal Products will operate according to the principle of the three knobs. You will operate with work, time, and resources in balance, and you will not change one of the knobs without changing at least one of the other two."

He waits for people to nod their assent or voice their commitment. Peter Newfeld does neither. He raises his hand and asks in his soft-spoken voice, "Do you mean that if engineering is properly in balance in terms of work, schedule, and resources, then if Sam or Mark wants to add something else to engineering's workload, he must agree to a change in other work, schedule, or resources?"

"You're absolutely correct," Ross replies, "unless you have already planned for the work, which is also known as a forecast, and therefore have already planned for the resources to do the work and have scheduled the work. In this case, the forecast is converted to an actual order for the work to be performed. You would release the resources to do that work according to the schedule. But if you have not planned or forecasted the work and if there is not enough resource to accomplish the change in work, the knobs are out of balance, and that out-of-balance situation must be resolved."

Mark Ryan's discomfort is visible. "Aren't there times when we must add work in engineering to satisfy customers? We do not always have a choice," he says.

"I disagree," Ross replies. "You always have a choice. Many companies do not have the process or the information to effectively make the choice. I'm suggesting that you establish a process that makes visible the choices that you have. Then make a decision."

Anita Cooper, the purchasing manager, raises her hand. "It is like when I go to a supplier for something I need inside lead time. My good suppliers will give me a choice. Often, they will say they can meet our new requirement if we give them relief on the delivery of one or more of the existing orders. Or they might say they can meet our delivery, but they must do it on overtime and we will have to pay a premium. So they ask for a premium special-handling charge. In essence, they are turning the knobs. And they are giving me a choice."

"That is an excellent example," Ross says. "It is interesting that we will deal with our suppliers in that manner, but we won't afford the same courtesy to our inside suppliers, that is, the engineering and manufacturing groups within our own company."

Mark is noticeably annoyed. "But no one ever says they can't get it done. They just say yes."

"There is a fundamental rule in manufacturing and engineering," Ross says. "This rule states that if you are not armed with the facts, the only answer you can give is yes." He explains that the crux of the issue is to have the information to know the consequences of saying yes. In other words, you need to have the information necessary to understand the business choices.

An important corollary is that with the right information, people almost never have to say no. Rather, they say, "Here are the choices and consequences."

Ross points to the three knobs on the screen again. "With the right information, what happens when we say yes without turning one of the knobs on purpose? I will tell you. One of the knobs turns by accident. We may make one delivery, but at the expense of the delivery of other orders. And this happens with no visibility and no conversation about which orders will slip. I like to call this the MBA process or the management-by-accident process."

Ross observes everyone in the room thinking about what he has said. He is unsure whether they have grasped the concept of the three knobs and are ready to commit to keeping the three knobs in balance.

"Let me try again," he says. "I would like this management team to agree that at Universal Products, if the work, the schedule, or the resources change, you will recognize the need to adjust at least one of the other two elements. Mark, will you support that?"

Ross has put Mark on the spot. Mark is not yet completely comfortable with the principle, but believes he has to trust Ross's experience. "I will support the principle with the caveat that we must have the information to understand the change," Mark replies.

"Great. Is everyone else okay with that?" Ross asks. There is no response. "Okay then, silence is approval. You heard the issue, you understand the issue, and you agree."

"Now I see how this 'silence is approval' works," Janis Novak comments.

No one voices disapproval, and Ross is ready to move on to the principle of regularly and routinely satisfying customer expectations.

■ ■ ■

The next topic, Ross knows, will generate discussion. "I will now introduce another fundamental principle of a best practice in the sales and operations planning process," he says. "Sales and operations planning is a demand-driven process. The objective is to *regularly and routinely* satisfy all customers' expectations all of the time."

Sam Wente, the sales director, leans back in his chair with a satisfied expression on his face. "I sign up for that one," he says loudly. "Ross, this is good stuff!"

"Be careful," Ross warns. "You may just get what you ask for. Any comments from anyone on the principle of regularly and routinely satisfying all customers?"

Ray Guy, the final assembly manager, quickly responds. "That's the rule we are operating under now. And it is causing us to do crazy things in manufacturing and final assembly. I don't buy it!"

Jim Simpson, the manufacturing director, is quick to second Ray's statement. "I agree with Ray, unless I don't understand the concept."

Mark Ryan intervenes before the discussion gets heated. He is impressed with Ross's ability to stir things up. "Ross, there is obviously more to this. Please go on."

Ross picks up Mark's cue. "First, let me try the phrase 'meet customer expectations.' Does anyone have any problem with that phrase?"

There is no response. "Silence is approval," Ross says.

"Not so fast," says Sam. "I would like to say 'meets or exceeds customer expectations.' We want to delight the customer."

"I won't argue with that," Ross replies. "Anyone else?"

No one has anything to add. But Ross is not ready to move off the point. "Sam, here is my question for you," he says. "What are your customers' expectations? Let's start with something simple, like delivery lead time."

Sam is a little slower in replying. "Well, for sure they want shorter lead times than we are giving them now. Mostly they want us to deliver when we say we will."

"Sam, I don't want you to think I'm picking on you, but I have two observations," Ross says. He tells the group that Sam responded the way most people in sales initially answer the question about customers' delivery expectations. The answer Sam gave was "shorter" lead times, yet that is of little value in planning. Part of the sales and operations planning process is identifying and quantifying customer expectations. Those expectations will vary by product, by market, and by customer. Not only do customer expectations vary between products, but they also change over time.

"Customer expectations are influenced by the competition, the economy, and who knows what else," Ross explains. "However, if we don't know what the customers' expectations are, how do we know if we are meeting them?"

Sam is a bit defensive. "I can quantify the expectations if that is what you are saying."

"That is great, Sam," Ross replies. "Understanding what customers want is part of being demand driven. If we know what customers want and expect, we can develop both strategies and tactics to support their wants and needs."

Ross sits on the edge of the table in the front of the room. "The second point I want to make, Sam, relates to your comment that customers want you to deliver when you say you will." He explains that there is another principle the Universal Products management team needs to agree upon — the people on the management team will *do what we say we are going to do.*

"This implies you will do whatever the task *when* you say you will do it," Ross says. He mentions that one of his daughter's college professors told her that the secret to success in business is to *"just do what you say you are going to do."*

"Think about that statement for a moment," Ross tells the group. "There's a lot of truth to it. Think about it from your personal perspective, in business or at home. When problems occur, it is often because we didn't do what we said we were going to do."

Ross pauses and looks at the management team. "Let me get a consensus on the principle. We will do what we say we are going to do. Any comments?"

Peter Newfeld's hand shoots up. "Let me see if I understand what you are saying using my previous example of engineering. Let's say I am in balance with work, schedule, and resources, and I am asked to do additional work. If I say yes, I must be able to do the additional work as well as meet all my previous commitments because that is what I said I was going to do."

"That's right," Ross says.

"And if I can't do all the previous work and the new work on schedule with the authorized resources," Peter continues, "I shouldn't say I will do the new work. The issue that the work cannot be performed on time surfaces by using these basic principles. This forces a choice or a decision."

"Wait a minute," Sam says, sitting upright. "It sounds like we just gave engineering the ability to say no to customer needs."

"That's a good observation, Sam," Ross replies, "but behaviorally we will agree as a team to not say no. Peter, and anyone else for that matter, should say, 'I can do it if…perhaps with additional resources' or '…perhaps if you change the schedule on some previous commitment.' The objective is to say yes, not no. Why? Because we have an overriding objective to meet customer expectations."

By the expression on Sam's face, it is obvious that the concept is beginning to sink in. "So in Peter's example," he says, "he would be predisposed to say, 'Yes, if….' With that response, it compels us to adjust the knobs, to make choices; in other words, to make an informed decision."

"Or to say no to the customer," Ross explains. "That is also one of our choices. I would hope it would be the last choice, but it is a choice nonetheless."

As Mark listens to the dialogue, he realizes that Ross is describing an effective management process using very simple principles, or mechanics. He raises his hand. "Ross, it is my observation that all of these principles you are asking us to agree on tie together."

"You are absolutely correct," Ross replies. "And, Mark, if you go back to the people, process, and tools diagram, most of what we have been talking about falls into the people circle. Yet companies spend most of their money on the tools circle. Just think how much you spent for your enterprise resource planning system. It's obviously not giving you the benefits you should be getting. Why?"

"Because we didn't address the people and process circles as we should have?" Mark answers tentatively.

"That's correct," Ross says. He shifts his focus to the rest of the group. "I am still trying to get you to agree to the principle of regularly and routinely satisfying or exceeding all customers' expectations all of the time."

He can see that the group is not truly ready to commit to that principle and says, "Maybe this example will help. Let's discuss zero defects." He explains that it is highly unlikely that companies are able to achieve zero defects 100 percent of the time, but the goal should be to continuously strive to achieve zero defects results in incremental and continuous improvements.

Ross shifts back to the matter at hand — getting agreement on the principle to regularly and routinely satisfy or exceed all customer expectations all of the time. "Bear in mind that this principle is a two-edged sword," he says. "Not only does it create a responsibility for the supply side of the business to operate and execute extremely well, but it also creates a responsibility for the demand side of the organization to appropriately create and influence customer expectations."

Ross turns toward Sam and continues. "Suppose the corporation siphons off cash to the point where a new product which you counted on for this year cannot be completed. Suppose you have already done a limited product introduction announcement. What should be done?"

"I would fight like hell to get the money from corporate to complete the product development and introduction," Sam replies forcefully.

"I agree," says Ross, "but for sake of argument, let's say you have tried that and corporate won't budge. What should be done?"

Sam is obviously thinking through the options and does not reply immediately. Finally, he says, "I guess I would have to change my customers' expectations. Be honest and let them know."

"That's exactly correct," Ross says. He's not through, however, illustrating his point. "Suppose you have a product that can be sold in greater volume than you have the capacity to produce. It appears that this capacity issue is going to be long term, and you will never be able to meet market demand. What should you do?"

Sam does not hesitate in answering, "We would have to decide who will get the product and who won't get the product."

Ross nods in agreement. "And presumably, you would communicate this decision to your customers and your sales force. In essence, you are choosing your customers, and you are committing to service them — to meet their expectations and to do what you say you are going to do."

Ross goes on to explain that choosing customers can be extremely difficult, and it is not what companies ideally want to do. Companies want to service the bigger market, but because of the constraints, such as capacity, they are forced into choices.

"If you do not overtly make the choice, what happens?" Ross asks.

Anita Cooper, the purchasing manager, thrusts her hand up. "Let me answer that because it happens to me with our poorly performing suppliers. The sales force sells me on the product. I order it, but I don't get delivery. The supplier is not doing what its sales force said it would do."

"And then what do you do?" Ross asks.

"I find an alternate supplier or go to engineering for an alternate item to meet the need. And I stop buying from the poorly performing supplier," Anita replies.

Ross slowly observes each member of the group. "What do you say? Can we agree on the objective to regularly and routinely satisfy all customer expectations all the time?"

Mark Ryan has sat quietly during this discussion. He feels it is time for him to assume a leadership role. "Let me answer. The answer is yes. This is our objective. But one last question. Ross, you continue to say 'regularly and routinely.' Why? What do you mean?"

"Good question," Ross responds. "By regularly and routinely, I mean that the supply side of the business is properly resourced or, in other words, properly prepared to handle the business. Consequently, manufacturing costs go down, material costs go down, transportation costs go down, quality goes up, and the quality of life for people on the supply side of the business is tremendously improved."

"Just the supply side? What about the demand side?" Mark asks.

"People on the demand side see similar kinds of improvements. Because the product is on time or available, they find it easier to sell. The salespeople's personal credibility with customers goes up. Their time is spent selling instead of expediting and apologizing. The people in sales feel better about their company and their jobs."

Ross scans the group one more time. "Any questions?" The room is silent. "If there are no further comments or questions, let's take another break. Ten minutes, please."

■ ■ ■

During the break, Mark Ryan observes his team. The room is humming with voices. Team members are grouped in clusters of two or three, animatedly talking about what they have learned so far in the session.

He overhears team members using words like "do what you say you are going to do," "the three knobs: work, schedule, and resources," "demand-driven customer expectations," and "regularly and routinely." Their conversations focus on how that would work at Universal Products.

Mark feels good about what he hears. The team obviously is taking the class and sales and operations planning seriously.

Standing by himself, Mark almost wishes that Jack Baxter, the corporate president, had been able to attend the session. It would have been good for him to learn the concepts of sales and operations planning directly.

Ross interrupts Mark's thoughts. "I had expected to get into the sales and operations planning process by now, but the dialogue with your staff was extremely important. I will start immediately after this break." Ross is obviously concerned about Mark's previous comment about getting into the meat of the process.

"You're doing fine," Mark replies. "That was an important exchange we just had. You know what you are doing. I will follow your lead."

"I have a concern about Susan," Ross says. He looks over at Susan Callahan, the planning manager. She is talking quietly with Ray Guy, the final assembly manager. "She has not said much during the discussions. You may want to talk with her during lunch to make sure she is okay with what is being presented."

"Will do," Mark replies.

"I think Peter is doing fine now," Ross observes. "Do you agree?"

"Absolutely," Mark says. "He is participating and asking good questions."

Ross excuses himself. "I need to use the rest room before we get started again." He leaves Mark observing his team, thinking about each member and how he or she will respond to this new way of doing business that is being introduced today.

■ ■ ■

Mark Ryan watches Ross Peterson as he reenters the room. He takes measure of the man as Ross stands at the computer and clicks through the first few visuals for the next section of the class. Ross demonstrates confidence, which Mark assumes comes from doing this kind of work for nearly fifteen years.

Ross glances at his watch. Mark does the same. It has been ten minutes exactly. Ross begins to speak in a loud voice. Mark's staff members are still talking. Slowly, their conversations trail off, and they take their seats.

"We will now finally begin the discussion of the sales and operations planning process, its characteristics, the essential elements for it to work, and roles and responsibilities," Ross continues.

He walks to the table where Susan Callahan, the planning manager, is seated. "Before we start," Ross says, lowering his voice, "I want to check with Susan to make sure she concurs with the principles we just discussed."

Mark looks up in surprise. He thought Ross wanted him to talk to Susan during lunch. Ross obviously has taken a different tack. Mark leans back in his chair, curious to see how Ross's approach works out.

"Susan, you have been very quiet," Ross says. "I know you are certified by the American Production and Inventory Control Society and understand most of what I have been presenting, but do you have any issues before I start?"

By her body language, Susan exhibits no evidence of discomfort. She answers Ross's question directly. "I've been quiet mostly because my department is doing what you have been saying. I am a little surprised that your assessment and this class have not acknowledged what we already do. As you know from my conversations with you and Nolan, I believe in the principles you are presenting, and I believe that my organization lives by them."

Mark is glad that Ross chose to approach Susan during the class session. Susan's response on one level is a challenge to Ross. Why didn't he acknowledge Susan and her department's expertise in planning? Mark wonders how Ross will respond to Susan's challenge.

Ross does not appear surprised or flustered by Susan's response. "Thank you for being so direct, Susan," he replies. "Let me take a moment to share my experience."

He turns away from Susan and addresses the group at large. "Often, the planning organization, or whatever it is called — materials management, supply chain management, production and inventory control, etc., knows what needs to be done, but has no control to make it happen. Susan, if all your people are living up to the principles that we have talked about this morning — *and* the organization did what planning told it to do, we would not be here today. Let me give you an example."

Ross explains that in almost every company he visits, there is some individual or group of people who the company views as being responsible for inventory. It is as if they work in shirts imprinted with a big *I,* which stands for inventory.

"If the inventory gets too large," Ross says, "management takes these people out back and flogs them. If the inventory is insufficient to support customer deliveries, management takes them out back and flogs them."

"Here is the issue," Ross continues. "These people, at any particular point in time, have the least control of inventory of anyone in the company." He explains that inventory is the result of what the company sells, makes, and buys. Planning does not sell, make, or buy anything. Therefore, the current inventory level is a function of what was sold, what was made, and what was bought.

Ross addresses Susan again. "Does sales sell what you tell it to sell? Does manufacturing make what you ask it to make? Does purchasing buy what you tell it to buy? Or do they make many independent decisions on all of those issues?"

Susan is quick with her answer. "I develop plans that manufacturing and purchasing should follow. My biggest problem is that I can't tell sales what to sell. So what I tell manufacturing and purchasing to do is overridden by what is being sold."

"You are saying that you do not actually control what happens in the factory or in purchasing," Ross says, "even though you and your planning organization operate to the principles we talked about this morning."

Susan nods her head in agreement.

"So, if Universal Products were to put in a process that got everyone in the organization to do what planning told them to do, would you consider that a good thing?" Ross asks.

"Yes, I would," Susan replies. "But I'm not sure anyone else here would agree to do only what planning told them to do."

Ross smiles. "Suppose it is not the planning organization that tells people what to do, but the executive management team, and perhaps the planning organization helps communicate the executive management team's decisions to the rest of the organization. Would that help?" Ross asks.

"Of course it would," Susan replies.

Ross turns to the group. "That is what sales and operations planning is all about," he says. "It allows the management team to decide what it wishes to do. It addresses the normal conflicts present in any manufacturing and engineering company and gets the people on the executive team signed up to 'do what they say they are going to do.'"

Ross goes on to explain that Effective Management, Inc. is often asked by planning organizations to consult with their companies. They know that the planning organization cannot succeed unless there is a sales and operations planning process in place. They look for help to get the management team to agree to operate with the fundamental sales and operations planning principles in an organized, common sense manner.

Ross addresses Susan again. "After the sales and operations planning design is complete, we will need to revisit whether you believe the entire organization will be operating under the fundamental principles. Let's move on."

Mark Ryan permits himself a sigh of relief. He was unsure where Ross was going with his questions to Susan. He recalls how Ross had told him during his last visit that he may ruffle feathers at times.

He is impressed with Ross's skill in bringing out Susan's perspective and setting the stage for what sales and operations planning is really all about. Mark thinks the group is truly ready to learn about the sales and operations planning process itself.

■ ■ ■

Ross wastes no time in starting to address the fundamentals of the sales and operations planning process. "How does the sales and operations planning process enable the management team to decide what it wishes to do in an organized, common sense manner and then communicate these wishes throughout the organization?" he asks the group.

Without pausing, Ross answers his own question. "By adhering to some basic operating principles, the sales and operations planning process forces opportunities and constraints to surface."

He explains that the management team then acts upon the issues in proper priority or focus. These actions are in concert, with all functions pulling in the same direction on the same priorities, which is called alignment. Also, all the appropriate departmental resources are working on the same priorities, which is called engagement. The process enables management to become *focused, aligned, and engaged,* working on the agreed-upon priorities to support the goals and objectives of the business.

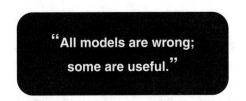

"All models are wrong;

some are useful."

Figure 9   Einstein's Wisdom

Ross shifts gears. He returns to the front of the room and clicks the mouse on his computer to advance to the next visual (Figure 9). "Let me now describe the sales and operations planning process. I want to start with a quote from Albert Einstein." Ross points to the photo of Einstein and reads the quote out loud: "All models are wrong; some are useful."

"The point I am trying to make," Ross says, "is that I will be presenting a fundamental model. To operate sales and operations planning effectively, every company must apply and adapt the model to its own business."

He goes on to explain that it is not uncommon for the implementation of sales and operations planning to highlight fundamental deficiencies in the current management processes. When this occurs, the individual managers or management team should not be blamed. Rather, the discovery of deficiencies should be used to create an understanding of what must be done to better manage the business.

Ross pauses to flip through the pages of the class notebook on the front table. He asks everyone to turn to page 30. As they do so, he clicks the mouse and advances to the next visual (Figure 10).

Ross tells the group that he refers to this graphic as the Kodak model. Originally, the model for sales and operations planning was presented as a time line that went from left to right. When Kodak implemented its sales and operations

Figure 10   Sales and Operations Planning — Basic Model (Copyright Oliver Wight International. Reproduced with permission.)

planning process in Mexico, the management team made the illustration circular. The original model did not show the product review, which was added later. "The management team felt, and I agree, that this model more appropriately represents the replanning nature of sales and operations planning," Ross comments.

Ross steps quickly through the process, using the circular model as a guide. Since sales and operations planning is strategy and demand driven, the process starts with a *product review*. The output of the product review is updated product development and launch plans and anticipated product end-of-life plans. This is followed by the *demand review*. The output of the demand review is an updated demand plan or forecast.

Next is the *supply review*. The output of the supply review is a supply plan, which supports the updated demand plan.

This is followed by the development of the resulting projected pro-forma financials across the planning horizon, which is the output of the *financial review*. For most companies, the planning horizon is at least eighteen months. Finally, the senior management team meets to make any necessary decisions and to agree upon the new plan.

Ross looks out at the group. "Hopefully, this sales and operations planning model looks and feels like organized common sense," he says.

He explains that he believes the circular model reflects the sales and operations planning process more accurately than a linear model because, once started, the planning process goes on forever.

"In fact, the term sales and operations planning is misleading in a small way," he says. "Sales and operations planning is actually a *replanning* process. Every month, or replanning cycle, the management team looks at the business as it knows it *now* and makes business decisions accordingly. I also contend that when sales and operations planning is done effectively, companies can discard their annual planning processes as they are traditionally conducted today."

Janis Novak, the controller, speaks up. "Wait a minute, Ross. I'm obligated, as is the corporation, to provide an annual plan or budget to the board of directors. We report our performance against that plan every quarter. This is a key part of my job. Help me understand what you mean."

Ross explains that the annual planning process, as it is conducted in most companies of any size, is flawed. It is a game. It is an administrative waste of time. Sometime between midyear and year end, the company goes to the marketing and sales organization and asks, "What are you going to sell next year?" The sales organization, knowing that its compensation will be tied to its answer, often provides a conservative, or low, number, in dollars or appropriate currency.

Management observes that the number is not as large as it hoped for and asks sales and marketing to resubmit another projection. Sales and marketing comes in with a less conservative number that management again rejects. Finally, sales and marketing typically will ask, "What number do you want?" Management responds, and sales and marketing reluctantly accepts the number even though it is not based on reality. Rather, it is based on management's desires or wishes. The supply side of the organization is then asked to develop the resource plan to support this optimistic company sales plan.

"Anyone who has ever spent any time in manufacturing or engineering knows that they must ask for far more than they expect to receive," Ross says. "Why? Because multiple entities are competing for a scarce resource called capital. If manufacturing and engineering's resource plan is cut, which invariably it will be, maybe, just maybe, the reduced resource plan will support the real demand, since no one believes the sales plan anyway."

Ross explains that meanwhile the finance organization is faced with a dilemma. The financial people don't believe the sales plan or the resource requests from the supply side of the business. Yet, they must develop a plan against which they will be measured. The general manager, or company president, will also be measured against the financial plan. From the corporate and board of directors' perspective, the financial plan is the general manager's performance commitment.

"The general manager is often deluded into believing he or she is actually contributing to the annual planning process in some positive manner," Ross says, "although often this is not the case. He or she receives poor information from personally motivated individuals. The best he or she can do is second-guess all the numbers and reach an agreement with finance and corporate."

Mark Ryan observes that on this topic, Ross speaks with the force of someone who has a strong belief. He certainly doesn't pussyfoot around, Mark thinks to himself.

No one attempts to interrupt Ross's monologue. "And, of course, all of this effort took multiple months to complete. The end result," he says, "is a new business plan, or budget, that is outdated before it is even published."

Ross explains that the planning started months before the new fiscal year, and things have changed during that time. The annual plan, or budget, ends up being a plan of wishes versus a plan based on reality, which renders it useless for operational planning. The annual plan, or budget, does not have sufficient detail or timeliness to be truly useful for operational planning, yet it is used as the basis for management review in a monthly, or quarterly, review process.

"Quite frankly, I am embarrassed that companies actually pay people a lot of money to do annual planning," Ross declares.

Universal Products' management team remains silent. Ross steps back and takes a deep breath. "Excuse me. I have gotten carried away. It is just that so often I see such wasteful management practices that I have grown to have strong feelings about some of them."

Ross pulls out a newsletter that has been lying on the front table. He tells the group that a telecommunications firm had been in the process of making significant changes to its organization and its management processes.

He points to the banner headline on the front page of the newsletter, which is published for employees, customers, and suppliers. The headline announces that the traditional annual budget preparation and budget negotiations will no longer be the planning process. Rather, the company will now rely on a process of rolling financial planning. "The basis for the rolling financial plan is a global sales and operations planning process," Ross says.

Realizing that there has been little discussion, Ross pauses. "Let me stop and see if there are any questions," he says.

Janis Novak, who started Ross's diatribe, raises her hand. "So how does sales and operations planning replace the annual planning process?" she asks.

"When sales and operations planning is conducted with discipline," Ross replies, "the annual planning process becomes a *significant nonevent*. It is *significant* because the resulting plans from the process create expectations on the part of the board of directors, the shareholders, Wall Street, and other financial constituents. It is a *nonevent* because the resulting annual plan is just another cycle of the sales and operations planning process."

Ross explains that when companies adopt a planning horizon of at least eighteen months, they have up to six sales and operations planning cycles, or six review sessions, before having to commit to next year's annual business plan/budget. He advances the computer to a new visual that illustrates the three to six cycles before committing to next year's annual business plan (Figure 11).

After studying the graph for a few moments, Janis speaks up again. "This graph implies that the operating numbers and the financial numbers are tied together. Does this mean that finance no longer forecasts?"

"That's right," Ross replies, "or at least not the way that finance currently forecasts." He explains that the company will have one set of operational numbers that tie directly to the financials and vice versa. In practice, however, finance's role in forecasting changes significantly. Finance becomes "another view" of the forecast. Finance serves as a devil's advocate, challenging and questioning the sales and operational numbers.

"If there are numbers that you can't believe, the issue surfaces during the sales and operations planning process," Ross says. "Through the process, the management team will arrive at consensus on the operational and financial numbers."

Sam Wente, the sales director, squirms in his seat. "Are you saying that finance has the authority to second-guess the forecast?"

"Authority is probably the wrong word," Ross replies. "I am saying that any member of the management team may challenge the forecast. The sales and operations planning process will ensure consensus on the forecast or demand plan

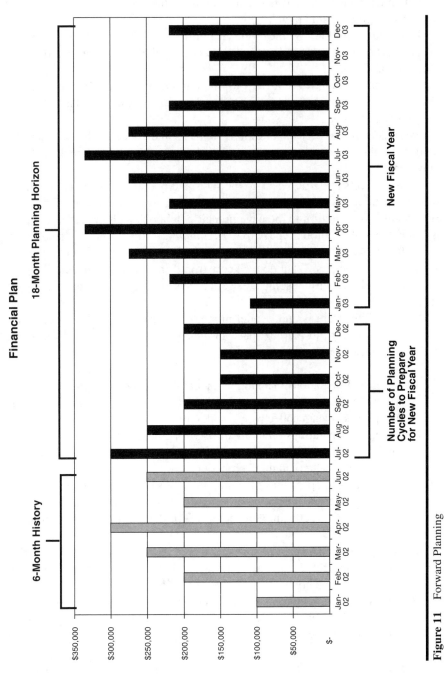

Figure 11   Forward Planning

each month. Once consensus is reached, all departments will operate to support the agreed-upon demand plan."

Ross pauses and surveys the room. He returns his attention to Sam. "This puts the pressure on you, Sam, to develop the best demand plan that you can. It *will be* challenged."

Before continuing, Ross decides to find out whether Mark Ryan is comfortable with what has just transpired. "Do you have any questions, Mark? Are you okay so far?" he asks.

Mark does not expect the question. He has some concerns, but decides that reticence is the best approach for now. "I'm doing just fine," Mark replies. "Let's move on."

Ross redirects the group back to the sales and operations planning model. "I want to spend a few minutes discussing characteristics of the process," he says. He asks the group to turn to the page in their notebooks with the definition published in the ninth edition of the *APICS Dictionary*. It fills the page in small type.

"I prefer using another definition," he says. "Remember, words and sentences are models of thoughts. What do we know from Einstein about models?"

"All models are wrong; some are useful," Susan Callahan, the planning manager, replies.

"That's right. Here is another definition, or another model," Ross says. He asks the class to turn to the next page in their notebooks, where the following definition appears:

- Sales and operations planning is a monthly management process that ensures that the company is *focused, aligned, and engaged* in those efforts the management team collectively decides are the priorities of the enterprise.
- Sales and operations planning deals with continuous change that occurs in the business and is a process to effectively manage ongoing change. In practice it is a "replanning" process.
- The sales and operations planning process is owned by the general manager. It is a cross-functional process and includes all the functions of the company. Correctly implemented, it is a demand- and strategy-driven process.
- The process addresses the management of key company resources in support of anticipated customer demands and expectations, new product development, and company initiatives.
- The sales and operations planning process provides senior management control of the business. It is sophisticated simplicity resulting in organized common sense.

"It is important to understand where sales and operations planning fits relative to the other planning and control processes that take place in a manufacturing or engineering company," Ross says. He refers to the books *Orchestrating Success* by Walter Goddard and Richard Ling, *The Marketing Edge* by George Palmatier and Joseph Shull, and *World Class Production and Inventory Management* by Darryl V. Landvater. These books describe the relationship of sales and operations planning within a fully integrated planning and control process.

"For our purposes," Ross explains, "we need to recognize that sales and operations planning integrates senior management with middle management cross-functionally. It serves to integrate management both vertically and horizontally."

He displays the next visual (Figure 12) and tells the group that sales and operations planning connects, or integrates, with the setting of the annual goals and budget, as previously discussed. It integrates with strategic planning and long-range planning in that it is the process which links strategy with action. Sales and operations planning directly links with demand planning and supply planning and sets the boundaries for the detail sales plan and master production schedule.

He notes that sales and operations planning is an aggregate planning process. Individual products are grouped into what are known as "families" to facilitate aggregate planning. That does not mean, however, that detailed planning, down to individual line items, is eliminated. "In a fully integrated planning and control system, both aggregate and detailed planning are done," Ross comments.

He sees inquisitive looks on the faces of some members of the group and goes on to explain that on a daily and weekly basis, the master scheduling process is the primary process for controlling the balance between demand and supply. It links detailed demand to detailed material and capacity planning, which in turn link to plant scheduling and supplier scheduling.

The function of plant scheduling and supplier scheduling is to set the daily and weekly priorities for suppliers inside and outside the company. An integrated master schedule for product development also must integrate with the manufacturing master schedule.

"Sometimes it is easier to understand what I have just said if you see some graphical representations," Ross explains. "I have other models for you to study. Compare the integrated planning model I have just presented with this second model." He advances the presentation to reveal another graphic (Figure 13). "This model is what Nolan and I normally find when we are called into a company."

"Now let's look at a model of a more ideal, and more effective, sales and operations planning process," Ross continues. He advances the computer to reveal the next graphic (Figure 14). "This model is an alternate presentation of the integrated business management process. Please remember the Einstein quote," he says.

"All models are wrong; some are useful," the class members repeat.

Ross smiles and says, "That's right." He explains that the model on the screen is often referred to as the "three-legged" model and is becoming more widely

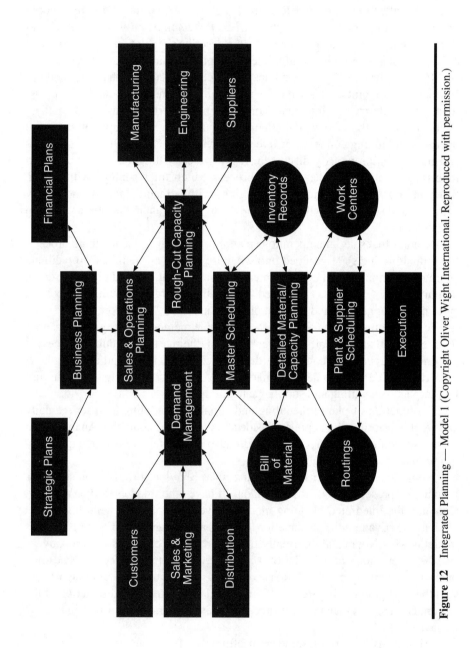

Figure 12 Integrated Planning — Model 1 (Copyright Oliver Wight International. Reproduced with permission.)

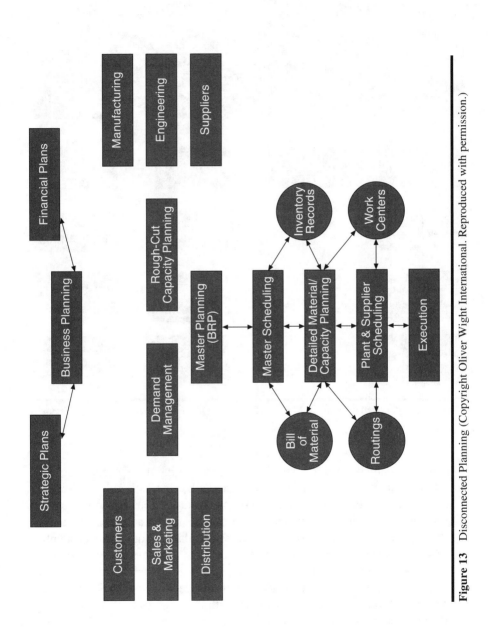

Figure 13 Disconnected Planning (Copyright Oliver Wight International. Reproduced with permission.)

Figure 14   Integrated Planning — Model 2 (Copyright Oliver Wight International. Reproduced with permission.)

preferred by many companies. This model directly communicates that sales and operations planning includes new products and other projects and programs referred to as *activities management.* Many managers believe the model demonstrates more effectively that sales and operations planning is a process for managing the business as a whole, not just a process of balancing demand and supply.

Ross asks the class to study the three models he has just shown. Clicking the mouse from one visual to the other, he says, "The important point with these models is that all the processes connect. All the models show the basic processes connected with lines or arrows. The model with the disconnected arrows is very typical of companies with planning and control processes that are broken or disconnected. Each function may have its own processes, but they are not working together."

Ross asks the class to note that the arrows go both ways. "The secret to successful integrated planning and control is the arrows," he explains.

Mark raises his hand. Ross's back is to the class. He is pointing at the two-way arrows in one of the models on the screen.

"I have a question, Ross," Mark says. Ross turns toward Mark. "When you and Nolan did the assessment, we limited the scope to sales and operations planning. Do you have any observations about the other processes shown in your models and how they function at Universal Products?"

"We did limit the scope of the assessment to sales and operations planning," Ross replies. "However, during the assessment, Nolan and I noted that you have an issue with master scheduling. Our expectation is that as you get demand and supply in balance at the aggregate level of planning for sales and operations planning, it will help you to begin to size your resources correctly. Once that happens, master scheduling will surface as one of the next areas you need to improve. Master scheduling is the process that connects management's choices to the execution system."

Ross sees Susan Callahan, the planning manager, shift uncomfortably in her seat. "In defense of Susan and her planning group," he continues, "master scheduling is an area that requires adherence to the principles we have been discussing. Without the discipline of proper operating principles, master scheduling is ineffective. There are also other areas which we noted were not functioning as well as they could be, but in the interest of time, we shouldn't try to discuss them today."

Mark nods his agreement, and Ross moves on to the basic characteristics of sales and operations planning.

■ ■ ■

Ross glances at his watch. It is 11:30 a.m. He feels the energy of the class winding down. It is a good time to introduce the basic characteristics of sales and operations planning before breaking for lunch. The introduction requires more quiet thinking and thoughtfulness by the group in order to assimilate the characteristics. After lunch, he expects that as people begin to think about applying the characteristics, there will be spirited discussion.

He asks the group to turn to pages 30 to 34 in the class notebook and to read the basic characteristics of sales and operations planning (Figure 15). He gives the class some time to quietly read the information.

After a few minutes, Ross tells the group that he wants to make additional points about some of the basic characteristics. He points to the first characteristic. "Remember the sales and operations planning diagram," he says. "Sales and operations planning consists of a product review, demand review, supply review, financial review, and an executive sales and operations planning meeting. These

1. The S&OP process is a series of steps. It is not just an executive meeting.

2. New product development and company initiatives are reviewed to understand and communicate any project or priority changes and whether projects are on schedule, on cost, and within scope.

3. The S&OP process is "owned" by the senior-most executive in charge. This person may have the title of general manager, managing director, president, or another title. S&OP is not a process that is relegated to middle management.

4. S&OP is a cross-functional management process with all management from all functions participating. The management team makes decisions that are in the best interest of the company, not necessarily coincident with the best interests of an individual department.

5. The S&OP process cycle occurs monthly, or more frequently as may be required. The process integrates planning and control at the middle and executive management levels of the company.

6. The management team agrees to operate with the following set of fundamental principles:

    ■ Strive to meet or exceed customer expectations all of the time.

    ■ Do what we say we are going to do.

    ■ If work, timing, or resources change from a balanced to an unbalanced condition, at least one of the other two components must be changed.

    ■ Never promise more than you can deliver.

    ■ Deliver what you promise, or communicate that you will be unable to deliver as promised.

    ■ Don't shoot the messenger.

    ■ Strive for open and honest communication.

    ■ Perform continuous, rolling replanning, rather than static annual planning.

    ■ Planning, execution, and communication must be synchronized.

    ■ Silence is approval, and all numbers and dates are valid.

7. The S&OP process includes both existing and new products. The output of the process

Figure 15   Sales and Operations Planning — Basic Characteristics

reviews and meeting are not conducted all at once. They are separate sessions that generally occur on different days."

He scrolls down on the computer to the fifth point and tells the group that some people question why sales and operations planning is a monthly process. Why can't it be conducted quarterly? "The answer is simple," Ross says. "Any less frequency than monthly will not provide adequate response to the dynamics of the business."

He explains that a planning and control system must be as dynamic as the environment in which a company operates. If it is not, less effective control methods will emerge. This is often called the *informal system*. When informal systems provides a picture of the present and future business across the planning horizon as best as it is known today.

8. The focus of S&OP is on the future. Performance measures, however, are reviewed to make problems visible and to stimulate continuous improvement.

9. The S&OP process is demand driven. It starts with an updated demand plan.

10. Demand and supply imbalances are identified and resolved each cycle.

11. Conflicts in work, timing, and resources are identified and resolved. Decisions are made. S&OP is not a reporting process; it is a decision-making process.

12. The approved S&OP plan is the plan that will be executed unless and until it is changed. It is expected that the plan will change and decisions will be made to enable the plan to be changed. A nondecision is a decision; it is a decision to stay with the previously agreed-upon plan.

13. Financial impacts as well as marketplace and operational issues are considered in the decision-making process.

14. The output of the S&OP process is one set of operational numbers. These are the numbers the management team has agreed to execute until changed.

15. Each S&OP cycle results in consensus, accountability, and commitment for the following deliverables across the planning horizon:

- Bookings Plan
- Sales/Demand Plan
- Production Plan
- Inventory Plan
- Backlog/Customer Lead-Time Plan
- Financial Plan
- New Product Development Plans
- Company Initiative/Project Plans
- Associated Resource Plans

16. The planning output of S&OP is fundamentally a simulation of the business. As such, it can be used for "what if" scenario planning and to develop contingency plans based on different business scenarios.

Figure 15 Sales and Operations Planning — Basic Characteristics (continued)

---

are deployed, executive management goes through the motions of planning, but its efforts have little direct impact on what actually is planned, sold, manufactured, and delivered.

Ross points to the seventh point projected on the screen. "Sometimes there is unneeded discussion about what new products to include in the sales and operations planning process," he says. "New products for sales and operations planning include those products recently launched, products in development, and new products anticipated to be developed or launched within the planning horizon. The product review also reviews products approaching their end of life."

He points to the eighth point, which involves performance measures. "We recommend using a balanced scorecard approach with performance measures," Ross says. He explains that Robert S. Kaplan and David P. Norton introduced the balanced scorecard approach in a *Harvard Business Review* article and a subsequent book several years ago.

"Here's how a balanced scorecard approach might be used in your company," Ross says as he advances the computer to the next graphic (Figure 16). He explains that discussions and performance measures for sales and operations planning should center on evaluating a company's effectiveness with markets and customers, finance and shareholders, employees and productivity, technology/innovation and product development, and internal improvement initiatives. The performance measures should focus on the performance that management is striving to achieve. The measures should also provide visibility as to how well operational processes within the company are operating and improving.

"Sometimes it is hard to visualize how performance measures are presented in the sales and operations planning process. Here is an example of what we call a balanced scorecard presented in a dashboard format," Ross says as he displays the next visual (Figure 17).

He explains that the colors indicate performance at a glance. Green means that performance is meeting objectives or standards. Yellow means that performance is outside the stated objective tolerances, but the issue is being remedied. Red means that performance problems are serious and require action or decisions.

Ross looks at his watch. It is a little after noon. He had not meant to talk into the lunch hour. "Let's break for lunch," he says. "If it is agreeable with you, can we start up again in forty-five minutes?"

No one answers. He assumes silence is approval.

The group members push back their chairs and head for the hotel restaurant, where a buffet lunch will be served.

■ ■ ■

Ross pulls Mark Ryan to the side as the group exits the meeting room. He tells Mark that he needs to take a walk to refresh, gather his thoughts, and mentally prepare for the afternoon. He will grab a quick bite from the buffet after his walk.

"Nolan will be available for discussion with your team," Ross says. "That will give your people a chance to talk without me present. Nolan is a key resource, as you will see when he presents this afternoon. Take advantage of what he knows."

"I understand your need to take a walk," Mark replies, "but before you go, I think it is important to express my concern about the amount of time being spent

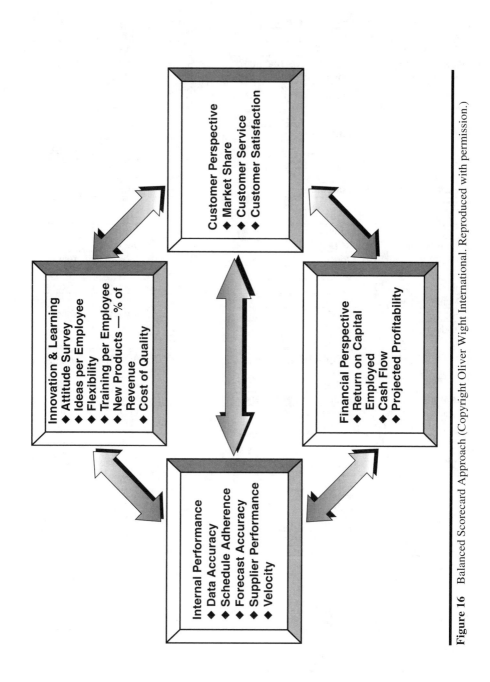

Figure 16   Balanced Scorecard Approach (Copyright Oliver Wight International. Reproduced with permission.)

Sales and Operations Planning	-3	-2	-1
Was everyone prepared?	Red	Yellow	Green
Were the right people present?	Red	Red	Yellow
Was the information at the right level of detail?	Yellow	Yellow	Green
Were the needed decisions made?	Yellow	Yellow	Green
Did we make efficient use of our time?	Yellow	Yellow	Green
Can we improve the S&OP process?	Red	Red	Yellow

Financials	-3	-2	-1
EBIT ($)	Red	Yellow	Green
Sales revenue to plan ($)	Green	Green	Yellow
Margin % to plan	Green	Green	Yellow
Operating expenses to budget ($)	Green	Green	Yellow
Cost drivers	Green	Yellow	Red

Supply	-3	-2	-1
Manufacturing revenue to plan	Yellow	Yellow	Red
Inventory value ($) and turns	Green	Green	Yellow
Supplier quality performance	Yellow	Yellow	Red
Initial test yields ($)	Yellow	Yellow	Red
Cycle times (days)	Yellow	Yellow	Red
Inventory record accuracy (%)	Green	Yellow	Yellow
Production plan vs. actual (%)	Red	Red	Red
Master schedule performance (%)	Red	Red	Red
Master schedule stability (weekly)	Green	Yellow	Red

Products	-3	-2	-1
New product introduction on-time performance (%)	Red	Red	Red
Cycle time to first customer prototype	Green	Green	Green
Cycle time to safety approval	Yellow	Red	Red
Average cycle time	Red	Red	Red
Project development costs	Green	Green	Green
Development resource load to capacity ratio	Yellow	Red	Red

Demand	-3	-2	-1
Forecast vs. actual by subfamily (units and %)	Yellow	Yellow	Yellow
Forecast vs. actual by top 30 sku mix	Green	Green	Green
Inventory performance by customer group	Yellow	Yellow	Red
On-time customer service performance (%)	Yellow	Yellow	Red
Bookings activity	Yellow	Yellow	Red
Past due customer orders	Green	Yellow	Yellow

Markets	-3	-2	-1
Total market forecast accuracy	Yellow	Yellow	Red
Market #1 market share	Green	Green	Green
Market #2 market share	Yellow	Yellow	Red
Competitive portfolio positioning	Yellow	Yellow	Red

Figure 17   Balanced Scorecard Approach for Sales and Operations Planning Measurements

on philosophical and conceptual discussions versus what is needed to get sales and operations planning started."

Ross understands Mark's concern. It is typical. He also knows that if people do not understand the process conceptually or the management philosophy that is required to support the process, they will never truly embrace sales and operations planning.

"It sounds to me like you think the process is *the* answer," Ross replies. "It is not. The process is only as good as how your people use it to make decisions. Just to be sure that you and I understand one another, I should explain that there are numerous people out there who profess to be experts at implementing sales and operations planning, but there are very few experts who can get you results quickly. Mark, at this point, the issue should not be the details of the process steps or the software presentation tools. The real results come from developing a strong understanding about a few key interactive management principles."

Mark visibly recoils at Ross's response, but Ross is not finished. "Quite frankly, Mark, your comments concern me a bit," Ross says. "I'm not certain you understand what will make the real difference in successfully implementing sales and operations planning. The real difference is in the people circle. If your management team does not understand the importance of people, if your team does not understand the importance of the behavior required to operate to some basic principles, you will end up with mediocre results at best. Perhaps you and I should spend some additional time one on one soon discussing the people requirements."

Mark does not like what he has just been told. Ross has accused him of not understanding the sales and operations planning process. Mark thinks it is a fairly straightforward process, and he understands more than Ross is giving him credit for.

Mark decides to push back. "Ross, I don't know whether to get angry or what. I am the reason you are here. I take exception to your comments. I believe I *do* understand the importance of the people circle."

Ross realizes that he has ruffled Mark's feathers, but he does not back down. "I am telling it like I see it. My only objective is to make you successful and help you get results in the shortest period of time. It is not my objective to make you happy. If you are uncomfortable with this, I know I can arrange for a major consulting firm to come in and make you happy. It will cost you more money, you will get fewer results, and it will take longer, but if that is what you want, I will make the call."

Mark is puzzled by Ross's behavior. Ross is working for *me,* Mark thinks to himself. He realizes that Ross has put him in an unusual situation. He has hired someone who is now criticizing his knowledge. He does not like it. In fact, he is angry.

Mark begins to respond to Ross's challenge, but draws back. Discipline kicks in. Long ago, he learned that to speak in anger damages relationships, sometimes permanently.

He thinks back to the morning's session. He was so pleased earlier. Why am I upset now? he asks himself.

The answer is simple. Ross told him some things he did not like to hear. Maybe Mark's staff is feeling the same way. His team may have been uncomfortable hearing some of the things discussed this morning. Is that not what Susan expressed earlier in the morning?

Mark decides that this is neither the time nor place to confront Ross. At some point, he will want to carry this conversation further. He also will want to make sure that Ross doesn't cross the fine line between motivating people to change and alienating them so much that they stubbornly refuse to change.

"I had better lighten up," Mark says to Ross. "I disagree with you, but for the moment will give you the benefit of the doubt. I will endeavor to continue to listen more and strive to understand the concepts more deeply. We *will* need to have that one-on-one session soon."

"The one-on-one session is already in the plan," Ross replies. "I need to get outside for some space. I hope you don't mind. We will have plenty of time to discuss this and other matters."

Ross heads for the door that leads outside, and Mark strolls into the restaurant to look for his group. The buffet line is empty; everyone is eating.

Mark quickly ladles soup into a bowl and serves himself a green salad. He sits at the end of a table next to Susan. He does not participate in the conversation. He listens with one ear, but is mostly preoccupied thinking about the confrontation with Ross.

Mark is now curious about Ross. He wonders what types of relationships Ross has formed with his clients. He also wonders whether he is married and where he lives. Mark is embarrassed that he has not asked these questions earlier.

He realizes that he knows very little about his management team as well. He has been so busy and pressured, he has neglected to learn more about the people who work for Universal Products.

Mark's feelings move quickly from anger to inadequacy. There are so many things he should be doing as general manager. Damn, we need to get this process started so we can begin to turn this ship around, he thinks to himself.

Meanwhile, Ross has been taking a leisurely stroll outside, viewing the foothills and breathing the Colorado air. He is still a bit irritated with Mark.

After working as a consultant for fifteen years, Ross finds himself less patient with company leaders. He is irritated that Mark assumes it will be easy to implement sales and operations planning. Mark is thinking that all his management team needs is to understand the steps, and then Mark will make sure they march to those steps.

But it is not that easy. Ross knows that the management team must be willing to use the information from the sales and operations planning process to make decisions about supply, demand, product development, and the resources required to support the company's plans.

Ross is reminded of a story he once heard a consultant tell. The consultant was working with the president of a client company. He reviewed the plans to implement a planning and control system. The president disagreed with the timetable. He felt it should be accelerated. "If I tell my people to do this, they will do it," he told the consultant.

The consultant asked the president if he would be willing to participate in a little experiment. The president said of course he would.

The consultant asked the president what side of the bed he slept on. The president said he preferred the left side. The consultant asked him to switch sides with his wife that night.

The next morning, the consultant dropped by the president's office and asked how the experiment worked out. "We started out on opposite sides of the bed," the president explained, "but then my wife decided she needed to sleep closest to the bathroom, and I decided I needed to be close to the bedroom door in case we had an intruder."

The consultant told the president that he had flunked the test, and he had to try again that night. The next morning, the president said he could sleep only a few hours on the opposite side of the bed because he got a kink in his neck. He wasn't used to the mattress on his wife's side of the bed.

The consultant instructed him to try again. It took the president four nights to sleep on the opposite side of the bed.

When the president reported his success at last, the consultant asked him, "Do you still think it will be easy for your people to change and adapt to a new way of doing business?"

■ ■ ■

Ross and Nolan meet for about ten minutes after Ross returns from his walk. Nolan will be doing some of the teaching this afternoon. They review points to be sure to make. Nolan updates Ross on the lunch discussion, and Ross updates Nolan on his discussion with Mark.

Nolan tells Ross that Janis Novak, the controller, and Jim Simpson, the manufacturing director, discussed during lunch whether the concept of never promising more than you can deliver conflicts with stretch goals. Nolan and Ross decide that Ross will address the issue before turning over the presentation to Nolan.

They walk into the meeting room together and are pleased to see everyone already seated, waiting for them to start.

"I understand that during lunch there was some discussion about stretch goals," Ross begins. "This is an important issue. Some of you are wondering whether stretch goals are in conflict with saying you will never promise more than you can deliver. My answer to this is not at all."

Ross explains that, first, it is important to differentiate between a goal and a plan. A goal is a target. A plan includes actions to achieve a goal.

Second, it is important to consider timing. Goals are usually set less frequently than the number of times the plan is reviewed, changed, and replanned. Goals are usually set at least annually as part of the annual business plan. Consequently, the quantified business plan is actually a set of goals for the year.

"If you do your homework correctly and if you utilize the monthly replanning process of sales and operations planning to help develop the annual goals, the annual goals will be realistic at the time you establish the business plan," Ross explains. "Some companies also wish to set another level of goals, sometimes referred to as stretch goals. These goals are typically more aggressive than the business plan goals."

"What happens if the business plan goals don't meet the shareholders' desires or expectations?" Janis asks.

"It is important to have visibility of the shareholders' goals and expectations, whether they match the current realistic goals and plans or not," Ross replies. "These higher level expectations should be viewed as the target or the goal you are trying to meet or exceed."

Ross explains that it is okay to set a higher level or "stretch" goal and to provide additional rewards should it be reached. The sales and operations planning process will identify the most likely scenario, however — the agreed-upon current realistic plan given the current action plans and assumptions.

During the sales and operations planning process, it may be recognized that the agreed-upon realistic plan will not achieve the higher level stretch goal. In this case, a *gap* has been identified and quantified. Also, the timing needed to fill the gap to achieve the stretch goal has been identified.

"Management can begin now to work on changes to the action plans that will be reflected in the updated sales and operations planning plans to fill the gap and achieve the higher goal," Ross says. "The changes in action plans will hopefully result in a realistic plan that meets both the business plan and the stretch goals. The key point is that through the process, you have identified the gap early so that actions can be taken sooner."

"Isn't that part of what strategic planning does? Set the stretch goals?" Ray Guy, the final assembly manager, asks.

"Yes, normally that would be part of the strategic planning effort," Ross replies. "Let me digress for a moment, though. Earlier I said that sales and operations planning makes the annual business planning process a significant non-event. By that, I meant the annual budgeting process. Sales and operations planning moves you to what is effectively a flexible budgeting process. Sales and operations planning does *not* replace strategic planning. We encourage companies to do strategic planning early in the year, usually around the end of the first quarter. The motive for this timing is to separate the strategic thinking from establishing expectations as part of putting the annual plan in place, which usually occurs toward the end of the year."

Ross explains that using this approach gives the management team six to nine months and six to nine cycles of sales and operations planning to address changes and implementation of strategies, including those strategies and tactics to attain stretch goals. When strategic planning is done late in the year, the annual business plan has a tendency to in reality be a stretch plan, which is a high-risk plan. This is caused by the executive team getting enthused about the strategic plan and stretch goals. The executive team tends to commit to plans that cannot be feasibly implemented in the time period covering the next fiscal year.

"Most shareholders, and Wall Street, want management to do what they say they are going to do," Ross says. "They want the management of companies to be reliable and credible. The annual business plan should be a realistic plan and, therefore, not an unrealistic stretch plan."

Ross clicks the mouse on the computer to display the next visual (Figure 18). Pointing to the graph, he says, "As I review a company's sales and operations planning process, I look to see that the numbers do not magically add up to the annual business plan month after month or add up to the stretch goal."

He explains that some companies are in the habit of taking any variances and moving them to the end of the year. It finally becomes obvious that the plan will not be met, but by then it is too late to take any effective action.

"It is important," Ross notes, "to find the gaps between the sales and operations plan and the business plan early. Remember that the business plan is a goal. Remember, too, that *bad news early is better than bad news late.* Conversely, *good news early is better than good news late.* When gaps between the sales and operations plan and the business plan are identified, the issue becomes whether there is enough time to take action and/or change expectations."

Mark Ryan wants to be sure that he understands what Ross has just presented and that his staff concurs with differentiating a realistic plan for the business plan and stretch goals. "I would like to restate what I just heard you say to make sure I understand you correctly," he says. "Each month, we come to a consensus on an agreed sales and operations plan for a minimum of eighteen months. That plan represents reality as we know it at the time. When it comes time to set next fiscal year's business plan, which is really a goal, we should be able to use the numbers straight from sales and operations planning. We conduct strategic planning early in the year. One of the outputs of the process could be stretch goals over the next few years. As we begin taking actions to support changes in strategy and to reach higher level stretch goals, these actions will be reflected in our updated sales and

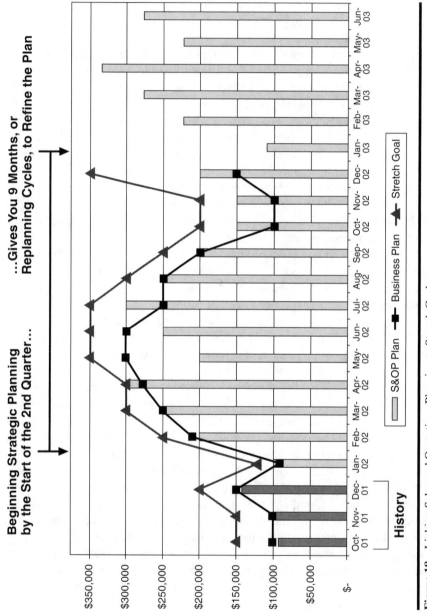

Figure 18 Linking Sales and Operations Planning to Stretch Goals

operations plans. If we are disciplined and approve only realistic plans, we will always be able to see the gap between the most recent sales and operations plan and the business plan and the stretch goals. Is that correct?"

"Maybe I should have you teach the class," Ross replies. "That is correct. Any questions?"

The room is quiet, but Sam is restless. Ross looks at him. "Do you have something you want to say?"

"Well, now that you ask, yes I do," Sam replies. He turns to Mark. "Based on what you just described, Mark, I trust that you are serious about approving and supporting realistic plans and goals in our planning process. But what about corporate? Every year, we provide a bottom-up forecast with the best information we have, and every year corporate says that isn't good enough. Will corporate support realistic plans, or will corporate make us change the numbers to support its view?"

Ross interjects before Mark can reply. "Sam, you make an excellent point. Let me give you my perspective, based on my experience with many companies." Ross explains that the more credible the bottom-up plans, the less likely that corporate management will override those plans. The monthly replanning nature of sales and operations planning helps to ensure that the bottom-up plans are more reliable.

"Quite frankly," Ross says, "it's part of Mark's job to represent this division and to ensure that corporate does not impose unrealistic plans or goals."

"I hear what you are saying, Ross," Sam replies, "but I will have to see it to believe it."

Mark is now moved to speak. "Sam, based upon the history of our company's behavior, I think your point is well taken. Clearly, this is an issue that we will have to deal with as we build realistic goals and plans. It's also an issue that I will have to resolve directly with corporate."

Ross holds up his hand. "Let's move on," he says. "Nolan is going to present some additional detail about the sales and operations planning process. During this presentation, he will attempt to get you to make as many key decisions as possible. These decisions will serve as guidelines for the process design."

Ross steps away from the front table. "Nolan, it is all yours," he says.

SALES AND OPERATIONS PLANNING REVIEW MEETINGS

Nolan Drake strides confidently to the front of the room. He appears to be ten years younger than Ross. He is nearly six feet tall and lean. His manner is easy and gentle. Without any preliminaries, he asks the group to turn to page 34 in the notebook and look at the visual (Figure 19).

"You'll remember this visual from this morning," Nolan says. "I'm going to begin at the point labeled 'start' and work my way around the process."

Nolan notes that the executive team has chosen for the company to be strategy and demand driven and has agreed upon an objective to meet or exceed customer expectations. The team also discussed that the process starts with a product review to identify any changes to product development priorities, update schedules, and ensure that projects are on time, on spec, and on cost.

"Once we understand what products will be available to sell and when," Nolan says, "we then update the anticipated demand. The demand review box in the model represents the process of reaching consensus on the forecast of anticipated demand. In the sales and operations planning process, it is strongly recommended that each process step have a process owner who is at the executive level and a process coordinator who is usually at the management level."

Jim Simpson, the manufacturing director, interrupts Nolan. "I am a little confused. Isn't the whole diagram a process called sales and operations planning? I

Figure 19   Sales and Operations Planning — Basic Model (Copyright Oliver Wight International. Reproduced with permission.)

thought Ross told us that the general manager, in our case Mark, is the process owner."

"That's right," Nolan replies. "The entire diagram represents the sales and operations planning process, and Mark is the executive owner. However, other processes also appear in the diagram; product review, demand review, supply review, and financial review all are also processes. You may choose to think of them as subprocesses that require process owners. Most general managers decide to assign owners and coordinators to the subprocesses. Some people call these subprocesses pre-sales and operations planning steps, meaning they occur before the executive sales and operations planning meeting. Did I make myself clear, Jim?"

"I understand," Jim says.

Peter Newfeld, the product development/engineering director, is quick to comment. "That means that the product review step needs a process owner. Is that person me?"

"It certainly could be you," Nolan replies. "Technically, it is whomever the general manager, Mark, wants. Often, that person would be the head of engineering. In some companies, it might be the head of marketing. Having said that, in this company, Ross and I both believe it makes sense for that process to be yours, Peter."

Mark quickly agrees and tells the team that Peter is the process owner for the product review subprocess.

Nolan moves on to describe the demand review subprocess. He tells the group not to think of it as just forecasting. It should be thought of as an integrated sales and marketing planning or replanning process.

The demand review itself is often a meeting of key sales and marketing management. One of the outputs of the process is the quantitative demand plan by product or product line. This results in an aggregate forecast by product family for sales and operations planning and a detailed forecast used as input to the master scheduling function.

Other outputs are an updated marketing plan and an updated sales plan. These plans are time-phased action plans for influencing the market and booking new business. Associated with these plans is an updated marketing and sales budget.

Susan Callahan, the planning manager, raises her hand. She wants to be sure that the group understands what Nolan just said. "So, Nolan, the planning organization would expect to get an updated forecast," she says, "but that forecast is tied to actions that the sales and marketing people are planning to do. These actions include such things as introducing new products, pruning the product line, emphasizing the sale of one product over another, conducting promotions, changing price, and lowering a bid on a large contract. Is that correct?"

"It sure is, Susan," Nolan replies. "I would like you to think about the forecast not as a guess about what customers are going to buy, but instead as a *request for product* that we wish to have available because that is what we intend to sell. We actually prefer to use the words 'demand plan' rather than 'forecast.' Forecast implies a guess or an estimate of what is going to happen. Demand plan suggests that specific action plans are in place to make the demand happen. In essence, it implies that you are going to plan the sale and sell the plan. In an engineering, or custom product, environment, think of it as a *request for resource or capacity* to satisfy the market demand."

Peter Newfeld, the engineering director, raises his hand. "For a product that already exists, we have a part number and a bill of material. How is a request for product or a request for resource communicated for an engineered or new product for which part numbers and bills of material do not yet exist?" he asks.

Nolan explains that tools and techniques have been developed for planning new and engineered products when the details of the product may not yet be defined. A planning bill, which is like a bill of material, is created for key materials and resources for the new or engineered product. The planning bill is used to provide a link between what it is believed will be sold and when and the resources required to meet the demand. There will be uncertainty in the planning bill, but as time passes and the order is received or the design is completed, the planning bill is updated to reflect the changes. As a result, the uncertainty will be reduced as time goes on.

It is important to make visible to the entire management team, on a regular and routine basis, what is likely to be sold and what new products are being developed. With this information, resource requirements can be determined and communicated to all functional areas.

"This is a very brief explanation, Peter, but for now I would like you to trust me that there are standard ways of handling both new and engineered product," Nolan says.

"I am fine for now," Peter replies.

Nolan points to the demand review box on the screen. He tells the group that each cycle of sales and operations planning results in a consensus demand plan. This plan, or request for product, will be updated during the next cycle.

"This implies that if we ask for product, we may get it," says Nolan. "If we don't ask for it, we won't get it. If we ask for it and don't sell it, we call it inventory. If we ask for it and it is not enough to support actual customer orders, we call it poor customer service. Sam, how do you feel about this notion?"

Sam hesitates before replying. "Well, I have some concerns. It is very difficult to forecast our business at the product level. I am not sure we can do that. And I want my people selling. I don't want them spending a lot of time in the office doing administrative tasks. I want their feet on the street. What you described sounds like another reason for them to stay in the office."

"Those are certainly legitimate concerns," Nolan says. "However, if you're going to meet your customers' expectations and gain or keep a competitive edge through delivery and availability, someone has to request the availability of product."

Nolan explains that some supply-side activities must be completed before the company receives a customer order if the company is to meet customer expectations. Depending upon the delivery time required and the time it takes to supply the product, it may be necessary to complete the entire product and put it into inventory in anticipation of a customer order.

"You do this with some of your products now, don't you?" Nolan asks. "Some products may be partially completed and then finished after receipt of the customer order. With others, you may start from a totally new design and build the entire product after receipt of the customer order. Depending upon the tactic you take, the lead time to your customer will be different. That lead time could range from immediately available to several months before product is available. Am I correct?"

Each member of the executive team nods their head in agreement. Janis Novak, the controller, adds, "And you should see just how much inventory we have. It is large compared to other companies where I have worked."

"So who is responsible for the inventory?" Nolan asks. He points to Susan Callahan, the planning manager. "Is it you, Susan, and if so, why do we have so much?"

"Everyone here believes that I am responsible," Susan replies, "but as Ross told us, I don't sell anything. I don't make anything, and I don't buy anything. So how could I be responsible for the inventory level when it is the result of those three things?"

"Who is doing the forecasting? How does the product get into inventory?" Nolan asks.

Susan is quick to reply. "For some of our inventory, we use a minimum/maximum approach. When the inventory goes below the minimum level, we place an order. We also use material requirements planning to tell us what we need to order and when. Unfortunately, we have inaccurate inventory records and bills of material. As a result, those of us in planning often end up guessing at what we will really need. This is especially true of purchased materials."

Anita Cooper, the purchasing manager, adds, "And truth be known, we in purchasing guess at what we will need also and will use our own forecasts to attempt to get a better volume price break and to make sure we don't run out of stock."

Nolan looks at Peter. "I'm sure you have a communications and planning process for engineering changes so that purchasing will not buy any additional raw materials and that bills of material will be updated so that planning can plan for those items being changed by engineering," Nolan says tongue in cheek, knowing full well there is no effective engineering change process.

Mark jumps to Peter's defense. "Where are you going with this, Nolan? We know our engineering change process, or lack of it, contributes greatly to the inventory problem. I thought we were talking about forecasts."

"Perhaps I am getting a little off track," Nolan replies, "but I mostly wanted to point out the disconnects, the lack of integration, starting with the forecast. Right now, you are using some material requirements planning with poor data and some minimum/maximum tactics. But there is little forward visibility. We know this will cause problems. That is a fact. Planning does some guessing at what is needed, and purchasing second-guesses those numbers. And I didn't even give Jim a chance to tell us that he makes different quantities than those requested by planning for a variety of reasons, all associated with manufacturing costs. I also did not discuss what an overloaded master schedule will do. The point is that inaccurate forecasts are not the only problem you will have to deal with to solve your inventory problem."

"Now, let's get back to the subject of demand planning," Nolan says. "I am a strong believer that those closest to the market and to the customers should know most about what the customers and the market want to buy and that they should be responsible for the forecast. Simply stated, the process owner of the demand review step in sales and operations planning should be the executive in charge of sales and/or marketing. In your case, since the same person is responsible for sales and marketing, that person would be Sam."

Sam squirms uncomfortably in his chair. "I am responsible for developing the forecast," he says, "but how does that help the fact that our business is difficult to forecast? I also want my salespeople selling, not being administrators."

"A partial answer to your question is that you need a demand coordinator, sometimes referred to as a demand planner or demand manager," Nolan replies.

He explains that the demand coordinator's full-time job is to make it easy for sales and marketing to contribute quality information to the demand planning process. He notes that Universal Products does not have a person who currently fills this role.

Most companies find they do not have to add head count to accomplish the demand coordination task. The reassignment of tasks usually enables a resource to be dedicated to demand coordination, although some companies may have to add head count for a short period of time while the process is being developed.

Sam asks Nolan another question. "I'm not sure that this is the place or time, but is that something that Justin Roberts in my marketing department could do? I know you interviewed Justin in the assessment."

Mark interrupts before Nolan can answer the question. "This is not the time for discussing specific organizational changes, Sam."

"Forgive me, Mark," Nolan says, "but I want to respond. Sam, someone with Justin's skills would be ideal. Having answered that question, Sam, I still haven't addressed the issue you raised about the difficulty in forecasting. We don't have the time today to discuss the demand planning process in detail, but we have a wealth of experience helping companies to improve their forecasts through people, process, and tools — the three circles that Ross introduced early this morning. Sam, it will not be as difficult as you think, if you put a dedicated resource, like Justin, on the task."

Janis Novak, the controller, interrupts. "Aren't you being a bit optimistic, Nolan? It has been my experience that implementing demand planning is not an easy task. And even when implemented, you still may have considerable forecast error."

"That's true to varying degrees, depending upon the company, the product, and the business situation," Nolan replies. He explains that in his experience, when products are found to be repeatedly difficult to forecast with a high degree of accuracy, the first step is to evaluate whether it is a people problem or a process problem that contributes to the inaccuracy. If it is neither, the company must make a tactical choice in how to deal with variability and the error.

"There are choices you must make," Nolan says. "Will we carry more inventory? Will we operate with spare capacity? Will we vary lead time and ask our customers to wait longer for delivery? Will we flex capacity internally or externally at higher costs? Will we even turn away some business?"

Nolan pauses for a moment. He scans the group. "Who decides and authorizes those tactics in your company?" he asks.

Ray Guy, the final assembly manager, is quick to reply. "Why, we do as a management team through the sales and operations planning process."

"Give Ray a prize," Nolan says. "You are absolutely correct. That is how it should be done."

Janis raises her hand again. "I have another question about demand. How do you handle emergency orders? It seems to me that most companies have situations they must respond to immediately regardless of the plan."

"Companies that truly do sales and operations planning well include emergency orders as part of their planning," Nolan says. "I had a general manager once tell a group of class attendees that the easiest part of their business to forecast was emergency, or quick response, orders. Every month, he could count on around 10 percent of his business to be emergency business. Once they started tracking and understanding the nature of the demand, they could plan for the capacity and raw materials to handle the emergencies. In essence, they made emergencies routine."

Sam raises his hand. "I want to be sure I understand my role," he says. "You are saying that I am responsible for the forecast of demand. In the sales and operations planning model, I am responsible for the demand review subprocess. I need a demand review coordinator, who also might be called a demand planner. Further, I should view the demand review process as a management process for marketing and sales. I believe you said it was an integrated marketing and sales management process that may culminate in a monthly meeting, presumably my meeting. And for now, I should trust that you can help put a process together that will work. Am I correct?"

Nolan nods his head in agreement. "You are correct," he says. "And when you are leading the demand review process, you will follow another principle: It is the responsibility of sales and marketing to not only represent the company to the customer but also to represent the customer to the company. By providing a realistic, credible forecast of anticipated demand, you are representing the customer to the company."

Sam leans his chin into his hand. "I never thought of it that way. I like the concept. Yes, I concur with the principle. Is this true for new products as well as existing products?"

"Yes, it is," says Nolan. "Let me give you one last concept before moving on to the supply review. I would also like you to think about the forecast as what you are going to sell. Since you are going to sell it, you need the product to satisfy customer expectations. That's why it is to be viewed as a request for product. But since it is also what you plan to sell, you are telling Mark and the other members of this team what you are committing to sell. We like to use the expression *plan the sale, sell the plan.*"

Sam, always mentally quick, sees the punch line coming and interrupts. "I know what principle applies: *do what you say you are going to do.* For me, it is to sell what I say I am going to sell. I expect that I should be prepared to discuss any and all performance variances to the demand plan each month since I am accountable for the planning and execution."

Nolan turns to the rest of the group. "What do you think, team? Is Sam's description okay?"

"Yes!" the team replies.

"Let's take a ten-minute break. Then we'll take a look at decisions we can make about the supply review subprocess," Nolan says.

■ ■ ■

Ross Peterson and Mark Ryan approach Nolan at the front of the room while the executive team members go in various directions for their break.

"That was a good job, Nolan," Mark says. "You were able to get Sam to agree on some things I did not think he would necessarily support."

"I agree," Ross says. "We could spend all afternoon on the subject of demand. However, we need to move forward fairly quickly with the rest of the process. Don't short the subject being covered, but be careful not to get off on tangents or we will run out of time. Mark, what is the latest we should conclude this afternoon?"

"I told people we plan on finishing by 5:30," Mark answers.

"We don't want to run much over that time anyway," says Nolan. "People will begin to lose attention by then."

Ross looks toward the door and says, "Nolan, let's go outside for a few minutes to get some fresh air."

"Will you excuse us, Mark?" Nolan says.

"Not a problem," Mark replies and decides he, too, would like some fresh air. He steps out in front of the hotel, where he will have a few minutes to himself. He finds a bench outside the entrance and sits down.

He thinks about the class so far. He is encouraged by how readily his staff has seemingly accepted the teachings of both Ross and Nolan. His team seems to have confidence in them. It helps that they both have hands-on, real-world experience in implementing sales and operations planning. They are not just presenting theory; they have done it themselves.

An added dimension is developing as well. Mark senses that a more personal relationship is building. That is a positive development. Mark wants to quickly implement sales and operations planning. His staff will need to readily adopt the advice and guidance of experts like Ross and Nolan. Strong relationships, based on trust, will be needed.

A gentle, cool breeze stirs the trees. Mark looks out past the parking lot to the mountains beyond. It is early afternoon, and the shadows from the pine trees are beginning to lengthen. In just a few hours the sun will go behind the mountains for an early sunset. Then, it will cool off quickly. Mark likes the climate in Colorado. The dry air makes sunny days warm, and the high altitude makes for cool nights.

His musings are interrupted when Ross sticks his head out the door. "We'll be starting in two minutes," he says.

Mark follows Ross into the meeting room. Nolan and Sam are having an animated discussion in a corner near the front of the room. Mark is pleased to see Sam engaged and asking questions. It is obvious that Sam is already thinking of how to implement the demand review process.

■ ■ ■

When the management team returns from the break, the sales and operations planning model is illuminated on the overhead screen. Nolan moves toward the screen and points to the supply review box at the bottom of the circular model.

"Now, we will move to the supply review subprocess," he says. "What do we need to do first to get the subprocess started?"

"We need an executive process owner," Jim Simpson, the manufacturing director, quickly replies.

"That's right, and who should that be?" Nolan asks.

No one answers. Mark realizes the reason for his team's reticence. Four managers from the supply side report to him.

"How do you decide a process owner when multiple managers report to the general manager on the supply side?" Mark asks. "We have Ray in final assembly, Jim in manufacturing, Anita in purchasing, and Susan in planning."

"What do you think the choices are?" Nolan replies.

"When we discussed the demand review process, the choice was easy because Sam is responsible for both sales and marketing," Jim observes. "What if there were two managers, one for sales and one for marketing? Who would have been the process owner?"

"Remember doing what you say you're going to do?" Nolan asks. "Think of it from the perspective of who is most likely to be held accountable. For example, on the demand side of the business, the process owner would be the primary person the general manager holds accountable to develop and sell the demand plan. In some companies, that might be the senior-most marketing executive. In other companies, it might be the senior-most sales executive."

Nolan explains that there is no absolute right answer, only choice. The process will work successfully — even when there is a separate sales organization and a separate marketing organization — as long as everyone knows their role and is held accountable. If the head of sales were chosen as the demand review process owner, then the head of marketing would participate in the process and vice versa.

"If I were general manager," Nolan says, "I would prefer to have one person I could hold accountable to do what they said they were going to do, but that is just my choice. It depends upon the people, their strengths, weaknesses, etc. I would prefer to have a single vice-president of demand."

"Vice-president of demand. That is an interesting title," Mark says.

Jim Simpson continues with the thought. "So if I relate what Nolan just said to the supply review, the process owner would be whomever Mark holds most directly accountable to produce and ship the product to customers. In our case, the shipment of most of the product goes through final assembly. So should the process owner be Ray?"

Ray Guy, the final assembly manager, does not agree. "I don't have any control over what happens in manufacturing," he observes. "And Susan is supposed to be coordinating all of this through planning. Shouldn't the process owner be Susan?"

Ross and Mark lock eyes. Ross gives Mark a slight nod of the head. Mark had asked Ross the same question during one of the breaks. They discussed the strongest and best-suited candidate in the supply organization. Mark is ready to make a recommendation.

"I have already given this choice some thought," he says. "Here is what I would like to do. Since final assembly is responsible for completing the product for customer shipments, I would like Ray to be the process owner for the supply review, with Jim participating. In practice, you both have to work together to deliver product to the customer. Also, based on the principles of total quality management that we practice, Ray in final assembly is actually a customer of Jim's in manufacturing, and both Jim and Anita in purchasing are suppliers to Ray. Ray is a supplier to the customers represented by Sam in sales."

Mark has more to offer his team. "I want Susan to be the supply review process coordinator," he continues. "She is responsible for supply planning, so that is appropriate. Please do not consider this a change in organization. All of you still report directly to me, and all of you will participate in the executive sales and operations planning meeting that Nolan will talk about a little later. In practice, Ross has advised me that if I had to find one person who was totally accountable for supply in our organization since I do not have a vice-president of operations, it would be me. I am counting on you working together to make this happen."

Eyes turn toward Jim to gauge his feelings about Mark's pronouncement. Jim quickly diffuses any controversy. "I'm pleased to have Ray as the executive process owner for supply in the supply review process," he says, "and I am certainly supportive of Susan being the process coordinator."

Sam, smiling, says, "But since there is truly no one person in charge of all of supply, the vice-president of supply must be Mark, who is also the general manager."

Anita and Jim both simultaneously say, "That makes sense to me."

Nolan intervenes. "Is there any other input on the process owner and process coordinator for the supply review?" he asks. The room is silent.

"Silence is approval. Let's move on," Nolan says. With the issue of subprocess owner and coordinator decided, he is ready to get into the supply review process in greater detail.

Nolan explains to the group that just as the demand review process is truly an integrated management process for marketing and sales, the supply review process is an integrated management meeting for the key functions in supply. This would include, but is not limited to, final assembly, manufacturing, engineering, quality assurance, purchasing, planning, and human resources.

Ray, who now finds himself as subprocess owner, asks, "What about key manufacturing supervisors?"

"You will need to decide who participates for yourself," Nolan replies. "The issue is to have neither too many people involved nor too few. I know that does not answer your question directly, but the answer depends on a number of things."

He explains that when a full enterprise resource planning and control system is up and running properly — meaning that it is truly integrated, it is probably unnecessary for supervisors to participate in the monthly supply review. They will be involved in supply review, but on an ongoing basis. As part of the integration with master scheduling and manufacturing scheduling, the supervisors will be involved in weekly supply review relative to performance to the master schedule and the manufacturing schedules. If a fully integrated planning and control system is not in place, there may be more value in having the supervisors participate in the monthly review process.

"But you do not need to decide that today," Nolan says. "Let's continue our discussion of the process." He tells the group that as part of the monthly supply review subprocess, the supply team reviews performance against the last agreed-upon supply plan. Some questions must be asked and answered: Did we do what we said we were going to do? If not, why not? What were the variances and why? What should we do, if anything, to correct the source of the variances?

"Sam will be doing the same thing on the demand side of the business," Nolan notes.

He advances the computer presentation to the next slide (Figure 20). "Here's an example of a performance measurement review format," he says. "Just like the sales and operations planning dashboard, shown earlier in the morning, a green, yellow, and red system is employed to show performance at a glance."

Supply Measurements	Month -3	Month -2	Month -1
On-time delivery (%)	Yellow	Yellow	Red
Build plan performance (%)	Green	Yellow	Yellow
Ship plan performance (%)	Yellow	Yellow	Red
Supplier delivery performance (%)	Red	Red	Red
Inventory to plan (%)	Red	Red	Red
Number of defects (%)	Green	Yellow	Green
Manufacturing costs plan vs. actual (%)	Green	Yellow	Yellow

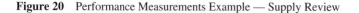

Figure 20   Performance Measurements Example — Supply Review

Nolan continues to explore the supply review subprocess. He tells the group that the performance review is followed by a review of the newly updated demand plan, or request for product. The purpose of this review is to determine whether the supply side of the business can support the changes in the demand plan and still maintain current resources and projected costs. A simulation of capacity, called rough-cut capacity planning, is commonly used to determine feasibility.

Nolan is quick to point out that rough-cut capacity planning is different from detailed capacity planning. Rough-cut capacity planning is known as a "first cut" at attempting to answer some questions: Do we have a reasonable chance to support the demand plan? Do we have sufficient resources to support the plan? Are our resources "sized" correctly? If the answer to any of these questions is no, the supply team is responsible for taking action or making recommendations to take action to solve the out-of-balance condition.

"In essence, rough-cut capacity planning is a 'what if' simulation that tests whether you can commit to support the new demand plan without changing one of the knobs we talked about before," Nolan says.

"When you use the term rough-cut capacity planning, are suppliers included in the simulation?" Anita Cooper, the purchasing manager, asks.

Nolan asks the group to turn to page 47 in their notebooks, which provides more details about rough-cut capacity planning. He explains that it is imperative to have the ability to perform multiple simulations quickly and easily. There are usually multiple planning options, and it is frequently desirable to test more than one production/supply plan alternative against the demand request for product.

Another principle of rough-cut capacity planning is the simulation of key resources only. "Not all resources are simulated," Nolan says. "Just the ones that are likely to cause problems."

He tells the group that key resources typically are bottlenecks or constraints. They may be resources that are difficult or expensive to change. He goes on to list typical categories of key resources: skills, materials, engineering, money, or any other item that may be a constraint in supporting the new demand request.

"And, yes, Susan," Nolan says, "they may include key suppliers as well as internal resources. Additionally, the key constraints may actually be key materials. These can be simulated as well as capacity."

Nolan explains that the objective is to first identify any constraints so that alternative approaches can be developed to support the demand. It would be unusual to find that all resources are constraints. Depending upon the volume and the product mix, it is typical to find a limited number of constraints during any particular period in time.

"Remember," Nolan says, "in a demand-driven organization with the objective to meet customers' expectations all the time, you should be predisposed to find a way to say yes to the new demand request for product. If it costs more to do so, the implications of supporting the plan should surface as a management issue in the sales and operations planning process. The cost of not meeting marketplace expectations may ultimately be far greater than the added cost to manufacturing or engineering."

Susan raises her hand. "If this is only rough-cut capacity planning, when is more detailed capacity planning performed?"

Nolan tells the group the detailed capacity planning is usually performed as part of the master scheduling process. The additional detail simulated typically includes testing resources for an expanded number of variables, including product mix, a more detailed simulation of resources, and specific days or weeks. Detailed capacity planning is commonly performed more frequently than once a month, usually weekly or sometimes even daily.

Nolan stops and surveys the room. He wants to make sure that the group understands the differences between rough-cut capacity planning and detailed capacity planning. He explains that for sales and operations planning, rough-cut capacity planning is performed monthly and at an aggregate level. For example, rough-cut capacity planning may simulate the demand of all product groups for the capacity of an entire work center, which may consist of three machines. In contrast, detailed capacity planning may simulate each machine in that same work center.

Nolan clicks the mouse to advance to the next slide (Figure 21). "Here is an example of a rough-cut capacity planning presentation for one resource," he says. The vertical columns represent requirements for the capacity in time periods. The bottom line represents demonstrated capacity. The middle line represents planned capacity, and the top line represents maximum capacity.

"The power of rough-cut capacity planning is its ability to demonstrate whether the resources are 'sized' correctly to support what we chose to do in the marketplace," Nolan comments. "It not only identifies problems of projected capability shortages, but it also identifies opportunities where there is projected capacity available. For master scheduling, additional detailed capacity simulations may be required to ensure that the detailed schedule is feasible and can be supported by the company resources."

Nolan looks at Jim, Guy, and Susan. He tells them that two books are required reading: *Gaining Control* by James Correll and Norris Edson and *Master Scheduling* by John Proud.

Jim Simpson raises his hand. "What about inventory and customer lead times? Are they considered in the supply planning process?"

"Yes, they are," Nolan replies. "In previous sales and operations planning cycles, you will set targets for inventory and customer lead times by product line or product group. The demand planning process could request changes in those

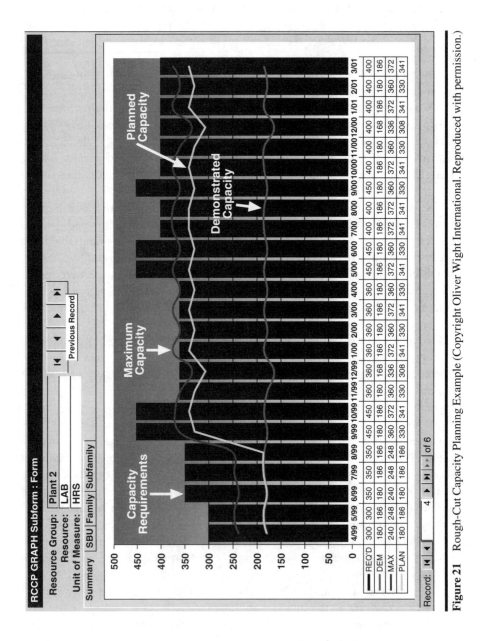

RCCP GRAPH Subform : Form

Resource Group: Plant 2
Resource: LAB
Unit of Measure: HRS

| Summary | SBU | Family | Subfamily |

	4/99	5/99	6/99	7/99	8/99	9/99	10/99	11/99	12/99	1/00	2/00	3/00	4/00	5/00	6/00	7/00	8/00	9/00	10/00	11/00	12/00	1/01	2/01	3/01
REQ'D	300	300	350	350	350	450	450	360	360	360	360	360	360	450	450	400	400	450	400	400	400	400	400	400
DEM	180	186	180	186	248	186	186	180	168	186	186	180	180	186	180	186	186	186	186	180	168	180	180	186
MAX	240	248	240	248	248	372	372	372	336	360	372	372	360	372	372	372	372	360	372	360	336	372	360	372
PLAN	180	186	186	180	186	341	341	330	308	341	330	341	330	341	330	341	341	330	341	330	308	341	330	341

Record: ◄ ◄ 4 ► ► ►* of 6

Figure 21 Rough-Cut Capacity Planning Example (Copyright Oliver Wight International. Reproduced with permission.)

targets along with their updated demand plan, or request for product. The load on key resources includes meeting inventory and lead time targets."

He explains that in response to requests for changes in inventory and lead time targets as well as the updated demand plan, the supply organization develops a volume production plan by month. This plan should (1) satisfy customer delivery requirements, or shipments; (2) conform as closely as possible to inventory targets; and (3) meet as closely as possible customer lead-time targets.

To achieve all three aims requires tactics that address how much inventory is required to support the desired customer lead-time targets. "The process for determining these tactics frequently is called 'where to meet the customer,'" Nolan says.

He further explains that determining the tactics is a key element of implementing a combined marketing–manufacturing strategy. It also is necessary for effective master scheduling.

"This could be the subject of another class," Nolan tells the group, "and we will have much discussion on inventory and lead time tactics as we work with you to develop your sales and operations planning process. For now, let's just acknowledge that we must decide what our tactics will be and set targets accordingly."

Susan raises her hand. "Before we move on, doesn't this whole conversation imply that the production plan could be different from the backlog of customer orders? Also, couldn't the production plan be different from what is planned to be sold?"

Mark admires Susan's approach. She already knows the answers to the questions she has asked, but she wants everyone else to hear the answers from an industry expert. She has some points to make, and she is going to let Nolan make them for her.

"You're correct, Susan," Nolan replies. "We call it the decoupling of demand and supply." He explains that, stated simply, decoupling of demand and supply involves choosing to produce at a rate different than the shipment rate or the bookings rate. To the extent that these rates are different, either inventory or customer lead time (backlog), or both, will need to be varied.

"The principle of decoupling demand and supply gives the supply side of the business improved control over two of the three knobs — the time knob, or schedule, and the resource knob, or people, equipment, etc.," Nolan says. "Even though the production plan is different from the customer order backlog when demand and supply are decoupled, the production plan still must support current orders on the books, or backlog, and the anticipated demand."

Nolan displays the next slide in his presentation (Figure 22). He asks the group to consider the point made by the graphic. It is a reality that demand fluctuates. It is also a reality that a level production schedule is most cost effective. Decoupling

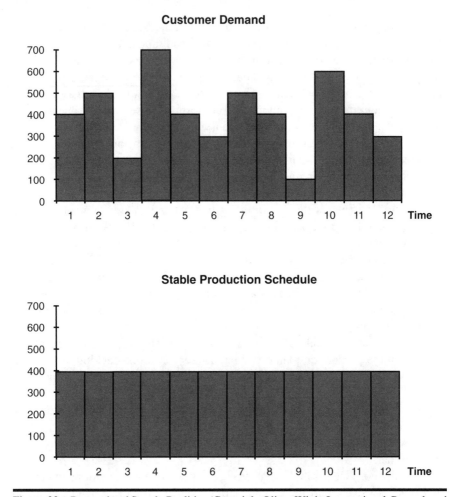

Figure 22 Demand and Supply Realities (Copyright Oliver Wight International. Reproduced with permission.)

demand and supply enables companies not to force demand to conform to a level production schedule. It also gives the manufacturing function the ability to produce more cost effectively.

Janis Novak, the controller, raises her hand. "When demand and supply are decoupled, don't you increase the risk of higher inventories?" she asks.

"That can occur," Nolan replies, "if inventory is not managed." He explains that sales and operations planning is a process to make sure that inventory *is* managed. He also asks the class to consider another risk. If demand and supply are *not* decoupled, companies risk higher manufacturing costs, higher material costs, and poor customer service. Sales and operations planning provides the means to keep inventory, costs, and service under control during the natural, ongoing changes in demand that occur in most businesses.

"How are inventory and customer lead-time targets established in sales and operations planning?" Susan asks.

"Good question," Nolan replies, "but I would like to defer answering it for now. We will spend considerable time on this issue during the two-day detailed class as well as during the implementation. For now, let me give you my quick one-word answer: *carefully*."

Seeing that Susan is not entirely satisfied, Nolan adds that some of the key considerations include:

- What is necessary to meet customer expectations
- What is necessary to be better than the competition
- The variability and accuracy of the forecast
- How quickly the supply side of the business can respond to change
- The cost of making change in the supply side of the business
- The financial strength of the company
- The current business situation

"If you take these, plus other considerations, into account with a large dose of common sense, you will come up with a starting point for the targets," Nolan says. "The company should then commit to continuously improve upon these targets over time."

"Does that imply you may have different targets for different product lines?" Susan asks.

"Yes, it does," Nolan answers. He explains that one practice employed by many companies is to use what is sometimes called a "peanut butter" approach, where one standard is used for all product lines. This practice usually results in two conditions that put the company at either a financial disadvantage or a service disadvantage. Poor utilization of inventory can be the result, or delivery lead times do not match market requirements on different product lines.

"Why does this peanut butter approach occur?" Nolan asks. "It is either a result of management by accident, meaning that management does not make a decision with regard to individualized targets, or it is the direct result of misguided senior management, which often occurs through what we like to call management by edict. Neither one of the two methods is truly professional management in my opinion."

Susan turns toward Mark and looks him straight in the eye. "Did you hear that, Mark?" she asks.

"Guilty as charged," Mark acknowledges. "But that is why Ross and Nolan are here. I want them to help us change some of our less-than-effective and inefficient practices, including my own."

Sam raises his hand. "Nolan, the supply side of the business has made commitments to shorten its cycle times and reduce its costs. Would the results of these efforts normally be reviewed in a supply review?"

Ray Guy, the final assembly manager, squirms in his seat. Reduced cycle times have not been achieved, and he is especially chagrined that someone on the sales side of the business is pointing out this deficiency.

Nolan ignores Ray's discomfort. He explains that the supply review provides an excellent forum to review the status of supply-oriented activities, such as cycle time reduction and cost reductions. The executive in charge of the supply review should be monitoring the progress of these activities at least monthly anyway. Some companies have introduced a performance measurement that addresses cycle time reductions.

Nolan searches through the presentation program until he finds the slide he wants (Figure 23). "This is a measure of velocity, often expressed as a velocity ratio," he says, pointing to the graphic. He explains that the objective of this measurement is to make visible how well nonvalue-added time is minimized in a process cycle. This measurement can be used to measure process cycles in all areas of a company, not just the supply organization. For example, it is useful for measuring order-entry processing time and invoicing processing time, as well as any other processes. Companies that utilize a lean or agile methodology consider velocity ratio a key measure of progress and success.

Ray Guy wants to shift the focus from supply issues to demand issues. He raises his hand. "I have a question regarding the process. How is the updated demand forecast communicated to the supply side of the business?"

"I meant to mention communication when I discussed the demand review process," Nolan replies. "There are two aspects that must be considered. One is the quality of communication; the other is the mechanics, or tools, used to communicate."

He explains that it is assumed that the demand review meeting will be attended by key marketing and sales management people as well as invited guests. These invited guests may include someone representing the product development or engineering function, finance, and the supply function. Usually, the supply planner represents the supply side of the business.

The supply representative does not attempt to influence the demand decisions in this meeting. The supply representative's role is to observe and hear the conversation regarding the updated plan, in particular changes to the demand request for product. This approach facilitates efficiency and understanding. The supply side does not have to wait for an official memo or e-mail to begin its analysis of how it will support the changes to the demand plan.

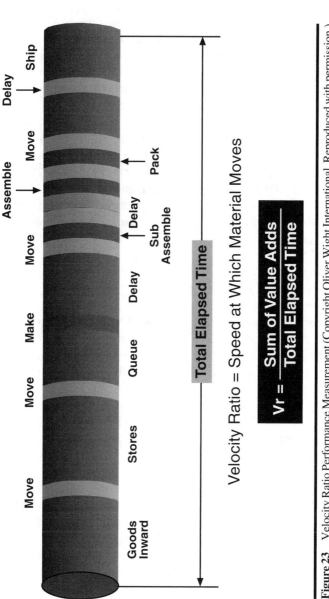

Goods Inward — Move — Stores — Move — Make — Move — Assemble — Move — Delay — Ship

Move — Queue — Delay — Sub Assemble — Delay — Pack

Velocity Ratio = Speed at Which Material Moves

Total Elapsed Time

$$Vr = \frac{\text{Sum of Value Adds}}{\text{Total Elapsed Time}}$$

Figure 23   Velocity Ratio Performance Measurement (Copyright Oliver Wight International. Reproduced with permission.)

The mechanics of communicating the demand plan depends on the availability of communications tools. The demand plan, or request for product, ideally is communicated via a database that is accessible by the supply side of the business. This database may be part of a communication and presentation tool specifically designed for sales and operations planning. It may be part of a forecasting software tool. It may be part of the enterprise resource planning system. It may also be as simple as a spreadsheet file.

Determining the tool that will be used is part of the detailed process design. Tools for sales and operations planning have been largely ignored by enterprise resource planning software suppliers. Some of the information needed to support sales and operations planning should be available in Universal Products' systems, but the reporting and presentation tools will need to be developed.

Jim Simpson, the manufacturing director, raises his hand. "In the discussion about the supply review, you showed us a sample of performance measurements. Will performance measurements be reviewed during the demand review, too?"

"Yes, they will," Nolan replies. He explains that the basic practice for all subprocesses is to:

- Review performance
- Discuss known changes
- Review the assumptions
- Review resource utilization (on both the demand and supply side)
- Determine any desired or recommended changes to action plans and resource changes
- Conduct both a qualitative and quantitative review and update of the plan

"The sales and operations planning process should be focused on the future," Nolan says, "but it should be pointed out that the past often influences the future."

He tells the group that performance measurements increase the accountability to achieve the plan. Each person is responsible and accountable to do what he or she said they were going to do.

Performance measurements have been found to fundamentally improve performance. Measurements of past performance provide a statistical basis for confidence or concern. If there has been high variability in performance in the past, it is only reasonable to expect high variability in performance in the future unless the cause of the variability is understood and corrected. Understanding past performance should have a significant influence on executive decision making.

"Do the demand review and supply review address the financial impact to changes in the plans?" Janis Novak asks.

"Yes," Nolan replies. "On the demand side, two views of the plan are reviewed. There is a review of volume changes in whatever unit of measure is meaningful to both the demand and the supply side of the business. There is also a review of pricing assumptions, which enables calculation of projected revenue over the planning."

"On the supply side," he continues, "the impact of changes to the plan on anticipated costs is used to calculate the projection of cost of goods sold as well as gross margin by product line."

Nolan also notes that, like the demand review, invited guests attend the supply review meeting. Those invited guests typically include representatives from finance, product development or engineering, and the demand function. The individual from the demand side would most often be the demand planner.

Peter Newfeld, the product development/engineering director, shifts uncomfortably in his chair. "Since it seems so many of the same people attend the product review, demand review, and supply review meetings, why can't there simply be one meeting? Wouldn't that be more efficient?"

Nolan explains that many companies have tried this approach, but the end results have been disappointing. While a single meeting may be better than no communication at all, the purpose of the reviews is diluted.

"Remember," Nolan says, "the purpose of the subprocess reviews is not just to communicate. The primary purpose is to serve as *functional management meetings.*"

Nolan tells the group that many of the topics that should be discussed in the demand review meeting are of little use to the supply side. Likewise, much of the discussion at the supply review is of little use to the demand side. It is a potential waste of some of the individuals' time.

Another critical reason not to combine the two meetings is the need for the supply side to have the time to analyze the demand request for product. The supply side needs time to determine whether and how it can support the updated demand request.

"In the absence of facts," Nolan says, and then he is interrupted by Jim Simpson.

"The only answer you can give is yes," Jim concludes.

"The supply side should not be forced to commit to a plan it can't achieve," Nolan says. "This often occurs when companies use a single review meeting, and then the supply side is unfairly criticized for poor performance."

Again he is interrupted by Jim. "For not doing what it said it was going to do," Jim says.

Mark and the rest of the group laugh. "Very good, Jim," Mark says. "I guess you must be learning something."

Jim laughs as well. "Mark, it's just that every day we do most of what Ross and Nolan say shouldn't be done."

Nolan does not want to lose momentum. This is an opportunity to point out how the sales and operations planning process should not be conducted.

"I have seen some companies conduct what they call a pre-sales and operations planning meeting," he says. He explains that an ineffective pre-sales and operations planning meeting is usually attended by a cast of twenty or thirty middle managers who represent most of the company functions. The meetings are long and typically degenerate into meaningless exchanges and name-calling. The reason pre-sales and operations planning meetings often fail is that neither demand nor supply is properly prepared. Both sides try to update their plans during the meeting itself, and there is no one with the authority to make a decision.

"Ross had one client," Nolan says as he turns to Ross, who is seated behind the rest of the class. "Ross, you tell it."

Ross stands and walks to the front of the room. "I had a client," he says, "that tried this approach. As I sat through one of these sessions, it became apparent to me that the most important part of the meeting was to try to second-guess what senior management would decide on an issue. Then the middle managers spent a great deal of time deciding what issues to present and not present to senior management for the executive sales and operations planning meeting. In essence, they were deciding what to hide from senior management. I was so upset with their behavior that I told them that if they worked for me, I would fire them all. *Open and honest communication* is a value that I believe all organizations should aspire to maintain. It is senior management's responsibility to develop management processes that facilitate and ensure open and honest communication."

"So what happened?" Susan asks.

Ross tells the group that the company's general manager had hired him because sales and operations planning was not delivering the expected results. Ross explained the consequence of the pre-sales and operations planning meeting to the general manager. He advised the general manager to discontinue it and follow the standard process steps and let the information speak for itself. The general manager followed Ross's advice, and the company ultimately developed an effective process that achieved the desired results.

"And no," Ross adds, "the general manager did not fire anyone, at least not over this issue."

"Let's complete the conversation on a separate pre-sales and operations planning meeting," he says. "In fairness, in large companies or large divisions, a pre-sales and operations planning meeting or step is often included as a formal step in the process." He explains that those companies that are successful with this approach utilize the pre-meeting to develop joint recommendations for critical decisions that surfaced during the pre-sales and operations planning steps.

The secret to making a pre-sales and operations planning meeting work well is to have only the people necessary attend the session. Who should those people be? It depends upon the issues that surface in the pre-sales and operations planning steps. In essence, the problem picks the people required to solve it. The outputs from a pre-sales and operations planning meeting are alternatives and a recommendation to senior management.

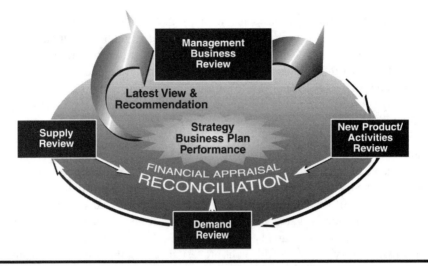

Figure 24   Integrated Business Management Model (Copyright Oliver Wight International. Reproduced with permission.)

"Here's another model that demonstrates what I mean," Ross says as he displays a new graphic (Figure 24). He tells the group that this model was developed in the European region of the Oliver Wight Companies. The model consists of the following five steps:

■ New products and activities review
■ Demand review
■ Supply review
■ Financial appraisal and demand/supply/inventory reconciliation
■ Management business review

Companies striving to improve their sales and operations planning processes use this model to help reinforce the importance of new products, programs, and projects in the management process. The financial appraisal and reconciliation step recognizes that senior management does not want to spend time working on detailed demand, supply, and inventory balancing issues. Those issues are expected to be resolved during the new products and activities review, demand review, and supply review steps.

It is not always possible to reconcile these issues. At times, additional resources must be authorized or management direction is required. In these cases, the issues are addressed by senior management in the management business review on an exception basis. This approach makes the decision-making process both more effective and more efficient, especially in larger companies.

Ross pauses for a minute. "I see this model utilized most often when the sales and operations planning process has matured to the point where it is truly the primary management process for the general manager and his or her staff."

Ross points to the first step in the process, the new products/activities review. He explains that the outputs of this step are updated new product plans, end-of-life product plans, and reporting of product development status. Status of key company projects, programs, or initiatives is also reported. A product/project coordinator facilitates this step.

The output of the demand review is the updated consensus forecast or demand plan. The purpose of the third step, the supply review, is to ensure that the demand plan can be met and that alternative supply plans are developed to support the plan as needed. Demand, supply, and inventory plans are synchronized.

The output of the fourth step, the financial appraisal and reconciliation, is critical. The finance organization compares the proposed sales and operations plans with the business plan and financial goals. The actions and activities defined as necessary to achieve the plans are tested against the company's business strategy. The purpose of this test is to ensure that company action plans are aligned with the company strategy. The outputs of this step are the key issues which require direction or decisions from the senior management team.

The fifth step, the senior management business review, is often referred to as the executive sales and operations planning meeting. The fourth step, financial appraisal and reconciliation, is often referred to as the pre-sales and operations planning meeting.

Ross asks the class to turn to page 61 in their notebooks. The chart on this page (Figure 25) describes each step in the process. Ross explains that in this model, the financial appraisal is in the center, to indicate that each step reviews the financial consequences of its plans. This model also shows reconciliation in the center. This implies that issues that can be resolved without senior management decisions are addressed in the appropriate reviews steps and recommendations to senior management are developed cross-functionally.

■ ■ ■

Nolan steps forward to continue his presentation, but Ross is not quite finished. "Let me make a few additional comments, if I may," he says.

Nolan steps back and gives Ross the floor.

"What happens when an unrealistic supply plan is allowed to be accepted?" he asks.

Susan Callahan, the planning manager, is quick to respond. "First, the dates in the communications system become invalid," she replies. "When the dates in the system are an invalid representation of what is truly expected to occur, it is an unrealistic plan. When the plan is unrealistic, people cannot rely upon the dates. They learn not to believe them."

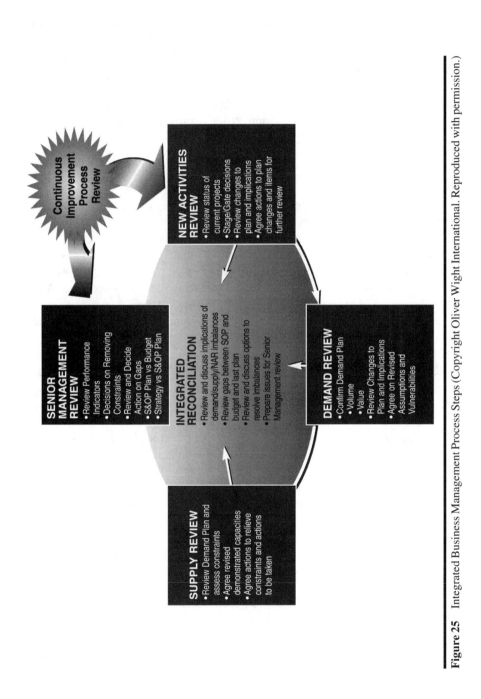

Figure 25 Integrated Business Management Process Steps (Copyright Oliver Wight International. Reproduced with permission.)

"Excellent, Susan," Ross says. "Let me create a scenario. The phone rings in the customer service–order entry area. It is a customer looking for her order. The customer service representative looks the order up on his computer and finds that it was supposed to ship last week. That is the date on the order, but the order has not been shipped. Here's the question. Does the customer service representative know when the order will ship or why it is late?"

"No," Susan responds quickly again. "He must find out the status."

"And how does he do that?" Ross asks.

"He calls someone in planning," Susan replies.

Mark is amazed by how quickly Susan answers. It is like watching a tennis match.

"And someone in planning goes to her computer system and looks up the order," Ross says. "What does she find?"

"That it was supposed to ship last week," Susan answers.

"Does she know when it will ship or why it is late?" Ross asks.

"No," Susan says. "She must find out the status."

"So she goes to final assembly to find out when it will ship," Ross says. "And when she gets to final assembly, Jim, what does she find out?"

Jim Simpson, the manufacturing director, is as quick as Susan to reply. "She finds out that the order is late, but of course, she already knew that," he says.

"Does she find out when it will ship and why it was late?" Ross asks.

Ray Guy, the final assembly manager, is quick to jump in. "Maybe," he replies. "It depends on whether final assembly has the parts and whether final assembly's work schedule is overloaded or not. If we are overloaded, and we usually are, we get the shipment date from our hot list that we use for priorities. If we don't have the parts, it is because they are late, and the planning person will have to find out when we will have the parts. After that, then maybe we can give her a ship date."

Anita Cooper, the purchasing manager, jumps in. "If final assembly doesn't have the parts," she says, "there is a good chance that the supplier is late in delivering. When that's the case, and it often is, I call the supplier to find out the delivery date."

"Ray, is it possible that your hot list of priorities will change as a result of the customer questioning why the order is late?" Ross asks.

"Not only is it possible, it is highly probable," he replies. "Assuming that purchasing gives final assembly a date when the parts will be delivered, we would tell planning, and planning would tell the customer service rep, who would then give a new ship date to the customer."

"Do you have only one customer calling to inquire about late shipments?" Ross asks.

Peter Newfeld, the product development/engineering director, laughs. "We have many, many customers calling about late shipments." He answers the logical next question before Ross can ask it. "And what that means is that we have multiple customer service reps going to multiple planners, who talk to multiple people in final assembly, manufacturing, purchasing, *and* engineering to determine the status of jobs and to expedite their customers' orders over other customer order. Each time a change is made in one area, it affects the schedule in most of the other areas."

"And that means when it comes time to develop the annual budget, you need to budget for more people in customer service and planning to keep up with the communication and administration of customer orders," Ross observes.

He pauses and looks at the team. It is time for him to make a point and set some expectations. He tells the group that when the management team allows unrealistic plans to be approved, there are many consequences. "Not only does it result in late customer deliveries," he says, "it also results in higher manufacturing and material costs, poor quality, increased inventory, and higher administrative costs than necessary."

Now it is time to articulate an expectation. A realistic plan on the supply side defines the quantity of product to be produced, the timing, and the cost. Dates should be credible. If a date cannot be met, that should be appropriately communicated, along with the reason why.

"By tracking the reasons, and using Pareto analysis," Ross says, "you can accumulate data that enable you to determine the root cause for late deliveries and then put corrective actions in place."

Ross turns to Sam. It is time to set another expectation. "Sam, marketing and sales has a leadership role to play here," he says. "That role is to help ensure the company agrees only to realistic plans. I have never known a professional salesperson who would knowingly lie to a customer. A professional salesperson knows that his or her only real asset is his or her personal credibility. If the company continually fails to deliver on its promises, or does not do what it says it is going to do, it hurts the credibility of the sales force and magnifies the effect of the missed deliveries."

Ross pauses. He wants the group to think about what he has just said. After a few moments, he adds, "When management approves unrealistic plans, it institutionalizes lying or at best misinformation. Unrealistic planning is mismanagement."

Mark Ryan is uncomfortable with Ross's last statement. "Aren't you being a bit harsh?" he asks. "I could interpret your words to mean that we or, more specifically, I am guilty of mismanagement."

Ross expected to ruffle a few feathers with his statement. He feels that a bit of discomfort will help begin to establish a motivation for changing management's behavior.

"Interpret the words as you wish," he replies, "but, no, I don't believe I'm being too harsh. In this day and age, there is no reason to operate with unrealistic plans. Every company has a choice to do it correctly or not."

All eyes turn to Mark to see how he will respond to Ross's indictment.

Nolan is quick to intervene. "Our purpose here today is to make you think," he says. "Think about how you are presently managing the business, and think about how you could manage the business more effectively. We will challenge your current practices. Our assumption is that you will institute new management practices, such as only approving realistic plans, because it is common sense to do so or, more specifically, organized common sense. We've just had a conversation about the current way the business is being managed. Does it make sense?"

The team, including Mark, is silent.

Nolan looks at his watch. It is time for a break. "Let's take ten minutes and then come back and talk about the financial review," he says.

■ ■ ■

Ross motions for Mark to join him and Nolan at the front of the room. They need to discuss logistics. Ross points to his watch. "We are running somewhat behind. To cover all the material we planned, we will probably need to go until at least six o'clock," he says. "How will that affect the dinner you planned?"

"We were on time until Ross came back up and interrupted my presentation," Nolan jokes.

Mark smiles. He likes Nolan poking fun at the more serious Ross. "Dinner won't be a problem," Mark says. "We can move it to 7:30. I am pleased with what has been accomplished. It has been worth taking the extra time. It has been good for us to see some of our behaviors in a different light."

Mark excuses himself to rearrange dinner. Ross and Nolan confer about the class material and the amount of time left. Nolan will cover the financial review, and Ross will present the sales and operations planning executive meeting. Ross will wrap up by presenting an overview of demand planning and then the sales and operations planning implementation steps.

It is a lot of material to cover in a few hours. Experience has shown, however, that if these topics are not covered with the executive team up front, the pace of the implementation slows as executives struggle to understand the concepts and methodology.

As Mark walks back from making his phone call, he is contemplative. He realizes that he is a significant reason why Universal Products has failed to meet its goals. In his zeal to be responsive to customers and corporate, he has regularly violated most of the principles and practices presented thus far today. The damage has not come from any single incident. It is the sum of all the small, singular incidents which occur on a daily basis that has caused the damage.

One month ago, after Mark's interviews with his executive team, he was confused as to why Universal Products was struggling to achieve its goals. Now, it is very clear why Universal Products is not operating effectively.

Rather than being discouraged, as he was one month ago, Mark is optimistic. He will have a tool that will enable him to influence change, and it does not appear that he will have to fight his team to implement change. From their dialogue today, the members of his executive team have shown that they are ready to operate in a new way.

Mark also feels an apology is in order. He understands now why Ross criticized him for focusing on sales and operations planning as a meeting. Sales and operations planning is much more than a monthly meeting. It is a methodology for managing and operating the business.

As Mark enters the meeting room, he is glad that Jack Baxter, the corporate president, was unable to attend the class. Mark wants time to assimilate what he has learned before discussing it with Jack. He knows that other divisions have operational problems similar to those at Universal Products. Mark makes a mental note to talk with Ross in the weeks to come about how best to introduce Jack to the essence of the sales and operations planning process.

■ ■ ■

Before Nolan can begin his presentation, Ray Guy, the final assembly manager, raises his hand. "Nolan, if you don't mind, I would like to state my understanding at this point to ensure that I heard correctly."

"Fire away," Nolan says.

"At this point in the monthly cycle, the demand review subprocess will have provided an updated demand plan or forecast, which is viewed as a request for product. Since Sam is responsible for the demand plan and responsible to execute the plan, there is no need for me to second-guess the demand plan. I also know that his performance will be visible to Mark and to all members of the team each sales and operations planning cycle."

Nolan nods his head. So far, so good.

"The supply review meeting compares our performance against what we said we would do," Ray continues. "We need to understand our performance to date because it may affect our decisions about the future supply plan. Also, we need to be prepared to discuss significant performance variances with Mark and the team. We understand the root causes for performance variances and develop a corrective action plan for problems identified. We develop a new supply plan in support of the updated demand plan, which may or may not require us to change resources. When we must adjust resources, we use the three-knobs principle of work, time, and resources."

Nolan smiles in affirmation.

"We have to understand the effect of the new plan on costs," Ray says. "Since we have participated as observers in the demand meeting and finance has been involved in both the demand meeting and the supply meeting, there should be little miscommunication or few surprises at this point. Do I have the gist of this correct?"

"Very good," Nolan replies, "and you have identified another principle of sales and operations planning. Once you get to the executive sales and operations planning meeting, *there should be no surprises.* The surprises have all been discovered and communicated in the pre-sales and operations planning reviews and communications."

"Well, that brings me to my question. It's about decision making," Ray says. "It's not clear to me what decisions are supposed to be made where in this cycle. It sounds like this process could reinforce the old 'command and control' management philosophy versus the more popular people-empowerment philosophy. Is that how the decision-making works?"

"If we are not careful," Nolan says, "sometimes we make it sound like all issues are being brought to the sales and operations planning meeting for resolution. In practice, this is not the case at all. In fact, sales and operations planning is a tremendously empowering process."

Ross stands up to address the group. "I have a personal experience that relates to your question, Ray. I personally believe that sales and operations planning is one of the most empowering things a company can do."

Ross tells the group that he once worked for a company whose senior executive was a micromanager. The senior executive believed he had to be involved in every detail of every decision. "It was only after we implemented sales and operations planning that I understood why the senior executive found it necessary to micromanage," Ross says.

He explains that without sales and operations planning, the senior executive was not confident that his executive staff was paying attention to the right things and making the right choices or decisions. He felt like he was the only one who understood the whole picture, and therefore he needed to be involved in the decision making. "And he was right," Ross says.

He tells the team that the sales and operations planning process gave the entire staff the whole picture and built the senior executive's confidence in his staff to identify the right issues and take appropriate actions. In short, sales and operations planning enabled the senior executive to let go of his participation in the detailed decision making. It enabled him to empower his staff. If empowerment isn't occurring at the executive level, it won't occur at any other level in an organization.

Nolan picks up the discussion of decision making. "Over the last decade, many companies have been flattening their organizations through downsizing, rightsizing, reengineering, restructuring, and other such cost-saving activities. In order for an organization to work effectively and responsibly in this environment, there must be an effective decision-making process. It's impossible for executives to be aware of everything and in control of everything at every level. It *is* possible to know that the company is in control and that decisions are being made in a timely and appropriate manner. Sales and operations planning can provide that visibility."

Nolan asks the group to think about sales and operations planning in the following way: The sales and operations planning process is really about setting boundaries within which the organization is expected to operate or to seek permission to extend beyond those boundaries.

An analogy is raising a child through his or her teenage years. Clearly, there are different rules and boundaries when the child is thirteen than when he or she is eighteen. Both the child and the parents struggle with changing the boundaries over that period of time, but if the parents hold on too tight, there will be relationship problems with the child. Parents have to learn how to hold on tight enough to ensure their teenager's learning, education, and safety without alienating their loved one.

In business, management has a forum, a vehicle, to allow for the dynamics of changing the boundaries of the decision-making process as business conditions change. That forum is sales and operations planning.

Nolan scans the group to see if they have understood. There are no puzzled looks. The team members' expressions are intent and focused. "Let's move on to the financial review," he says.

■ ■ ■

"By now, you probably know the first question I am going to ask about the financial review subprocess," Nolan says.

"Who is the executive process owner for this subprocess?" Jim Simpson, the manufacturing director, replies.

All heads turn toward Janis Novak, the controller. "I guess that would be me," she says.

"And who is the logical person to be your financial review coordinator?" Nolan asks. "Remember, this person will most likely be involved in the demand review subprocess and the supply review subprocess."

"Actually, I am fortunate," Janis says. "I have a couple of very good candidates, but I would prefer not to name the individual now."

Ross has coached Mark to take definitive action whenever he sees an opportunity to move the process forward more quickly. "So when can we expect you to name the coordinator?" Mark asks.

"I can make that decision by Tuesday of next week," Janis responds.

"Are both of the individuals scheduled for the sales and operations planning class tomorrow and the next day?" Nolan asks.

"They are," Janis replies.

"Good," says Nolan. "Now, Janis, I would like some help. Please describe what you think the financial review should look like."

"I have a vision of how finance fits into the process," says Janis. She tells the group that she has worked in companies that used a sales and operations planning process, although they did not call it that. However, the process and principles appear to be the same. The processes already existed in the companies when Janis joined the firms, and she played a role as part of the finance team.

"Here is how I see it working at Universal Products," Janis says. "The finance review subprocess coordinator will participate in the demand review and supply review meetings. If for some reason she does not directly participate, she must be in the communication loop to receive results from both reviews. I am using the word *she* because both of my candidates for the role are female," Janis tells the group.

She goes on to explain that the coordinator makes sure that projected pricing issues are discussed and agreed upon in the demand review and that projected cost issues are discussed and reviewed in the supply review. She has the ability to question and challenge issues in both the demand and supply reviews, but will accurately represent the financial choices of both. She is not empowered to make decisions for demand or supply.

Nolan thinks this is a good time to get the group's validation. "Is the group okay with what Janis just said?" he asks.

Sam Wente, the sales director, says, "It sounds great to me!"

"I like what I hear," Jim Simpson, the manufacturing director, says. "So far, as Janis has described it, finance has not tried to dictate *its* answer to pricing and cost issues."

"Janis, go on, please," Nolan commands.

Janis tells the group that the finance review coordinator will keep her personally advised of any significant issues or major changes since the last sales and operations planning cycle. That way, Janis will know what is happening and will not be surprised by any of the plans, changes, or issues.

The coordinator will be responsible for taking the quantitative output of the demand review and the supply review and generating the company projected proforma income statement, balance sheet, and cash flow analysis. She also will develop a month-by-month financial projection that demonstrates the effect of any changes to the plan.

"What is the planning horizon for the financial projection?" Anita Cooper, the purchasing manager, asks.

Before Janis can reply, Peter Newfeld, the product development/engineering director, speaks up. "I can see where you get revenues, cost of goods sold, and gross margin, but where do you get input for the SG&A?" he asks.

"Let me answer Anita's question first," Janis says. "The month-by-month projections would be for the full planning horizon. The projected pro formas will be summed by quarter and by fiscal year, but the data will cover the full planning horizon by month."

Janis explains that there is an important issue to consider which Ross brought up earlier. The financial projections, the output from the sales and operations planning process, are the numbers that are used to communicate current expectations. One of finance's responsibilities is to compare the current plan, or the reality today, against the annual business plan.

Gaps that should be discussed in the sales and operations planning meeting will surface in this comparison. These gaps often drive actions that will be reflected in the next sales and operations planning cycle.

Janis turns to Peter. "Now to address your question," she says. She explains that Universal Products has an approved SG&A plan from the annual plan and from the previous sales and operations planning process. If there are going to be changes to the basic SG&A plan or assumptions behind the plan, they will surface through the process.

It is one of finance's responsibilities to make sure that issues or changes surface. That is one of the reasons why finance participates in the pre-sales and operations planning subprocess reviews.

"Say, for example," Janis says, "that engineering finds it needs to allocate more resources for the support of existing products. This issue should surface, and finance must take that into consideration when developing the company pro-forma financials."

Mark wants to clarify what financial information will be communicated to corporate. "Will these be the same numbers you send to corporate?" he asks.

"No, Mark, not yet," Janis replies. "The numbers I present to corporate are what we as a team, with your approval, agree upon in the executive sales and operations planning meeting."

Ray Guy, the final assembly manager, shifts in his chair. "Janis, sometimes the supply organization will be compelled to propose alternatives to meet changes in demand. The decision on those alternatives will be made in the executive sales and operations planning meeting, and they will clearly affect the financial plan. Since you are developing the pro forma before the sales and operations planning meeting, how will you deal with the financial impact of the proposed alternatives?"

Mark takes a moment to look around the room. Nolan is standing next to where Ross is seated. Ross catches Mark's eye and smiles because of what is happening. The team is developing ownership and understanding simultaneously. The high-level framework for the sales and operations planning process is being defined by the staff.

Janis clearly has the floor, and the team is engaged in the discussion. "You bring up an important point, Ray," she says. She tells the group that in one of the companies where she previously worked, the chief financial officer attempted to put precision into the projections. This created a great amount of work and did not allow for easy handling of alternatives.

"I thought the time expended was wasteful," Janis comments, "since we started with a forecast of demand that was less than precise. Adding precision at the end of the process did not make sense to me."

Janis explains that in the other company where she previously worked, rough-cut financials were developed as part of the sales and operations planning process. The finance team spent more time on analyzing the financial effects of the different proposed alternatives. In essence, "what if" simulations were developed for the different alternatives.

"I believe the first company was tied into a mentality of legal financial accounting, whereas the second company had a much better understanding of management accounting," Janis comments.

"How did you interface with the general manager?" Mark asks.

Janis tells Mark that the results of the financial simulations were available as part of an information package communicated to the general manager and other participants prior to the executive sales and operations planning meeting. The analysis included a comparison of each alternative against the annual plan previously submitted to corporate. This information helped the general manager and other executives in the decision-making and authorization process.

"I would like to make another point," Janis says. "Sales and operations planning is an authorization process. The discipline, as we used it, was to authorize resources for budget changes through the sales and operations planning process."

She explains that the executive team did not approve a plan without authorizing the necessary resources to achieve it. This is what Ross and Nolan have referred to as "only approving realistic plans." Picking up on comments from Ross and Nolan about boundary setting, Janis adds that the amount of resources approved became a boundary within which to operate.

Peter grins at Janis. "How do you know so much about sales and operations planning?" he asks.

"I was the financial review coordinator at both companies. I learned through experience," Janis replies.

"And does the process really work?" Sam Wente asks.

"Oh, yes!" Janis exclaims. "I was surprised that we didn't have a similar process at Universal Products. I don't believe sales and operations planning is an option. I believe it is something we must do and do well!"

"Is there a financial review meeting?" Justin Roberts, the marketing manager, asks.

Janis responds that in the first company where she worked, there was no meeting. It was just an exercise in cranking out and communicating the numbers. In the second company, a brief meeting was conducted after the financial simulations were completed. The result of the financial review meeting was often a specific recommendation developed from the alternative plans.

Ross stands to comment on what Janis has just said. He explains that in the sales and operations planning model developed by the Oliver Wight group, which he showed earlier (Figure 24), this is the reconciliation step or the fourth step in the process.

Janis continues with her discussion. The financial review meeting participants included the demand planner, the supply planner, the financial coordinator, and the controller. Others, including the general manager, were invited. They attended from time to time when there were critical financial issues.

Generally, these other executives did not find it necessary to attend. They were kept well informed during the subprocess reviews and with the information package that was distributed prior to the executive sales and operations planning meeting.

Mark smiles approvingly at Janis. He is impressed with her knowledge of the process. He will have a valuable resource during the implementation. He also knows that he needs to select a sales and operations planning coordinator, and he is strongly leaning toward appointing Janis.

Nolan walks to the front of the room. "Well, Janis, thank you for giving my presentation. Let me just show a couple of examples of the financial information that can support the sales and operations planning process." He shows the group two more graphs (Figures 26 and 27).

"Does anyone have any other questions or comments?" Nolan asks while the group studies the examples. "If not, then let's take a ten-minute break," he says. "And for planning purposes, it looks like we will be running closer to a 6:30 finish."

Mark approaches Janis during the break. "I am so pleased and impressed," he says. "I didn't know you had this level of knowledge about the process."

"Thanks, Mark," Janis replies. "I have good knowledge of the financial part, but am not as strong in understanding the entire process," she explains. "I did not

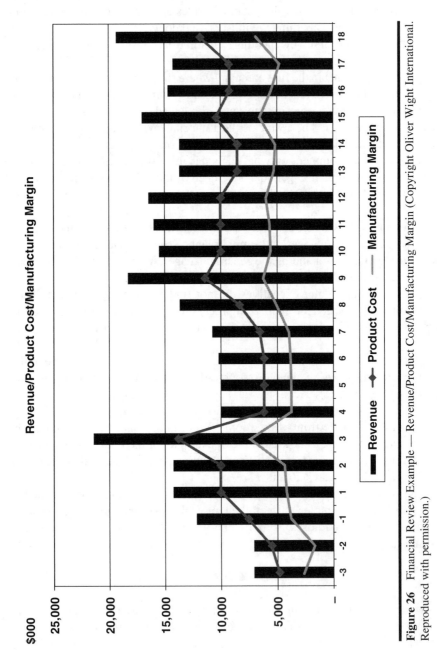

Figure 26   Financial Review Example — Revenue/Product Cost/Manufacturing Margin (Copyright Oliver Wight International. Reproduced with permission.)

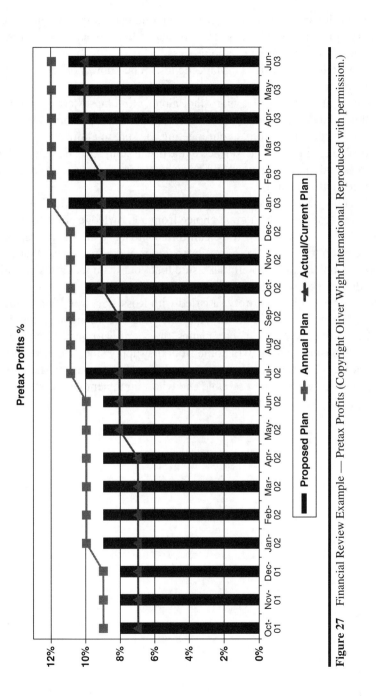

Figure 27 Financial Review Example — Pretax Profits (Copyright Oliver Wight International. Reproduced with permission.)

implement the process, nor did I actually participate in the executive sales and operations planning meeting. I know little about demand planning or supply planning, but I do know my part in the process."

"Don't sell yourself short," Mark replies. "You know more about the process than the rest of us."

Janis excuses herself, leaving Mark alone. Ross taps Mark on the shoulder. "We'll be addressing the executive sales and operations planning meeting next," Ross says. "Remember, that's your meeting. Be sure to allow questions or issues that you feel are important to surface in the discussion. Also, be prepared to name your sales and operations planning coordinator or tell your staff when you will announce your selection."

"What do you think about Janis being the coordinator?" Mark asks.

"I think that would be a great choice from a knowledge point of view," Ross replies. "However, you need to be comfortable that she has the proper chemistry with the rest of the team. From my observations, it doesn't appear that chemistry will be a problem, but we will make sure that your team members provide input on candidates before you name the specific individual."

Mark does not look entirely satisfied with Ross's answer. "Mark, there is no right answer as to who should be your sales and operations planning coordinator," Ross explains. "In many companies, the coordinator may be on the demand side of the business. Some will come from the supply side, and others will come from finance. The choice is really up to the general manager. The coordinator needs to be someone who is reliable and whose judgment you trust."

SALES AND OPERATIONS PLANNING EXECUTIVE MEETING

As the group members take their seats after the break, Ross stands at the front of the room. He will make the presentation about the executive sales and operations planning or management review meeting.

"Before we proceed, do you have any questions about the sales and operations planning subprocesses?" he asks.

"I am beginning to have a number of questions," Anita Cooper, the purchasing manager, says, "but I believe they are at a greater level of detail than you plan on handling in this session."

"That's a good sign, Anita," Ross replies. "We cannot cover all the details in one day. At best, we can help you all gain the same high level of understanding and see that you commit to your individual roles and responsibilities."

"So when do all the detail questions get answered?" Ray Guy, the final assembly manager, asks.

"Some of the questions will be answered in the next two-day education session. More will be answered during the design workshop. Even more will be answered during the first three cycles of using the process," Ross replies.

He explains that detail questions will be answered as issues arise during the operation of the first three cycles. Sales and operations planning is not something that needs to be massively engineered prior to operating the process.

"You will learn through doing," Ross says. "We will provide coaching and advice, but you will address the business issues yourselves. We cannot dictate the answers."

"I am somewhat passionate on this subject," Ross continues. He explains that he has seen many companies hire lots of consultants only to implement sales and operations planning unsuccessfully. First of all, most companies and consultants do not have hands-on operational experience with sales and operations planning. Many consulting companies and software suppliers are also more than happy to enter into a contract to supply something that is not well understood. It is viewed as continuous consultant employment — or at least employment until the client company realizes it is wasting time and money.

"You are taking some pretty tough shots at other consulting firms," Mark says. "Isn't that a little self-serving?"

"Perhaps you are right," Ross replies, "but to the extent that it is self-serving, the point I'm making is that I believe in a win-win philosophy." He notes that what drives Nolan, himself, and others in their firm is helping companies to implement sales and operations planning as quickly as possible. "We focus on time to results," he explains.

He tells the group that it is common to be invited into companies after they have been attempting to implement sales and operations planning for more than one or two years. These companies have spent millions of dollars on multiple consultants who have been continuously employed.

"There is a common thread among these companies that explains their failure," Ross comments. He explains that usually the executive staff and the consultants do not have a common understanding of what is to be accomplished. Management has hired consultants to implement the new management buzzword of the day, not to change the way of managing the business.

"How can that happen?" Mark asks.

"Very simply," Ross replies. He explains that business publications publish articles on an initiative or methodology that has worked for one or more companies. These articles provide an overview at best. They pique the interest of other company executives, who decide that if it works for someone else, it will work for them. They announce the new company initiative.

This is a common occurrence with almost any type of company initiative, from total quality to time-based competition. All of the initiatives that get press are valuable in their own right, but only if fully understood and implemented in the most appropriate way for the company.

The big void in most companies is lack of management understanding. That's why the following approach is being used with Universal Products:

1 Understanding
2. Design

3. Tools
4. Implementation

One client refers to this implementation approach as "schools, rules, and tools." The main point this client makes is that "schools," or understanding, must come first.

The late Oliver Wight, the acknowledged pioneer in integrated planning and control, used to say, "Commitment without understanding is a liability." He was absolutely correct. Without proper understanding, new initiatives may actually do more harm than good.

"Consider the tools requirements for sales and operations planning," Ross says. "Because minimum tools are needed to support the process, implementation can be accomplished three or four months after the senior staff and middle management team have been educated and have a true understanding of the process."

Ross explains that most of the elements of the sales and operations planning process are being done in some way, shape, manner, or form today. The implementation effort mostly requires sharing of information, working cooperatively to come to consensus on the plans, and simplifying and improving upon current activities.

For this reason, implementation need not be tremendously expensive, nor should it take an inordinate amount of time. The most important thing to focus on is to operate using the fundamental principles. This involves changing management behavior and is best accomplished through on-the-job coaching.

Mark recalls Ross telling him these things in their first meeting. It is important, he feels, for the entire group to hear Ross's perspective. It is born of experience.

"Thank you for the explanation, Ross," Mark says. "I have heard Ross's take on this before, but I wanted all of you to hear it, too." Turning to Ross, he says, "I must say, you were a little more bold with your comments this time."

"When I'm passionate, I can get carried away," Ross responds.

"Let's get going with the presentation on the executive sales and operations planning meeting," Mark says. "Ross, why don't you play the role of general manager and describe what you think the executive meeting should look like."

"I would be pleased to do so," Ross replies. After taking a few moments to prepare his thoughts for playing the role of general manager, he looks up and says, "First, I would like you all to consider that I am role playing. I am playing the role of the new general manager of Universal Products, Inc. Sorry, Mark, but that is my new role." The group chuckles.

Ross forges on. "Based upon my previous experience," he says, "no matter what my problems are in the marketplace, whether they are product performance, quality, price, delivery, customer service, or whatever, I know that I personally cannot solve the problems. I know that I must rely upon a team that shares the same values, vision, goals, and objectives as I do."

He tells the group that he also knows he cannot succeed by attempting to operate the enterprise with an annual business planning process. The annual plan can be used for overall direction in goal setting and strategy development. He also has enough experience to know that the traditional annual planning process is mostly a series of minor league games played between him and his staff and a major league game played between corporate and himself.

"I know that the development of an annual plan is necessary but not sufficient for my division's success," he explains. "I further know that micromanagement through daily and weekly interference with those who are tasked to get the work done rarely adds value. It mostly adds to the chaos and reduces the effectiveness and efficiency of the organization."

The group nods knowingly in support of Ross's last statement. Ross continues his monologue by explaining that he has come to recognize that he must quickly gain some level of control of the business. This control must be from a company perspective — not just a sales perspective, an operations perspective, an engineering perspective, or a financial perspective. In order to gain control from a company perspective, he needs a process.

He has learned enough about sales and operations planning to know that it looks and feels like organized common sense, and that is hard to argue against. He also knows that he has to establish an environment that enables the management team to make appropriate decisions and provide the proper strategic direction. Effective decision making and strategic direction require that all of the company functions appropriately and actively participate in the sales and operations planning process.

He has given some thought to how to establish an environment that enables effective decision making. He has determined that management behaviors that are not contributing to the whole entity will surface during implementation and operation of the sales and operations planning process itself. And if he is an astute enough listener and facilitator, he will also be able to determine the reasons for the poor behavior.

He also expects to find that people issues will not usually be the cause of lack of performance. The culprit will be lack of commitment by the company to honor the fundamental principles or processes. In other words, in the company's attempt to conform to the fundamental businesses or processes, the tools may be lacking to accomplish the task.

With those insights, Ross knows that he must establish a regular and routine monthly management process. The management process must integrate and synchronize the efforts of the individual functions of the company. His objective for the monthly management process is to ensure focus, alignment, and engagement on the right things throughout the company.

Ross has also concluded that if the monthly management process is conducted correctly, constraints that preclude the company from achieving its objectives will surface. Ipso facto, the process will identify those areas where management must take action to succeed.

In thinking about implementing this monthly management process, he has a fear that the company management team will fail in its efforts. This fear is offset by knowing that an industry best practice has evolved over approximately twenty years. The best practice is called sales and operations planning, and it is designed to accomplish the objectives Ross has just articulated.

In his review of the best practice standards, he has concluded that he must take responsibility and process ownership in order for the process to be implemented successfully. He cannot delegate ownership or responsibility. Delegation will ensure that the process fails.

He understands that the process involves multiple levels of management through the pre-reviews of product development, demand, supply, and finance. However, these reviews alone will not ensure that constraints that could prevent the company from achieving its objectives will surface.

By ensuring that company initiatives are integrated in the process, the key constraints will truly surface. This will involve reviewing the priority, status, and resources committed to company improvement projects at least once per month in the executive sales and operations planning meeting.

Ross, in his role as general manager, does not personally want to handle all the details of the sales and operations planning process. He does want a process to be developed in which he has ultimate confidence that it is working properly.

Ross recognizes that a sales and operations planning coordinator must be selected to work out the details and ensure that the process is working and improving. Consultants have advised him that, except in large corporations, the coordination position is not a full-time job. The logical candidates for this position are the demand coordinator, the supply coordinator, and the financial review coordinator. The sales and operations planning coordinator will ensure that reconciliation and problem solving occur.

The consultants have further advised him that in the early stages of the implementation, the sales and operations planning coordinator also serves as the project leader for the sales and operations planning implementation. Once the process is implemented, the sales and operations planning coordinator serves as the facilitator of the ongoing process.

The role of the general manager during the implementation is to serve as process owner and implementation champion. The general manager is personally responsible for the successful implementation and operation of the sales and operations planning process.

Ross stops and takes a deep breath. "How are we doing?" he asks. "Any questions?"

No one answers for a moment. Finally, Anita Cooper, the purchasing manager, asks, "How are you able to stand there and recite all of that?"

Ross smiles and says, "Through years and years of experience in implementing sales and operations planning in many companies. I take your question as a compliment. Thank you."

Ross continues by saying that it is important to have a picture of what a successful process looks like. When the process has been implemented successfully, all of the participants have an appropriate level of understanding and commitment.

In any successful process, at any instant in time, there is an agreed-upon company plan. The plan was agreed upon in the last sales and operations planning cycle. It was agreed upon through consensus and acceptance of accountability and commitment to a bookings plan, sales/shipment/demand plan, production plan, inventory plan, customer lead-time/backlog plan, new product development plan, company initiative plan, and the resulting financial plan.

"We use one set of operating numbers to manage the business," Ross says. "We operate under the principle that we will all do what we say we are going to do. This means we will achieve the current plan or advise if it cannot be met and clearly understand the reasons why."

He pauses. The executive team members nod their heads, indicating that they understand these fundamental principles.

Ross explains that as the general manager, he expects to spend four hours or less once a month in the executive sales and operations planning meeting. He expects that the pre-review meeting steps will have identified the changes to the current, previously approved plan. The rest of the month, he should be free to do the things that provide the greatest benefit to the company. This rarely includes micromanagement.

He expects that normally forty-eight hours prior to the executive sales and operations planning meeting, he will receive a package of material. Ideally, he would prefer that the material be e-mailed to him. He also expects that prior to the meeting, the sales and operations planning coordinator will brief him to highlight the issues, concerns, decisions that will need to be made, and direction required to be given.

Peter Newfeld, the product development/engineering director, interrupts. "Our e-mail system is not yet reliable. Do you recommend other approaches?"

"Twenty years ago, when this process was first developed, e-mail did not exist," Ross notes. "Any method of getting the information to the meeting participants that works for you is okay."

Ross pauses and steps back from the table. "Let me digress for a moment," he says. "At some point today, some of you must have had the desire to say, 'We already do this.' And my response is, 'Of course you do.'"

He tells the group members that they already perform most of the functions that were introduced today. However, they are done independently and separately — not as an integrated, synchronized process and not as a team.

Picture any team sport. The players must work together as a team to win. Whether it is football, baseball, basketball, doubles tennis, volleyball, or soccer, long-term success is based upon working together.

"Sales and operations planning is about taking all those things you already do, filling in the things you do not currently do, and integrating them. Keep it simple. It really is organized common sense," Ross says.

He takes a deep breath and asks if there are any questions.

Mark Ryan is surprised that his team has no questions. Then he notices Ross's behavior. After asking if there were any questions, he immediately looked down at the computer and began flipping through visuals. His head was down. His body language said not to ask him any questions. Earlier today, when he asked a question, he would walk into the center of the room. Mark concludes that Ross knows they are behind schedule and does not want any questions asked.

Ross stops at an overhead that is a list of sales and operations planing questions (Figure 28) and says, "Let me describe conceptually the executive sales and operations planning meeting." He explains that every company tends to have a little different meeting agenda. This is the general manager's meeting, and he does not want to attempt to be too prescriptive. He encourages clients to establish a standardized agenda that supports answering the questions in the overhead, not necessarily in the order shown.

1. What has changed since last month?
2. Are we on plan financially?
3. How are we performing to our company goals and key performance indicators, that is, the "balanced scorecard" performance measurements?
4. What new or different risks do we need to understand or consider?
5. What decisions need to be made or approved in this S&OP cycle?
6. What decisions will we be compelled to make within the next few months?
7. How are the individual product families or product groupings performing?
8. Are we on schedule, on cost, on scope with our product development efforts?
9. How are we performing to company initiatives? Are we on scope, on schedule, on cost?
10. Do we have any resource constraints, and how well are we utilizing our key resources?
11. Are we comfortable with the plan across the entire planning horizon?
12. Is there any reason to revisit our strategic plans or company goals?
13. What did we do well in this cycle of S&OP? What might we improve?

Figure 28   Sales and Operations Planning Questions

Ross walks up to the projection screen and stands on tiptoe to point to the second question. "From the general manager's perspective, this question is critical," he says.

He explains that financial expectations have been created in the annual business plan and then are updated and confirmed quarterly. The general manager must know whether the expectations are being met to date. The general manager also must know the financial projections for the rest of year. If there are variances, the general manager must know what caused the variances to date and what is causing the variances in the future financial projections.

"One word of caution," Ross says. He explains that the presentations of the financial projections and past performance should be an overview, which represents the sum of the detail work done in the subprocess pre-meetings. The detail understanding of the issues behind the financial numbers will be demonstrated as the other sales and operations planning questions are answered during the meeting.

"Another word of caution," Ross says. He explains that many general managers have difficulty waiting for the more detailed financial explanation and recommendations as they emerge during the executive sales and operations planning meeting. Impatience can result in not making fully informed decisions.

"It is important to see the whole picture," Ross says. "Sales and operations planning is about solving problems and taking advantage of opportunities. You cannot do so if you don't have visibility of the total picture."

Ross points to the third question on the projection screen. "Remember our discussion of the balanced scorecard earlier today?" he asks as he displays the visual that was presented earlier in the day (Figure 29).

He explains that once sales and operations planning is fully operational, company goals and objectives, key performance indicators, and key process metrics will have been defined. Performance can be compiled in a dashboard to easily see variances.

Ross returns to the list of sales and operations planning questions and points to the seventh item. He tells the group that the family-by-family review is a key part of the sales and operations planning process and is reviewed in summary in the executive sales and operations planning meeting. In a few minutes, he will discuss this subject in greater detail.

He asks the group to turn to page 50 in their notebooks, which shows a sample executive sales and operations planning meeting agenda (Figure 30). He explains that the sample agenda is intended as a starting point. It is expected that a fundamental agenda will be established. This fundamental agenda should remain fairly consistent, but the issues will change from meeting to meeting as issues that must be addressed in the executive sales and operations planning meeting surface.

Mark raises his hand. "In order to answer the questions you just showed us in a quality manner, the subprocess pre-meeting steps obviously must be done well," he says.

Sales and Operations Planning	-3	-2	-1
Was everyone prepared?	Red	Yellow	Green
Were the right people present?	Red	Red	Yellow
Was the information at the right level of detail?	Yellow	Yellow	Green
Were the needed decisions made?	Yellow	Yellow	Green
Did we make efficient use of our time?	Yellow	Yellow	Green
Can we improve the S&OP process?	Red	Red	Yellow

Financials	-3	-2	-1
EBIT ($)	Red	Yellow	Green
Sales revenue to plan ($)	Green	Green	Yellow
Margin % to plan	Green	Green	Yellow
Operating expenses to budget ($)	Green	Green	Yellow
Cost drivers	Green	Yellow	Red

Supply	-3	-2	-1
Manufacturing revenue to plan	Yellow	Yellow	Red
Inventory value ($) and turns	Green	Green	Yellow
Supplier quality performance	Yellow	Yellow	Red
Initial test yields ($)	Yellow	Yellow	Red
Cycle times (days)	Yellow	Yellow	Red
Inventory record accuracy (%)	Green	Yellow	Yellow
Production plan vs. actual (%)	Red	Red	Red
Master schedule performance (%)	Red	Red	Red
Master schedule stability (weekly)	Green	Yellow	Red

Products	-3	-2	-1
New product introduction on-time performance (%)	Red	Red	Red
Cycle time to first customer prototype	Green	Green	Green
Cycle time to safety approval	Yellow	Red	Red
Average cycle time	Red	Red	Red
Project development costs	Green	Green	Green
Development resource load to capacity ratio	Yellow	Red	Red

Demand	-3	-2	-1
Forecast vs. actual by subfamily (units and %)	Yellow	Yellow	Yellow
Forecast vs. actual by top 30 sku mix	Green	Green	Green
Inventory performance by customer group	Yellow	Yellow	Red
On-time customer service performance (%)	Yellow	Yellow	Red
Bookings activity	Yellow	Yellow	Red
Past due customer orders	Green	Yellow	Yellow

Markets	-3	-2	-1
Total market forecast accuracy	Yellow	Yellow	Red
Market #1 market share	Green	Green	Green
Market #2 market share	Yellow	Yellow	Red
Competitive portfolio positioning	Yellow	Yellow	Red

Figure 29   Balanced Scorecard Approach for Sales and Operations Planning Measurements

1. Outstanding action items
2. Special issues
3. Performance reviews
4. Review of assumptions and vulnerabilities
5. Family-by-family review
6. New products
7. Company initiatives
8. Review of minutes
9. Critique of meeting

Figure 30   Agenda — Executive Sales and Operations Planning Meeting

"That is a great observation, Mark," Ross replies. He explains that the general manager should expect that the fundamental issues will have surfaced in the pre-meetings. As a result, new action plans and recommendations would be presented at the executive sales and operations planning meeting for the management team's concurrence and approval.

"It also seems to me," Mark says, "that good meeting discipline will go a long way to make the process work well. For example, I assume minutes will be kept so that we all remember what we decided and why."

"That's correct," Ross replies. He adds that the minutes should include who was assigned each action item and when it was agreed that the action items were to be completed.

"Good meeting minutes will help keep you from revisiting the same subjects without taking action," Ross notes. "You want to avoid meetings that resemble the movie *Ground Hog Day*. Without recording who is expected to perform the action item, recycling of discussions will occur."

■ ■ ■

Ray Guy, the final assembly manager, changes the subject. "So if Mark is the sales and operations planning process owner, who should be the process coordinator?" he asks.

Eyes turn toward Mark Ryan, the general manager, but Ross does not give up the floor. "Let me share different companies' approaches to the sales and operations planning coordinator," he says.

He tells the group that some companies choose the demand planner to be the sales and operations planning coordinator. Others choose the supply planner. Some will choose the new product/activities coordinator. Still others choose the financial review coordinator. "There is no right choice," Ross says. "It is simply whomever the general manager selects."

He explains that a statistical sampling across a broad range of companies would reveal that about 50 percent of the coordinators come from the supply side of the business, 30 percent from the demand side, and 20 percent from finance. Most coordinators are selected from the supply side of the business because of the fact that the supply chain management group, materials management group, or planning group usually does some of the same work required for the sales and operations planning process. Also, sales and operations planning often evolves from the production planning process.

The trend toward tapping coordinators from the supply side is changing, however. More general managers are selecting coordinators from the demand side to emphasize the demand-driven nature of the process. Some general managers choose coordinators from the finance side because they tend to be skilled in developing models and simulations. Also, theoretically, representatives from the finance group are more neutral when there are conflicts between supply and demand.

"So, what do you think makes sense for Universal Products?" Ross asks.

Susan Callahan, the planning manager, says, "I think in our company it should be someone from finance. I say this not because I don't want the task in planning, but mostly because Janis has previous experience. It might help us to reduce the time to benefits."

Peter Newfeld, the product development/engineering director, quickly says, "I agree."

All eyes are on Janis Novak, the controller.

"Would you be willing to serve as the sales and operations planning coordinator?" Mark asks.

Janis hesitates before replying. "As long as the team realizes that much of the work will be delegated to the finance subprocess coordinator, I am fine with it."

Ross scans the group. "Any other comments?" he asks. There is no reply.

"Silence is approval," Mark says. "Great!" He is pleased with what just occurred. Ross did what he said he would do. He made sure the group was supportive of Janis as the sales and operations planning coordinator. He believes Janis is the correct choice. Her knowledge of the process will help shorten the implementation time.

Ross is ready to move on, but Jim Simpson, the manufacturing director, isn't. "As part of the preparation for this session, some of us reviewed *The Oliver Wight ABCD Checklist for Operational Excellence,* specifically the section that covers sales and operations planning. In the previous discussion, you mentioned that we should answer two questions: (1) What did we do well during the sales and operations planning cycle? (2) What should we improve? Should we use the checklist to evaluate our progress?" he asks.

Ross advances the presentation slides. While doing so, he says, "Most companies will periodically evaluate the implementation progress by using the checklist. Thank you for bringing that up. I meant to mention it before. To refresh your memories, here are the sales and operations planning best practices provided in *The Oliver Wight ABCD Checklist for Operational Excellence, 5th Edition.*"

Ross lets the group study the list of best practices (Figure 31) for a few minutes and then looks at his watch. "This is a good time for a ten-minute break," he says. "When we come back, we'll talk about the family-by-family review."

5-2 SALES AND OPERATIONS PLANNING

The sales and operations planning process focuses on customer requirements, supports the annual business plans, and aligns the entire organization in support of business strategy. The S&OP process is action oriented, where management aggressively resolves problems to maintain balance between market demands and available resources.

5-2a   There is a concise written sales and operations planning policy that covers the process, purpose, activities, participants, and expected results. Additionally, there is a well-documented procedure that details the pre-S&OP, S&OP, and post-S&OP activities. Specific roles and responsibilities are assigned, understood, and accepted.

5-2b   Sales and operations planning is truly a process, not just a monthly meeting. The process has a clear focus on intermediate to longer term time periods; detailed product and customer issues consume little time. There is not a fixation on points such as year end, where the process becomes shortsighted. One of the final steps in the process is the executive approval meeting.

5-2c   Defined activity dates are set well ahead to avoid schedule conflicts. In case the sales and operations planning regular participant is unable to attend the monthly meeting, he or she is represented by someone who is empowered to speak for the function. This also applies to emergency meetings.

5-2d   A formal sales and operations planning packet is circulated at least twenty-four hours prior to the meeting. This packet includes the agenda, objectives, past performance, assumptions, product family reviews, major program updates, and minutes from the last meeting. The agenda should clearly identify all issues that will be raised for review and decision as a result of the pre-S&OP process steps.

5-2e   For each product family, plans are reviewed in the units of measure that communicate to all functions most effectively.

5-2f   New product development as well as major program and project schedules are reviewed during the sales and operations planning process. These reviews concentrate on the impact of all major initiatives on resources, revenues, and costs. Changes in launch dates, promotions, etc. are also discussed.

5-2g   All participants come prepared to the sales and operations planning meeting. There are pre-meeting activities by function that need to take place: sales and marketing to prepare a demand (sales) plan, research and development (engineers) to prepare a new product plan, operations (manufacturing) to prepare a supply (production)

Figure 31   Sales and Operations Planning Best Practices (From *The Oliver Wight ABCD Checklist for Operational Excellence,* 2001. Reproduced with permission.)

plan, and finance to prepare a revenue and cost plan. Corrective action plans must be developed to rebalance available resources with changes in market demand when needed.

5-2h   The presentation of information includes a review of both past performance (minimum of three months) and future plans (typically eighteen to twenty-four months) for: sales, production, inventory, backlog, shipments, and new product activity.

5-2i   Inventory (finished goods) and/or delivery lead-time (backlog) strategies are reviewed each month as part of the process.

5-2j   There is a process of reviewing and documenting assumptions about the business and reviewing the alignment in support of the business strategy. This is done to enhance the understanding of the business and represents the basis for future projections.

5-2k   Sales and operations planning is an action process. Conflicts are resolved and decisions are made, documented, communicated, and implemented. Consensus is reached on a single, current operating plan.

5-2l   Any large and/or unanticipated changes are communicated to all functions prior to the sales and operations planning meeting. Disclosing surprises in the meeting without communicating to others is considered unacceptable behavior.

5-2m   Minutes of the meeting are circulated immediately after the meeting. This is typically done within twenty-four (maximum forty-eight) hours of meeting closure.

5-2n   The mechanism is in place to ensure that aggregate sales plans agree with detailed sales plans. There is consensus from all participants in the meeting.

5-2o   The mechanism is in place to ensure that aggregate operations plans agree with detailed operations plans (master schedules). There is consensus from all participants in the meeting.

5-2p   Rough-cut capacity planning is used to validate the reasonableness of the sales and operations plans. Required changes to these plans are made prior to release.

5-2q   The resulting sales and operations (production) plans are communicated to the master scheduling function at least monthly.

5-2r   Time zones have been established as guidelines for managing changes. In the near term, there is an effort to minimize the changes in order to gain the benefits of stability. In the mid-term range, changes are expected but are reviewed to ensure that they are realistic. In the long term, less precision is expected but direction is established.

5-2s   There is a computer-based simulation process supporting sales and operations planning that permits the evaluation of various levels of demand, supply, inventory, backlogs, projected shipments, and resulting financials.

5-2t   Tolerances are established to determine acceptable performance for: sales, engineering, production, and finance. These are reviewed and updated regularly. Accountability is clearly established.

5-2u   The entire business is included in the sales and operations planning process. The sum of the product families can be reconciled to the revenue and profit plan.

5-2v   There is an ongoing critique of the sales and operations planning process.

Figure 31   Sales and Operations Planning Best Practices (continued)

■ ■ ■

Mark Ryan pulls Ross aside. "Thank you for the way you handled the sales and operations planning coordinator issue," he says.

"Be sure you talk with Janis to make sure you are comfortable with her choice for the financial subprocess review coordinator," Ross replies. "As a practical matter, the coordinator will be doing most of the legwork needed to make the process function appropriately."

"Thanks for your advice. I'll do that," Mark says.

"As you may have already figured out, we're running somewhat behind. I will likely have to cut the demand planning discussion short today," Ross says. "I'll let Sam know and suggest that he may want to attend that discussion on the second day of the managers' class."

"That's a good idea," Mark says. "Even if Sam can't make that session, it would be good if you met with him and had a general one-on-one discussion on the subject. I'm sure he is planning on Justin Roberts in marketing to be his demand planner. I am comfortable with that."

"Nolan interviewed Justin and is comfortable with that choice as well," Ross replies, "as long as Justin is dedicated to the task. The demand planning function is not a part-time job."

"I would like for you to work with Sam on that issue," Mark says.

Nature has been calling Ross for several minutes now. "Mark, if you will excuse me," he says, "I need to take a quick break before we get started."

As Ross leaves the room, Mark has a moment to reflect. He is beginning to realize how much work will be needed and how important it will be to change Universal Products' historical modus operandi. On the surface, what has been taught today seems obvious. But if it is so obvious, why don't more companies do it well?

Mark concludes that it is all about people and discipline. The senior staff will have to be motivated to operate the process well.

That's where I must come in, Mark thinks to himself. He knows that he must take a strong leadership role if sales and operations planning is to be implemented in time to have an impact on this year's performance.

■ ■ ■

The senior managers are back in their seats waiting for Ross when he returns from the rest room. As he walks to the front of the room, he already is talking. "We are about to discuss a key part of the process. We call it the family-by-family review."

He explains that the family-by-family review is where the integration of demand, supply, and finance comes together, both quantitatively and qualitatively. Perhaps more importantly, the family-by-family review is where specific performance can be measured, decisions made, and actions assigned.

Jim Simpson, the final assembly manager, is tired of sitting. He decides to stand in the back of the room. "Ross, we have looked at demand, supply, and finance in the pre-sales and operations planning steps and presumably made some decisions already," he says. "What decisions would be made in the executive sales and operations planning meeting?"

"You are indeed correct," Ross replies, "but the cross-functional executive management team has not looked at and approved the integrated effect of changes in demand and supply." He explains that, for the most part, the subprocess reviews involve updating the previous plans and developing recommendations for the company. These plans and recommendations need to be agreed upon and decided upon collectively as an integrated management team.

"Bear with me, Jim, and I think this will become more clear," Ross says. He asks the group to consider why it is called a family-by-family review. The demand and supply information has been aggregated into specific product groupings. Since the executive team is not going to look at every individual product, the information must be presented in a manner that is meaningful.

These product groupings, typically called product families, are often aggregated in a manner similar to how they are presented in the company promotional catalog. They could be aggregated by product line or product brand, for example.

Ray Guy raises his hand. "But doesn't that present a problem for the manufacturing and engineering side of the house? The catalog groups things the way sales and marketing sells things, not the way we make or design things. I know I would prefer to have the products grouped by manufacturing resource center."

"And I would like to group product plans by business unit," Janis Novak, the controller, says. "We don't necessarily add the numbers up the way products are presented in the catalog either."

Ross holds up his hand to stop further comment. "The need for different product groupings by functionality, of course, is the reality of the situation," he says. "It is also one of the issues that must be resolved in the process design step. How will you group products for aggregation purposes? Let me give you some additional considerations."

He explains that the group may also choose to look at product families in the following ways:

- Demand streams (for example, international and domestic)
- Demand patterns (for example, seasonal and nonseasonal)
- Delivery and availability objectives (make to stock versus make to order)
- Raw material type

- Resource capability
- Manufactured or sold location
- Other groupings

"One of the dangers is allowing yourself to get into an endless debate over product families," Ross says. "If you have a reasonable set of software tools to assist you, you should be able to design the aggregation of the information so that different people can look at the information in different ways. And please remember the pre-sales and operations planning steps."

He explains that it is quite normal in the demand review to observe and discuss the information in the way most meaningful to sales and marketing, for example, by customer, territory, brand, and market segment. The information in the supply review may be aggregated in a manner more meaningful to manufacturing, engineering, and purchasing.

"And remember our discussion on rough-cut capacity planning," Ross adds. "For those simulations, information is grouped by key resource." He clicks the mouse to bring up a graph (Figure 32).

"Once the information exists from the pre-sales and operations planning steps, Janis, you should be able to present it in whatever manner you need for financial management purposes," he notes.

Ross turns to the group. "Please, everyone, listen to what I am about to say," he says. "Do not let this slow you down! Make a decision and get on with it."

He explains that once the process is started, the participants in the process will want to change how they choose to look at the information. The format of the information may be different in each step of the process.

"I recommend that for the executive sales and operations planning meeting, you look at the information in a way that allows the review of inventory and backlog or customer lead time," Ross says. "The information should be presented in the manner that the general manager prefers to see the data."

Mark raises his hand. "This should not be a major issue for us," he says. "Most of our products can be grouped in a manner that communicates well for both demand and supply. We will group the products for financial purposes the way corporate has dictated. There are only a few areas that will cause a debate."

"That is normally the case," Ross replies. "This was a much bigger issue about ten or fifteen years ago, when software tools were not as readily available or capable."

He tells the group that the enhanced ability to perform rough-cut capacity planning simulations has also greatly reduced the debate about product groupings. Ross's personal preference is to group products in the executive sales and operations planning meeting the way that they are marketed. This approach helps to ensure that discussions are more focused around customers, markets, and growth.

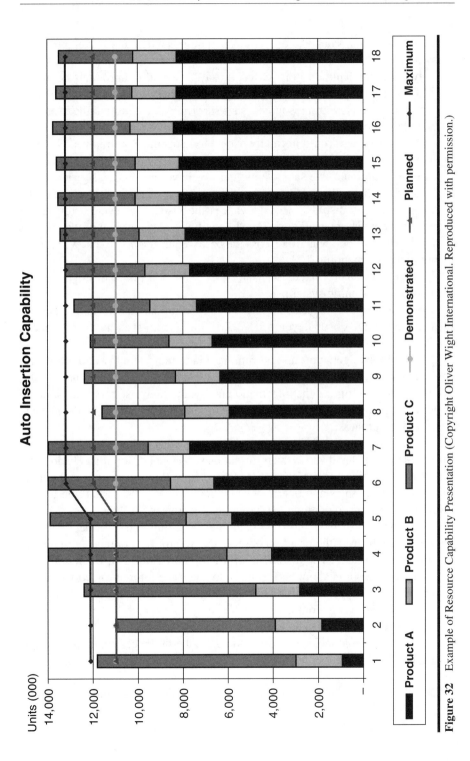

Figure 32 Example of Resource Capability Presentation (Copyright Oliver Wight International. Reproduced with permission.)

"As I have said, sales and operations planning is a demand-driven process," Ross comments.

Ray raises his hand. "In that case," he says, "would the products be aggregated for capacity planning through rough-cut capacity planning in the supply review process, and would resource issues surface by exception in the executive sales and operations planning meeting?"

"That is what we would normally expect to happen," Ross replies. He looks around the group. There are no further questions.

"Let me continue," he says. "Now that we have our products grouped and aggregated, perhaps the best way to demonstrate the process is to look at an integrated information display." Ross advances the visuals to reveal a format for viewing the demand plan (Figure 33). "I do not plan to go into all of the nuances of this format, but I do want to discuss the basic requirements so that we all have a common understanding."

"Where does this format exist?" Janis asks. "We don't have this in our enterprise resource planning system."

Ross answers that most companies start by using spreadsheets. A database presentation tool has been developed by EMI. It is a template with the format and graphics built in.

"This template gets you up and running much more quickly and allows for easier maintenance each month," Ross says. "I suspect that after some months, you will want to program the information into your enterprise resource planning system. But please do not attempt to do that until after you have implemented and stabilized the process."

Ross explains that every company takes a somewhat different approach to the information format and views the information somewhat differently. He does not recommend waiting for the normal lead time from the information technology group to start the sales and operations planning process. "We want you to start sales and operations planning next month, not next year," he says.

Janis nods her thanks, and Ross continues. Pointing to the format displayed on the screen, he asks the group to observe that the format contains both history and future projections. The historical information provides a base reference and facilitates a discussion about performance to date. The future projections should cover the agreed-upon planning horizon, which is recommended to be at least eighteen months. Many companies use a twenty-four-month horizon, and some even use a thirty-six-month horizon.

The format should include fields important to the subprocesses. In the example on display, the fields important for the demand side of the business include:

■ Bookings (quantity and timing of product demand at anticipated order receipt)

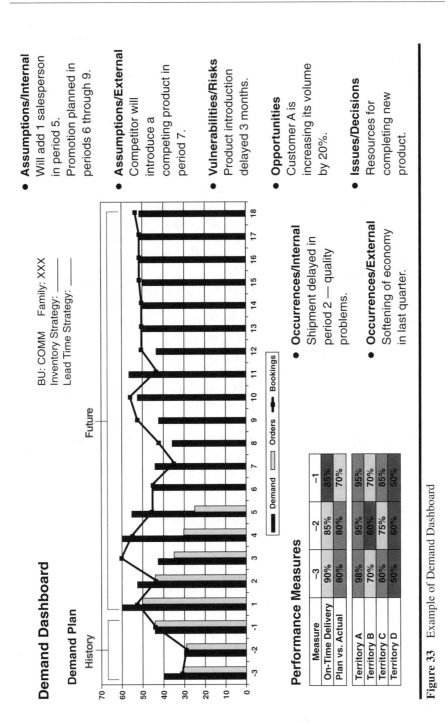

Figure 33 Example of Demand Dashboard

- Demand (anticipated quantity and timing of when the customer wants the product)
- Customer orders (orders received not yet shipped presented by current planned ship date)

Ross displays the next visual (Figure 34). In addition to the demand information, this format includes key supply planning fields, such as inventory, production plan, anticipated shipments, and total customer backlog.

Ross points to the top of the visual. He explains that these are reference fields that show the manufacturing strategy, delivery lead times, and inventory targets. MTS means make to stock. If it is a make-to-order strategy, the acronym is MTO, and if it is an engineer-to-order strategy, the acronym is ETO.

Jim Simpson, the manufacturing director, raises his hand. "There is a lot of quantitative information in that format," he observes. "I assume the information can be presented in both units and dollars."

"You are correct, Jim, and you make a very important point," Ross responds. "The financial projections come from the integrated operational numbers. There is no need for a separate, independent financial forecast. Isn't that right, Janis?"

Janis smiles and nods her head. "You are totally correct," she says.

Jim is not ready to move along yet. "So if we update the information in that agreed-upon format or template every month and are prepared to discuss collectively the reason for changes, we should be in control of the business?" he asks.

Before Ross can respond, Sam Wente replies. "To the extent that we commit to make the numbers happen, we will be in control of the business. If I say that my sales group will sell a specific volume and product mix, I need to manage my sales team to make it happen. If you and Ray say you will produce to a specific production plan, you must manage your people to make it happen."

"That's another way of saying 'do what you say you are going to do,'" Jim comments.

Susan raises her hand. Others in the group want to add to the discussion, but Ross recognizes Susan. She has been quiet, and he wants to hear what she has to say.

"If we review the variances of actual sales to planned sales and actual production to planned production, we will see the effect of those variances show up as a change in inventory or backlog/customer lead time. This is where Ross told us earlier that inventory is a result. The person with the big *I* does not get taken out back and flogged. Do I have that right, Ross?"

"You *all* have it right," Ross says, smiling.

Ross recognizes Janis. "We will be looking at the product family information," she says, "but when we do the company financial status and projections, the data come from this format. By adding up the dollars for each family, I get the total company financial numbers. Is that right?"

Demand/Supply Synchronization

Family: XYZ	Mfg. Strategy: MTS	Inventory Strategy: 2 Weeks	Lead Time Strategy: 3 Days

Synchronization — Demand & Supply — Units

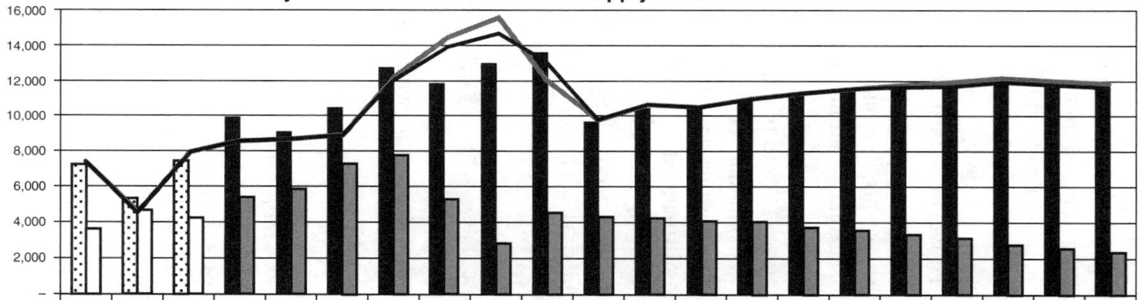

	-3	-2	-1	1	2	3	4	5	6	7	8	9	10	11	12	13	14	15	16	17	18
Total Build-Actual/Plan	7,303	5,297	7,551	9,852	9,024	10,374	12,657	11,897	12,971	13,649	9,587	10,413	10,090	10,774	11,183	11,449	11,521	11,534	11,727	11,598	11,510
Total Inventory-Actual/Plan	3,636	4,687	4,201	5,383	5,841	7,216	7,784	5,267	2,742	4,450	4,214	4,216	4,067	4,015	3,773	3,596	3,374	3,079	2,782	2,516	2,307
Total Demand-Current Plan	7,343	4,246	8,037	8,670	8,566	8,999	12,090	14,413	15,496	11,941	9,823	10,412	10,239	10,826	11,425	11,626	11,742	11,829	12,024	11,864	11,720
Total Ship-Actual/Plan	7,343	4,246	8,037	8,670	8,566	8,999	12,028	13,917	14,578	13,099	9,823	10,412	10,239	10,826	11,425	11,626	11,640	11,608	11,796	11,649	11,512

- **Assumptions**
  Plant maintenance in period 5.
  Supplier quality problems will be resolved in period 2.
- **Opportunities**
  Improve output 10% on machine 6 during maintenance
- **Occurrences**
  Supplier quality issues in period 2.
- **Vulnerabilities/Risks**
  Completion of planned maintenance on time.
- **Issues/Decisions**
  Imbalance periods 5–6. Delay planned maintenance? Or increase inventory build prior to shutdown.

	To Plan
Demand	
Supply	
Inventory	

Figure 34 Example of Demand/Supply Synchronization Dashboard

"Once again, you all have it right," Ross replies.

Mark raises his hand. "And the format gets updated in the pre-sales and operations planning steps," he says. "We do not do the updating in the executive sales and operations planning meeting. All the demand input, supply input, and financial input is completed in the sales and operations planning cycle. Conflicts surface and the obvious need to resolve specific problems and to pursue business opportunities is pointed out through the integrated view."

"Again, that is correct," Ross replies. "However, I must point out what must already be obvious."

Anita Cooper, the purchasing manager, interrupts. "For us, the format is blank today. We must populate the format with reasonable numbers to get started. I think that is going to be our biggest problem."

Peter Newfeld adds to Anita's observation. "Some of the data exist in the business plan," he says. "Some of the data exist in updated engineering and manufacturing schedules. Some exist in our enterprise resource planning system. I think I now see the role of the demand, supply, and financial coordinators."

"That is true," Jim says, "but a lot of the data you mentioned are inaccurate. For example, the enterprise resource planning system shows a lot of past-due dates. In reality, we cannot ship anything in the past. That means it is important to keep the information up to date, or it will not give us an accurate indication of what will be happening."

"And if the information is not kept up to date," Janis says, "I will be back in the financial forecasting business."

"If that happens, we will continue to struggle, just as we are struggling today," Mark says.

He pauses and observes his team. He wants to make a point. "Remember the three overlapping circles from this morning — people, process, tools? This format or template that we've been discussing is a *tool*. The pre-sales and operations planning steps and the executive sales and operations planning meeting are part of the *process*. And keeping honest and up-to-date information that is tied to what we are really going to do is the essence of the *people* circle."

Peter Newfeld raises his hand. "To add to what you just said, Mark, if we pick our families and key resources reasonably well," he says, "we can make decisions that will literally be tied to specific product actions in sales, marketing, engineering, manufacturing, finance, purchasing, etc. There really is an integrated set of *actions* that keep us — what did you call it, Ross? — aligned, focused, and engaged. In essence, we are synchronized."

"That's right," Ross says, "the words I used are focused, aligned, engaged, and synchronized."

He tells the group that another key point should not be overlooked. During the implementation of sales and operations planning, it is not unusual to find that the data in the enterprise resource planning system are not accurate or kept up to date.

When this occurs, it should drive a continuous improvement action to ensure that the data in the enterprise resource planning system are accurate.

"Earlier, I was asked if other improvements that were needed surfaced during our assessment," Ross says. "One of the classic problems we find with companies, and we found in your company, is that the dates in the enterprise resource planning system are not current and therefore are incorrect."

He explains that two problems occur when the dates are incorrect in the enterprise resource planning system. First, the customer service organization cannot trust the dates in the system. This forces customer service to contact the appropriate people to determine when customer orders will ship. The second problem that arises from incorrect dates in the enterprise resource planning system is that all capacity calculations are incorrect. Without correct dates, the system cannot accurately calculate in which time periods the capacity is really required.

"So, in essence, you have implemented with effort and expense a system that is not providing sufficient information to effectively and efficiently run the business," Ross concludes. "Sales and operations planning will not fix this problem, but the problem will certainly surface so that it can be addressed with appropriate actions and activities."

Ross pauses and takes a deep breath. He smiles at the group. "It's a good time for a short break. When we come back, we'll discuss the sales and operations planning process a bit more. Then, we will learn about demand planning and the sales and operations planning implementation. Take ten minutes, please. Sam, can I see you just for a moment, please?"

Sam walks to the front of the room. "What is it, Ross? I didn't say anything wrong, did I?" he asks.

"Oh, no!" Ross replies. "I just wanted to create some expectations with regard to the demand planning subject we are going to cover after break."

Ross tells Sam that the discussions have lasted longer than anticipated, but have been crucial to gaining understanding and commitment to the process. They won't be able to cover demand planning and demand management in the level of detail that was originally anticipated. Ross will only be able to give a very brief overview.

He suggests that Sam plan on attending the second morning of the middle management education session. Demand will be covered in greater detail during that session. He also suggests that they plan on meeting one on one for a few hours next week to discuss demand management and answer any questions Sam might have.

Sam tells Ross that he will make himself available to attend the second morning of the middle management education session. "That would be Tuesday morning," Sam says. "And if you are available early Wednesday morning, around seven o'clock, we could meet one on one."

"That's great," Ross replies. "There will be an added benefit of your attending the middle management session. It will send a positive message about your commitment to your sales managers."

Ross and Sam leave the meeting room together. Ross sees that Mark and Janis are having a serious discussion outside on the balcony. He decides not to interrupt them.

Mark has been asking Janis her impressions of the session. He wants to know whether she thinks the management team has really bought into the process.

"I'm really excited," Janis says. "As I told you before, I never implemented sales and operations planning. I worked in an environment where it already existed. But I have seen more enthusiasm here today than I ever expected for a one-day session. I believe everyone is understanding and starting to be on the same page."

"How do you feel about Ross and Nolan?" Mark asks. "Is the chemistry okay with the group? Do you think the staff will listen to them as they coach us?"

"They certainly have been able to reach our group today," Janis replies, "but I also think that we should reserve judgment until after the managers' session. They will be working with them as well as with us. I suspect Nolan will relate better with the managers, and Ross will relate best with the senior staff."

"Janis, I'm looking forward to working with you on implementing this process," Mark says. "I believe the potential of sales and operations planning transcends Universal Products. It could be potentially important for the entire corporation. If I'm correct, I'll need your help with corporate."

He tells Janis that he will be keeping Jack Baxter apprised of Universal Products' progress in implementing sales and operations planning. He asks Janis to keep the corporate finance group apprised as well.

"This process has the potential to greatly improve the total company's performance and to simplify the reporting requirements between the divisions and corporate," Mark says.

"I agree," Janis replies. "I'll keep corporate finance in the loop. If I see anything you should be aware of, I will certainly let you now. And, Mark, I am also looking forward to working with you on this. This should be interesting and fun. I need to freshen up before we start. I will see you later."

Mark watches Janis walk inside. He believes she will be a wonderful asset on this project. He admires her intelligence and appreciates her willingness to introduce sales and operations planning to him. She has developed strong relationships with the corporate finance group. With her strong communications skills, she'll be able to explain sales and operations planning to corporate finance.

Mark is anxious to begin the sales and operations planning process. He wonders what the current sales plan and operations plan will look like when they are first populated in the template format Ross presented. He knows the two plans won't be synchronized. He makes a note to get some advice from Ross on how to best manage the executive team to agree on a synchronized demand and supply plan.

7

INTEGRATING PRODUCT DEVELOPMENT AND INITIATIVES

Ross stands and begins to talk before everyone in the group is seated. "Earlier, I indicated that the management team, and especially the general manager, should expect to be able to answer some questions: Are we on schedule, on cost, and on scope with our product development projects? How are we performing to our strategic initiatives?"

He tells the group that in order to answer those questions, a couple of considerations need to be reviewed and discussed in designing the flow of the monthly sales and operations planning process.

"Excuse me," Peter Newfeld, the product development/engineering director, interrupts. "Before we get into that, Ross, how many days should it take for the process cycle each month?"

"There is not an absolutely correct answer to your question, Peter," Ross replies. He explains that the process needs to be completed within one month. The earlier in the month the cycle can be completed, the better. The earlier the process is completed, the more time it provides to implement changes to the current plan. This additional time may also allow more choices in the decision-making process.

If the process cycle time is shorter, the data are more current when reviewed at the executive sales and operations planning meeting. Shorter process cycle times enable the management team to concentrate on the entire planning horizon instead of just the current month.

"An interesting phenomenon takes place when the executive sales and operations planning meeting is held close to the end of the month," Ross says. He tells the group that the closer to the end of the month, the greater the chance that the discussion will focus on the performance this month and the plans for next month. The review of future months across the planning horizon is neglected.

A rule of thumb that has worked successfully with many clients is that the cycle should be completed by the tenth working day of the month. When just getting started with the implementation, the process will often take longer and will extend beyond the tenth working day of the month. As the management team becomes more proficient and efficient in operating the process, the cycle time is typically shortened and can be accomplished by the tenth working day of the month.

"It is important to keep the process cycle as short as is practical," Ross says. "When the cycle is too long, significant changes frequently occur during the process cycle. This adds confusion and extra work in updating plans already agreed upon in the earlier pre-sales and operations planning steps."

Nolan, from the back of the room, comments. "I have found that the most important issue isn't the time of month that the cycle is completed, but rather the total time to complete the cycle. If the full cycle is done within days rather than weeks, it goes much more smoothly."

Ross nods his head in agreement and then turns his attention back to Peter. "Peter, during the implementation section of the class," he says, "I will talk more about the sales and operations planning cycle relative to product development and company initiatives. How you handle these issues will influence the timing of the process steps."

Ross pauses for a few moments and walks into the center of the room. "Let me share what I believe most general managers are hired to do," he says. He tells the group that general managers are hired to do three things:

1. Run the business effectively and efficiently
2. Grow the business
3. Improve the capabilities of the business

"If a general manager accomplishes these three items, increased profits are the inevitable result," Ross says.

The discussions about sales and operations planning thus far have focused on running the business effectively. This is accomplished by integrating and synchronizing supply, demand, initiatives, resource, and finance management.

When a company has a process in place and the management team operates the process using the fundamental principles, conflicts and constraints are identified. Identifying conflicts and constraints enables the management staff to *act* as a focused and aligned team in achieving a common set of objectives.

"Well, guess what?" Ross says, moving away from the group and back to the table in the front of the room. "As we speak, conflicts and constraints exist in product development, in company improvement initiatives, as well as in manufacturing!"

He explains that in his experience, every company in existence has more opportunities for product development and company improvements than it has resources. He tells the group about the book *Leading Product Development* by Steven Wheelwright and Kim Clark. This book details the problems and opportunities related to product development. In an earlier publication by Wheelwright, he observed that companies routinely overload their product development resources by as much as 100 percent.

Ross turns toward Susan Callahan, the planning manager. "Susan, quickly answer this question: If you overload a resource by 100 percent, what percent of the load can we expect to get out of the resource?"

As quickly as the wink of an eye, Susan replies. "At best, you will get 50 percent of the planned output. In practice, it will be less than 50 percent because of wasted time and effort expended every day in changing priorities, doing extra coordination, and holding expediting meetings. This says nothing of the extra management attention expended to control the situation."

Peter raises his hand. "Ross, I would be interested in your opinion of what I am about to say. Engineering companies are notorious for overloading their resources. They overload a resource and add project managers to control the project. Having worked in that environment, I find that people spend more time answering questions for multiple project managers than they actually spend working on product designs. But companies rarely look at the overhead burden that unnecessary project management takes away from the bottom line."

"I concur with your observations," Ross says. "It is my experience that engineering companies have a great tendency to overload their critical resources, and when their resources are overloaded, the response is to add expediters. Some of these are very expensive expediters called project managers. The more project managers that are added, the worse it gets."

The reality, Ross explains, is that all companies have multiple product development projects and multiple company improvement initiatives. To prevent overloading of critical resources, an aggregate resource management process is needed for both product development and company improvement initiatives.

Management must be responsible for identifying, prioritizing, and providing resources for product development and company initiatives. Once specific projects and initiatives are determined, they need to be managed using the same principles discussed earlier.

"When companies effectively manage the resources that support product development and company initiatives," Ross says, "this is where they can truly gain a competitive advantage."

"I think I understand the issue," Mark says, "but how significant a problem is it?"

Ross explains that, in his experience, companies ask the product development function to do more than it is resourced to do. They also continue to pile one company improvement initiative after another on an already overloaded organization.

"The result," Ross says, "is what I call the 70 percent syndrome. The company gets 70 percent of everything and 100 percent of nothing. This is also known as *mediocrity*."

He reads a quote by Wheelwright and Clark from *Leading Product Development*:

> Product Development touches everything the business does. By the time a new product reaches the market, it will have passed through every function, to one degree or another, in the business.

"When you consider that product development impacts every function in a company," Ross says, "the processes need to be integrated with the management process of the company. The need for integration is *very* significant for any company with dynamic products and markets. Remember, sales and operations planning is really a replanning process."

He explains that in some companies and some industries, it is extremely important to integrate product development into the sales and operations planning process. In industries and companies that market technology-related products, the technology changes extremely quickly, which causes product life cycles to be extremely short.

"If a company does not have its product development and product launch integrated with its demand, supply, and inventory plans, chaos reigns," Ross says.

Susan Callahan, the planning manager, interrupts. "Isn't this the same conversation we had this morning about the three knobs: work, time, and resources?"

"Exactly," Ross replies. He explains that just like the other company functions, product development and company initiative resources must be kept in balance and aligned. When one of the three knobs changes, at least one of the other two needs to change.

"We would like that to happen in a managed and controlled manner," says Ross. "So the question becomes how to integrate the management of the product development and company improvement initiatives into sales and operations planning."

He asks the group to turn to the pages in the class notebook that show examples of process flow models that can be used to incorporate product development and company initiatives into the sales and operations planning cycle (Figures 35 and 36).

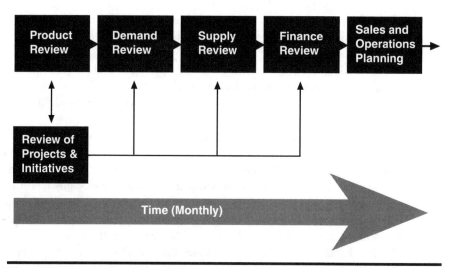

Figure 35   Model of Process with Review of Products and Initiatives (Copyright Oliver Wight International. Reproduced with permission.)

"Remember what Einstein said," Ross says. "All models are wrong; some are useful."

He tells the group that several key issues should be considered when designing the monthly management process. These issues often are best addressed by answering the following questions:

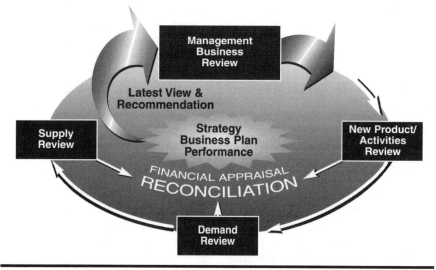

Figure 36   Integrated Business Management Model (Copyright Oliver Wight International. Reproduced with permission.)

- Who keeps the list of potential opportunities, that is, product development and company improvement initiatives?
- Who will do aggregate project resource planning?
- Who needs to be involved in determining priorities and resourcing?
- Who will manage the individual projects?
- How will the executive team be informed, and what role should it play?

"We aren't going to attempt to answer those questions today, or even in the first couple of cycles of sales and operations planning," Ross says. "You should answer the questions by cycle four of the process. However, I do want you to agree today that, as a minimum, the executive team will receive a high-level status report on product development and company improvement initiatives during the sales and operations planning process. Also, I want you to agree today that the senior management team will not allow the approval of plans that are unrealistic."

Peter raises his hand. "Let me see if I understand. We have multiple projects. Elements within those projects will change, and they need to be managed. I assume that we would use project management practices and project management software tools."

"Yes," Ross says.

"And project managers?" Peter asks.

"Yes," Ross replies. "They play a key role in the management process." He feels that clarification of a previous comment is in order. "My observation earlier about project managers meant to convey that if your management process is broken, *adding* more project managers may not or, more boldly, will not be the right solution."

"Ross, let me add to what I believe I understand," Peter says. "Projects and priorities may change. So, too, will the number of projects. As change occurs, we must manage the resources to make sure we complete 100 percent of what we *choose to do* on schedule, on cost, on scope. To accomplish this result, someone needs to do rough-cut capacity planning or, as I interpreted what you said, *aggregate project resource planning* for nonmanufacturing resources. This planning will identify any conflicts or constraints."

"So far, so good," Ross says.

Peter continues. "As a management team, we must do aggregate project management. In our monthly process, the conflicts or constraints identified through aggregate project resource planning need to be resolved. Since sales and operations planning is designed to do just that, it makes sense to integrate the product development and company improvement initiatives into the process. Therefore, the integration needs to be included as part of the process design and implementation."

"That's what needs to be done," Ross says.

Anita Cooper, the purchasing manager, raises her hand. "Aggregate project planning and aggregate project resource planning are new terms to me. I think I know what they mean, but could you explain in a little more detail?"

Ross reminds the group that the concept of rough-cut capacity planning was introduced earlier today. Most people think about applying rough-cut capacity planning to manufactured products. Manufactured products require key work center resources to build the product. The key work centers traditionally include bottleneck resources in manufacturing, engineering, and key suppliers.

The rough-cut capacity planning process adds up, or aggregates, all the work required to be done at a key resource center. The sum is compared against the available or planned capacity. This comparison is time-phased, meaning that the requirements and the availability are shown in specific periods of time over the agreed-upon planning horizon.

"If the available capacity is significantly out of balance from what you wish to produce or wish to be prepared to produce, then you have identified a management issue that needs to be addressed," Ross says.

Anita interrupts again. "I think I understand," she says. "For work that is not the traditional manufacturing of products, like product development and company improvement initiatives, the same principles apply. Rough-cut capacity planning is performed for the key work centers or resources required to do the work. It's just that there is a different name when the concept is applied to nonmanufacturing functions. It is then called aggregate project resource planning instead of rough-cut capacity planning."

"You understand correctly, Anita," Ross says. He explains that there is a reason why a different name is used. Aggregate project resource planning usually uses base information from whatever project management tool or software is being used. If the project plans are kept current and resources are loaded into the system, then the requirements can be added up by resource. These resources, typically engineering resources and indirect personnel, are not traditionally included in the rough-cut capacity planning of manufactured products. Therefore, they require a specific planning process that is separate from the rough-cut capacity planning process for manufactured products.

Ross's observation piques the interest of Susan Callahan, the planning manager. "Should the aggregate resource planning for new products and company initiatives be done by the same planning organization that is used for manufactured products?" she asks.

"That would be highly desirable, but not mandatory," Ross replies. He explains that it would be especially desirable when the same resources are shared for manufactured products and project work. Engineering typically falls into this category. The fact that engineering is a shared resource causes a lot of frustration when engineering is overloaded by projects.

"That's the truth!" Peter says. "Engineering signs up to do a number of product development projects, only to find that the company sells more products with greater engineered content than expected. Engineers are pulled off product development work to do the customer order work. The project work does not get done and, quite frankly, the future of the company is mortgaged. The real issue as I see it is insufficient engineering resources."

"And management in its infinite wisdom says we cannot have more people because it is not in the budget," adds Ray Guy, the final assembly manager. Ray looks at Mark and ducks his head. "Whoops. Sorry, Mark," he says softly.

Anita does not allow Mark to reply. "It's the three knobs again. In Peter's example, he changed the work but did not change the resource. This forced the time or schedule to move out."

Sam Wente, the sales director, voices his frustration. "And the schedule for new products moves out, and moves out, and moves out, and moves out again and again."

Mark holds up his hand as a signal to stop the comments. He does not want the group to focus on the negative. He wants to keep the managers focused on the positive — that they have the power to change the current situation.

"And team, that is why we are here," he says. "We know our process is broken. We are going to fix it. We will include not only standard manufactured products in the implementation, but also company improvement projects that are strategic to Universal Products. We will commit to operate with the same fundamental principles, whether it is for manufactured products, new products, or strategic company initiatives. We will not approve unrealistic plans."

Ross stops and sees the group members nod their heads in affirmation. "Now," he says, "I want you to consider for a moment the issue of timing for the implementation. You will need to be careful not to try to do too much all at once."

"The three knobs at work again," Mark observes.

■ ■ ■

"Before we move on to demand planning and sales and operations planning implementation, I want you to consider the stakeholders of the process," Ross says. He explains that managing new product development and strategic company initiatives is often the most demanding aspect of the sales and operations planning process. It is also where the most leverage is gained.

Both product development and company improvement initiatives should connect directly to Universal Products' strategy, and the strategy needs to connect directly to company goals. Company goals need to be balanced to ensure long-term success. The company goals must meet the needs of multiple stakeholders.

"And meeting the needs of different stakeholders is where real management skills are required," Ross observes, looking directly at Mark Ryan, the general manager. "Mark, every general manager has multiple stakeholders," Ross says, "and at least on the surface, these stakeholders have conflicting objectives or expectations."

"You mean that I must satisfy shareholders, customers, employees, suppliers, and the public community at large. And I must satisfy all of their needs simultaneously with integrity."

"That's what I mean," Ross replies. "And I ask you, is that an easy task?"

Mark laughs. "Clearly not," he says and explains to his team that customers all want continuously improving products that are high quality and furnished at continuously reduced prices or reduced total cost. The shareholders want continuously improving financial returns with fewer deployed resources, that is, at greater levels of return on invested capital, or profit. Employees want improving opportunities, better working conditions, greater compensation, and more opportunities for personal growth. Suppliers want increased prices for providing added value and improved profit returns. The community and society at large expect companies to be good neighbors to the environment, contribute to social causes, and be positive contributors to the well-being of the community.

"On any given day, all of these expectations can feel like they are in conflict," Mark comments. He pauses to see if the group is following his logic. From the expressions on people's faces, he feels further explanation is needed.

"Take a relatively simple issue, like cost and price, for example," Mark says. "To remain competitive, we must lower our prices or figure out how to deliver product at a lower total cost to the customer. Let's say we are forced to lower our prices."

"This is a real issue for us right now!" Sam Wente, the sales director, interjects.

Without missing a beat, Mark continues. "If we lower our prices but cannot lower our costs, then the shareholders are unhappy," he says. "If we lower our prices by reducing wages or postponing increases in wages, then the employees are unhappy. If we reduce costs by forcing lower prices from our suppliers, then they are unhappy. If we reduce costs by reducing our environmental controls and by declining to participate in community functions, then the community is unhappy."

Ross interrupts. "Some time ago, I listened to a division general manager at Hewlett-Packard describe his job to a group of people." He walks to the flip chart, picks up a pen, and draws a large triangle (Figure 37). "The general manager drew this illustration."

Ross explains that this general manager told the group that his job was living inside the triangle, trying to simultaneously satisfy all three stakeholders. To add to the challenge, the general manager had to operate within a set of values and company policies relative to people, the environment, and the community. Those were conditions of his job.

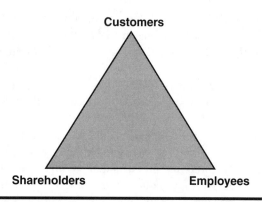

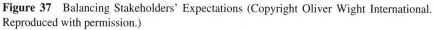

Figure 37 Balancing Stakeholders' Expectations (Copyright Oliver Wight International. Reproduced with permission.)

The general manager learned that he needed to stay near the center of the triangle. If he strayed too close to the shareholders, it could be at the expense of the other stakeholders. If he strayed too close to the employees, it could be at the expense of the other stakeholders. The same goes for straying too close to customers.

"I have observed at Universal Products and at many other companies that the management team does not spend its time wisely," Ross comments. He explains that it is common for management teams to spend their time on what should be routine day-to-day business tasks. Consequently, product development and company improvement initiatives do not receive the attention of management or the prioritization that they require.

"It's the three knobs at work again," Ray Guy comments.

Mark smiles approvingly at Ray. He believes his staff is really beginning to understand.

"Ross, you're correct," Mark says. "That is obviously why you want to make sure we develop an *integrated* sales and operations planning process. The sales and operations planning process should make the day-to-day operation of the business regular and routine, to use your words. And when this happens, the management team can then spend its time on the things that will grow the business, improve our capabilities, and help ensure our long-term, continuous success."

Before Ross can respond, Anita Cooper, the purchasing manager, interjects. "Ross, a few minutes ago, you said a general manager's job was to do three things: (1) run the business well, (2), grow the business, and (3) increase the company's capabilities. From this discussion, I see where sales and operations planning can be an enabling process for the general manager to accomplish these objectives. The process also recognizes the multiple stakeholders. I also now see how the balanced scorecard fits as part of this process. The balanced scorecard needs to consider the multiple stakeholders and the long-term success of the company."

"Thank you, Anita," Ross replies. "You have summed up perfectly."

Janis Novak, the controller, raises her hand. "I would like to say that during my previous experience with sales and operations planning, we did not do what Ross is presenting. The companies only dealt with the day-to-day issues of manufactured products in the sales and operations planning process. We only loosely tied in product development and did not address company initiatives at all."

"That's a good observation, Janis," Ross replies. "Many companies have implemented an abbreviated sales and operations planning process, and the results they achieve are abbreviated as well."

Ross clicks the mouse on the computer to advance to the next visual (Figure 38). "During our previous discussion," he says, "we showed how demand and supply information can be formatted in a template. Here's an example of how information on product development and strategic company initiatives can be presented."

Ross points out that some companies have thirty or forty projects. In such cases, the project status indicator may take up a whole page. The purpose of showing the templates is to provide a quick start for designing the information presentations for sales and operations planning.

"Before we move on, I have one more observation to make relative to integrating new products and strategic company initiatives," Ross says. He explains that sales and operations planning is typically implemented in phases. Some companies choose to implement the demand, supply, and finance subprocesses first. After these subprocesses are working effectively, they then will integrate new products and strategic company initiatives.

If a company does not have its demand, supply, and inventory plans balanced and aligned, the day-to-day, week-to-week experience of the employees is chaotic. Everyone works extremely hard, long hours only to find disappointing results.

The disappointing results cause management to direct the people to work extremely hard and many long hours to fix the problem. Unfortunately, while people are working on the day-to-day problems, they do not have the time to pay attention to the company's future needs and requirements. Strategy, key initiatives, and product development often suffer. Because it is rarely possible to focus on the future needs of the company when demand, supply, and inventory are not aligned, companies often choose to first bring into balance the demand, supply, inventory, and financials before integrating product development and other company initiatives.

"Often, there is tremendous benefit in improving the day-to-day management," Ross says. "But the greater benefit that has more leverage and, in my

Product Review Dashboard

Project	Schedule	Resources	Current Milestone/ Gate #	Planned Milestone/ Gate #
New Product A			10	9
New Product B			2	2
Enhancement 1			2	2
Custom design 1			1	4

Current Review Projection	$1,100,000
Current Review Projection	$700,000

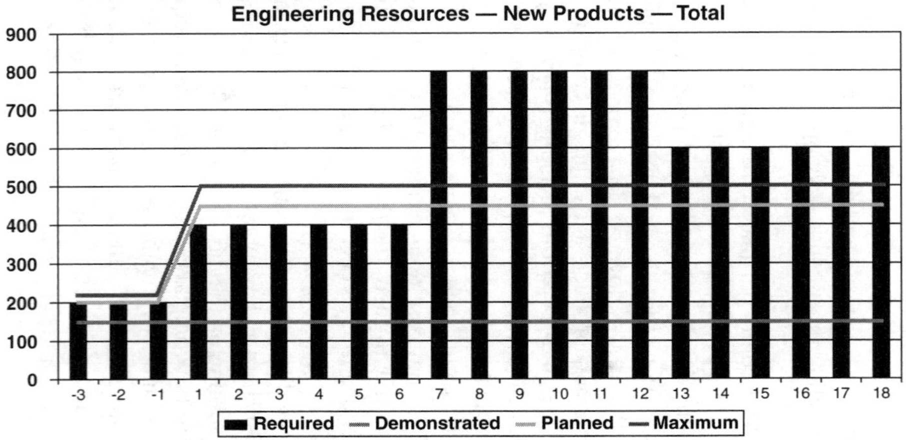

Engineering Resources — New Products — Total

Legend: ■ Required — Demonstrated — Planned — Maximum

- **Assumptions**
  Custom Design 1 will be delayed 2 months. Customer notified. Design for New Products A and B is stable.

- **Vulnerabilities/Risks**
  Will not achieve revenue goals unless outsource or add internal engineering resources.

- **Fixes/Recovery Plans**
  Outsource Custom Design 1.
  Add 3 internal engineering resources for New Products A and B.

- **Issues/Decisions**
  Add resources or delay launch schedules.

Figure 38 Product Review Dashboard (Copyright Oliver Wight International. Reproduced with permission.)

opinion, is more important to the long-term success of a company comes from the new product development projects and the strategic company initiatives. The sooner you integrate them into your process, the sooner you will realize far greater benefits."

Ross glances at his watch. "Let's take a five-minute break," he says. "Then we'll tackle demand management."

■ ■ ■

Mark Ryan watches as his staff files out of the room. He sees and feels enthusiasm.

He is pleased that his entire team seems to grasp how sales and operations planning will help them to more effectively run the business. He also is pleased that the details of sales and operations planning have been covered thoroughly enough to establish a basis for accountability.

Mark's enthusiasm is tempered by the realization that significant management issues that have been masked in the past will inevitably surface during sales and operations planning. He fears that his team will not be pleased with what the process reveals.

He knows that his entire executive team is unhappy with Universal Products' current performance. On the upside, when significant management issues surface — if Mark is skilled enough to keep his team members focused on what is causing the issues — maybe they can successfully solve the problems that are hindering Universal Products.

That will be key, and it will take all the interpersonal skills that Mark possesses. He knows that when under pressure, his staff members will be tempted to place blame on someone else or some other functional area. He must not let that happen.

Today has shed light for Mark on another realization which, until now, he has been loathe to admit. He now knows why Universal Products did not achieve significant benefits from implementing the enterprise resource planning software. During the implementation, the focus was on the tools circle. The process and people circles were neglected.

Mark sees Ross enter the room and motions for him to come over. "Ross, let me make an observation. We are at a high point in the day right now, in my opinion. It's getting late. I don't want to diminish our benefits from today's session, which have exceeded my expectations. How much more must you cover today?"

"You and I are in sync," Ross replies. "I was planning to tell the group that we'll do an abbreviated discussion on demand management and implementation of sales and operations planning. We will cover both topics extensively in the managers' class. The executive team is welcome to attend those parts of the session. We should be able to finish up in a little over an hour."

"Will we get what we need out of that hour?" Mark asks.

"Yes, you will," Ross replies. He promises that he and Nolan will spend time with the executive staff, either collectively, individually, or both, after the managers' class. Ross and Sam already have arranged to meet Wednesday morning, and Sam has made a commitment to attend the demand management section of the managers' class. During his one-on-one session with Sam, Ross intends to work with him to develop a plan for Sam to move forward in implementing a demand management process.

"That's great!" Mark says.

Ross walks away to coordinate with Nolan, leaving Mark to resume his introspection. Even though he is concerned about how his team will respond to the significant issues that sales and operations planning will make visible, Mark feels a measure of comfort in knowing he can rely on the skills and experience of Ross and Nolan. He is pleased that Janis advised him to contact Effective Management, Inc.

8

DEMAND MANAGEMENT FUNDAMENTALS

Ross watches the managers as they file into the room. They are beginning to look tired. Several people stretch to twist the kinks out of their backs before taking their seats. Ross decides to launch right into the subject of demand management and makes a mental note that he and Nolan will need to keep nonessential discussion to a minimum.

Without a preamble, Ross says, "Earlier today, Nolan presented the demand review step in the sales and operations planning monthly cycle." Ross reviews the highlights of Nolan's presentation to ensure that the group has the proper grounding for the presentation on demand management. He reminds the group that sales and operations planning is a demand-driven process and that a primary step in the monthly process is to update the demand forecast or request for product. The output of the process is an agreed-upon demand plan, which represents what the company will be prepared to ship to satisfy customers' demands. This shipment plan is also the revenue plan from shipments.

Therefore, the demand plan, the shipment plan, and the sales or revenue plan are all one and the same. If services are a product, the service requirements and projected revenues should be included in the plan and should be made visible as a separate family or at least as a separate demand stream.

"The purpose of our discussion of demand management this afternoon," Ross says, "is mostly to emphasize the importance of demand planning and demand management. If you understand the importance, then you will ensure that demand management receives the proper amount of attention during the implementation."

He explains that the emphasis on demand management should not be construed to mean that supply planning is not equally important. In his experience, he has found that most companies dedicate resources to supply planning, just as Universal Products does with its planning organization. Most companies, however, do not dedicate the same level of resources to demand planning and demand management.

"Is that what you found during our assessment?" Sam Wente, the sales director, asks.

"Nolan assessed your demand management capabilities," Ross replies. "He found the classic situation where there are significant resources in supply planning and expediting, but virtually none in demand planning."

This news does not sit well with Sam. "We update our forecasts for Mark every month," he says.

"Ross, may I respond?" Nolan asks from the back of the room. The group turns to look at him.

"Sam, toward the end of each month, you update that month's forecast only," Nolan says. "The update shows only the revenue you believe will be generated. Quite frankly, this is an exercise that only helps Janis and Mark tell corporate what to expect for that month's bookings and sales from the division. It is of virtually no use to anyone else. And if you will excuse my bluntness, I doubt it is of any real use to corporate. I strongly suspect it is of little or no use to your sales effort. In fact, it could be viewed as extra, nonvalue-added work by the sales people. It is just something that has always been done. Don't mistake what you are presently doing as demand planning or demand management. It is not."

Mark Ryan makes a mental note that Nolan can be just as frank as Ross. They certainly don't pull any punches. He is interested to see how his team will respond to Nolan's indictment of the forecasting process.

Janis Novak, the controller, jumps in. She defends the current process. "Corporate needs to know what is happening to communicate to the analysts, the directors, and ultimately the shareholders," she says.

Nolan responds calmly. "There are much better ways to do that with less effort," he replies. "One of the real benefits of sales and operations planning is the information that the finance organization receives. The output is one set of operating numbers, and the information that the corporate finance organization needs is contained in those numbers."

"Yes, I know," Janis replies, "but it may not be as easy as you make it sound. Corporate must accept those numbers, and that means we need to get corporate involved so that its expectations are met by the process."

"I agree," Nolan says.

Before anyone else can comment, Ross steps in, remembering his resolve to keep the discussion and presentation laser-focused on the demand management

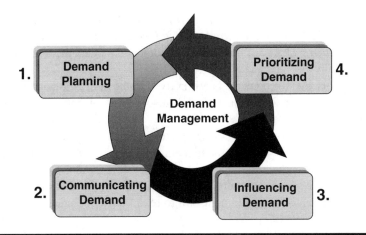

Figure 39   Demand Management Process Model (Copyright Oliver Wight International. Reproduced with permission.)

material. "Let's make a note, Nolan, to continue this discussion with Sam and Janis in one-on-one conversations," he says. "Now that we have criticized your current process, let's show you what are considered to be the best practices for demand management."

Ross tells the group that there are four key elements of demand management. He displays a visual to illustrate the elements (Figure 39).

"Done correctly, demand management is really integrated marketing and sales management," Ross observes. He explains that many companies think of demand management as forecasting, or guessing what will happen in the future, but it is more than that. It includes all areas that ultimately affect demand for products or services, including all marketing and sales activities, which range from marketing strategy to order promises.

Ross has found that when a company does demand management well, it usually does marketing and sales management well. Likewise, companies that develop effective processes for integrating marketing and sales management with supply management tend to do well in the marketplace.

He quotes Philip Kotler's definition of demand management from his book *Kotler on Marketing*:

> Marketing's main thrust and skill is *demand management,* namely to influence the level, timing and composition of demand in pursuit of company objectives.

"To my mind, this is the best definition of demand management to be articulated to date," Ross comments.

Sam Wente, the sales director, raises his hand. "Earlier you referred to a book entitled *The Marketing Edge: The New Leadership Role of Sales and Marketing in Manufacturing.* Does this book deal with demand management as you are presenting it today?"

Ross replies that the book deals primarily with the integration of demand planning with the rest of the organization. It also deals conceptually with demand management.

"So yes, it does, Sam, but not completely," Ross says. "I understand that a more comprehensive book on demand management principles is in the process of being written."

Ross tells the group that there are several reference books on sales and marketing management that would be useful to read. These include:

- *Kotler on Marketing,* by Philip Kotler
- *The Executive in Action,* by Peter F. Drucker
- *Strategic Selling,* by Robert B. Miller and Stephen E. Heiman
- *Conceptual Selling,* by Robert B. Miller and Stephen E. Heiman
- *Revenue Management,* by Robert Cross

Sam turns to Nolan, who is in the back of the room. "You really ticked me off earlier," he says, "but your points are well taken. I have the feeling that implementing demand management as you describe it is a journey, not a destination. I can see implementing the demand planning process, and once that process is integrated into sales and operations planning, demand management should become a driver for continuously improving our marketing and sales efforts. I can already see that it will create visibility of information that we did not have before, which will enable us to address some of the realities all of us have preferred avoiding or not confronting."

"Sam, you've got it! Absolutely correctly stated!" Ross says.

Mark smiles approvingly at Sam. He has come to know that when Sam becomes committed to something, he stays committed. It appears that Sam understands that his sales and marketing group needs to be fully engaged in the implementation. Since sales and operations planning is a demand-driven process, Sam's role is going to be vital.

Ross points to the overhead on the screen. "Let's get back to the four elements of demand management. I'm going to explain each element."

He shows the group another visual (Figure 40) and uses the laser pointer to circle the first three items: demand planning, communicating demand, and influencing demand. "The better you perform these three items, the less the level of activity required in performing the fourth, prioritizing demand," he says.

"Do not underestimate your ability to influence demand," Ross continues. He

1. **Demand Planning:** A process to provide (1) a monthly update of marketing and sales plans and (2) a formalized, updated demand plan (also known as a request for product and a forecast) over the agreed-upon planning horizon as part of the monthly sales and operations planning process. The process includes feedback to the sales force on what they are expected to sell and what will be available to sell.

2. **Communicating Demand:** A process that links the demand planning process to the supply planning, master scheduling, and sales and operations planning processes. This involves communicating in the formats and planning horizons required to support each process. The process includes mechanisms for continuous communication and updates of the demand plan between the monthly sales and operations planning. Continuous communication and updates help to ensure responsiveness and flexibility in serving customers and markets.

3. **Influencing Demand:** This process is the essence of marketing and sales and oftentimes is referred to as execution. The ultimate objective of marketing and sales programs is to influence customers to buy products and services in such a way that it supports your company's goals and objectives. This involves managing the classical marketing mix of product, price, promotion, and place. Conversely, influencing demand involves influencing your company to do the right things for the customers and markets.

4. **Prioritizing Demand:** This is a process for prioritizing demand when volume or timing of supply is insufficient to meet demand. This process involves use of communications processes and planning analysis tools to determine priorities and to communicate how the resource in scarce supply is to be deployed. Prioritizing demand typically results in some customers receiving preference over other customers in terms of delivery quantity and lead time. It also may result in some customers receiving the product and others customers not receiving the product.

Figure 40   Four Elements of Demand Management

reminds the group of the book *Revenue Management* by Robert Cross. The book focuses on influencing demand in a capital-intensive industry where (1) the ability to change supply in the short term is difficult and (2) optimal resource utilization is a condition for profitable operations.

Susan Callahan, the planning manager, stirs in her chair. "Ross and Nolan, how you describe demand management sounds like people and behavior issues again," she comments.

"That's a good observation," Ross replies. He explains that the demand planning process is a key part of sales and marketing management. The communications process is required to ensure that customers and markets will receive what is sold — that their expectations will be met. Influencing demand really involves executing the demand plan and dealing with day-to-day fluctuations in demand, and prioritizing demand involves dealing with the inevitable out-of-balance situations — large and small.

"And you're right, Susan," Ross says. "While tools enable you to process, analyze, and present the demand information more readily, ultimately it comes down to people developing the sales and marketing plans, communicating the plans, and making the decisions required to influence and prioritize demand. It's all about people and behaviors."

■ ■ ■

Sam Wente's back is sore, and he's tired of sitting. He walks to the back of the room and leans against the wall. "So what do we need to do to implement a quality demand management process?" he asks.

Ross looks at Nolan, and Nolan steps forward to answer Sam's question. He tells the group that the most effective place to start is to implement a closed-loop demand planning process. By a closed-loop process, he means that a sales and marketing plan for each product family or grouping is developed. Performance to plan is measured by product, by customer or market, and by sales and marketing responsibility to attain understanding of the customers and markets, accountability, and corrective action. The marketing and sales organization is responsible for developing marketing and sales plans that include action plans, assumptions about the business, and the quantification of the demand plan by product in units and dollars.

When the demand plan is integrated into the sales and operations planning, the actions required to achieve the desired results are defined through the management process. By comparing the planned results versus the desired results, gaps are identified. Sales and marketing action is needed to close the gaps. The management process deals with how to best close the gaps.

Nolan nods at Ross, who displays the next graphic (Figure 41). Ross draws the group's attention to the chart. "Nolan's explanation assumes that there is a plan against which to compare. It may be the annual business plan, stretch goals from the strategic plan, or both," he says.

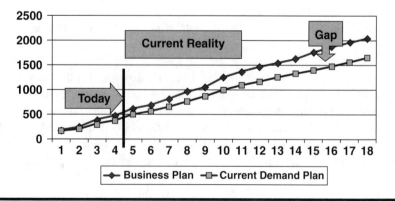

Figure 41   Gap Management

He tells the group that in helping companies to implement sales and operations planning, he and his colleagues have found that the need for a quantified strategic plan in support of company goals usually surfaces during the process. This is particularly true in small- and medium-size companies.

Often a strategic plan exists, and may be referred to as the long-range plan, but sometimes it exists only in the mind of the entrepreneur, who periodically may reveal portions of it to others in the organization. In these cases, sales and operations planning becomes the stimulus to improve the development and communication of the business and strategic planning processes.

By measuring performance to plan, variances are determined and analyzed. When the variances are analyzed, the findings stimulate an understanding of the effectiveness of the current marketing. This new understanding, in turn, becomes a stimulus for change.

Susan Callahan, the planning manager, has joined Sam in the back of the room. Leaning against the wall, she asks, "And I assume it also becomes a primary input for updating the forecast. If you have significant variances and you choose not to change the marketing mix, then you must change the plan."

Anita Cooper, the purchasing manager, chimes in. "This sounds likes a proactive version of the three knobs. If you expect something to change, you must change something."

Before Ross and Nolan can reply, Sam Wente speaks up. "I agree," he says, "and to implement a closed-loop process, we need to consider the three circles — people, process, and tools. We need a demand planning process supported by whatever tools are required. The information that surfaces through the process will require the marketing and sales organization to make management decisions that will ensure we meet our commitments. This is the people circle at work again."

Peter Newfeld, the product development/engineering director, drops his class notebook on the desk to get Sam's attention. "And that brings us back to 'do what you say you're going to do.'"

The group laughs, and Ross says, "By George, I think you've got it!"

Mark Ryan decides it is time for him to make an observation to the group. He has tried not to interject himself too much into the discussion so that his team will feel comfortable discussing and thinking through the sales and operations planning process. He has been careful not to be judgmental about anyone's thought processes because everyone learns at a different pace.

Now is the time to add perspective, however. "Everyone wishes they had a better view to the future," Mark says to the group. "Wouldn't life be considerably easier if we could see the opportunities and problems coming ahead of time instead of after the fact?"

Everyone nods their head in agreement.

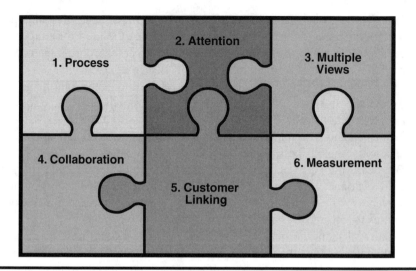

Figure 42   Best Practices — Demand Planning

"I guess that puts the onus on me to make sure we implement a quality process," Sam Wente, the sales director, says. With barely a pause, he asks, "So, Ross, what must I do to make sure we implement a quality demand planning process?"

"To answer your question sufficiently will require a separate seminar and significant coaching," Ross replies, "but I can give you a summary of the best practices." He asks the group to turn to the section on demand management in their notebooks, specifically the page entitled "Demand Planning Best Practices." He advances the slide presentation to reveal a new graphic (Figure 42).

"I will briefly give an overview of each best practice," Ross says. "This overview will give you a basic understanding of what is necessary to have a quality demand planning process."

Ross points to the upper left part of the illustration, which refers to process. "One of the first keys to a quality demand planning process," he says, "is to establish a repetitive process for updating the demand plans." He explains that the objective is to make the updating of demand plans regular and routine. It should become a natural part of the sales and marketing functions in the company. It should not be considered extra work, but rather part of the work that a professional sales and marketing organization performs.

He notes that Universal Products will need to define its demand planning process. Every company's process will differ somewhat based upon the sales and marketing organization and the way the company chooses to market its products. In designing the process, consideration should be given to:

■ How the sales and marketing organization is managed, including who is accountable for each function within the organization
■ Who within the organization has the ability to influence demand
■ Information required to manage the sales and marketing functions
■ Common information that will be used to develop the product forecast

Ross reinforces a previous point, that the aggregate product family demand plan needs to be updated monthly, and the update should cover the agreed-upon planning horizon. Part of the update involves the demand review step in the monthly sales and operations planning process.

There will be times when the product family demand plan will need to be updated more frequently than on a monthly basis. During the month, as more is learned about customers' demand and the marketplace, the plan needs to be updated and communicated to the supply organization.

Ross points out that the individual detailed item forecasts will be updated in a continuous ongoing process and reviewed at least weekly. In that review, the sum of the detail forecasts is compared to the aggregate product family forecast to see if it is within acceptable tolerance of the current plan. If it is not within tolerance, additional analysis and updating of the aggregate product plan may be required.

Ray Guy, the final assembly manager, and Jim Simpson, the manufacturing director, voice their concern at the same time.

"Do you mean that sales can change its forecast at any time?" Jim asks.

"That doesn't seem any different than what we do now," Ray adds.

"What I'm talking about is much different from what you do now," Ross replies. "Today, you respond only to orders, not to the forecast. Today, you do not adequately decouple demand from supply."

He explains that decoupling allows the supply organization to choose to produce the product in different quantities and timing than the orders that are received. It enables the production organization and suppliers to be in better control of their operations.

"Remember that the forecast should be considered a request for product. *Asking for product does not ensure it can be provided.* That is a separate decision," Ross says. "From a business perspective, you should be predisposed to say yes to customers. An updated demand plan provides visibility. It enables the manufacturing and engineering organizations to be prepared to say yes to customers and to execute effectively and efficiently."

Susan Callahan, the planning manager, raises her hand. "In essence, the planning is done based upon the orders we have plus the demand we see coming. This is expressed and communicated in the form of a demand plan or a forecast of anticipated demand. We want the best information we can have at any time. If we don't allow the demand plan to be updated as opportunities and problems occur

— even in between the monthly sales and operations planning cycle, then we cut ourselves off from the visibility and ability to respond. We should not have to wait for a monthly meeting to update the plans."

Peter Newfeld, the product development/engineering director, shakes his head vigorously in disagreement. "But what if we can't meet the requested delivery date because we don't have the resources in that time period?"

Susan looks to Ross. Ross nods his head and looks at Susan in acquiescence.

"That's why we need to decouple demand from supply," Susan replies. "Perhaps we can schedule work earlier to utilize our current capacity. Perhaps we can schedule out some other work. We may be doing work at risk to a forecast, but it may be a better risk than not being able to meet the customer demand and customer expectation. If we simply can't meet the need, we have a demand management issue to change the expectations of the customer or the marketplace."

Sam Wente, the sales director, walks back to his seat. "This is how I see it, Peter," he says. "If sales increases the forecast during the month, the increase has not been reviewed and approved by management, meaning all of us. But the request has been communicated to planning, which I guess puts the request into the master schedule. Let's say that planning reviews the request and finds it is impossible to meet the customer's requested delivery. Planning communicates to sales to let us know not to sell what we can't deliver, or it will give us a chance to review other customer orders to potentially change priorities, depending upon what is in the best interest of the company."

Sam's explanation does not alleviate Jim Simpson's concern. "But like Ray said, this sounds like what we are doing today. We are changing priorities every day on work already in process."

Mark is pleased with the conversation. Jim and Ray are articulating real issues that will inevitably surface when Universal Products begins to utilize best practices for sales and operations planning.

"The difference between what Susan and Sam explained and what we currently are doing is simple," Mark says. "We do not have forward visibility today. We aren't looking out two months in the future, let alone eighteen months, as Ross and Nolan have recommended. We chase and change orders only after they are received. The demand for these orders could have been communicated earlier and influenced earlier, if needed. Jim, Ray, and Peter, I see how forward visibility and decoupling demand and supply will be a tremendous help. The key is to gain visibility through the demand plan, decouple demand from supply, and allow sales to request forecast changes as soon as the need is identified, even before we receive the order."

Mark pauses to look at his team. "But how do we do all of that, Ross?" he asks.

Ross explains that the subject the group has been talking about chiefly involves master scheduling. Master scheduling is the key process that connects the decisions made in sales and operations planning to the supply chain. It is the link between planning and execution from the executive perspective.

"Mark, you and I have talked briefly about master scheduling," Ross says. "It is something you do not do well today, but will need to do. Susan's group does some limited decoupling of demand and supply, but only on occasion and only through brute force."

Susan turns to address Mark. "Mark, we are willing and anxious to do master scheduling as Ross and Nolan teach it. To make it work well, we need at least a *reasonable* forecast of demand. We have the master scheduling software that was part of our enterprise resource planning implementation. We are ready to do proper master scheduling if we can get a reasonable forecast of demand and if we choose to operate to the best practices and principles that we have discussed today."

Mark nods his head in acknowledgment. He understands Susan's message.

Ross clears his throat. "Since I've been mentioning some books as references, let me also tell you that there is a definitive book on master scheduling. Some people think of it as the bible on master scheduling. The author is John Proud, and the book is entitled *Master Scheduling: A Practical Guide to Competitive Manufacturing.*"

He pauses for a moment and then says, "Let's move on. We have said that demand management is a process that should be used in the management of sales and marketing. It requires a monthly management review and requires the ability to communicate product forecast changes as needed so that decisions and action can occur."

He explains that the demand planning process involves a series of steps that communicate changes in demand and changes in market conditions that may have an influence on demand. In a company like Universal Products, the communications process involves the following:

- Inputs from the sales organization on customer and market activities
- Inputs from the marketing organization on product development, marketing mix changes, and assumptions about market factors affecting the business
- Visibility of major projects that could have a significant effect on demand
- A forecast for service and spare parts

"In short, you will need to identify the key inputs into the process and design the process to pull all the information together into a company demand plan," Ross says.

He explains that on a monthly basis, the plan is reviewed and approved through the sales and operations planning process. During the month, minor changes are communicated and handled as part of the day-to-day business. Significant changes during the month will require the management team's review and approval.

Sam shifts in his chair. "This seems like a lot of work," he says. "I am assuming that is why you mentioned earlier today the need for a full-time demand planner."

"You're right, Sam, and that brings me to the next demand planning best practice," Ross replies. He tells the group that the most common reason why companies fail in implementing demand management is insufficient *attention* to the process. The reliability of the demand plan will not improve if the work is not done.

"It is a very simple fact," Ross says, "yet most companies do not have a demand planning function. You, too, will need to overcome this hurdle."

Ross explains that attention to demand planning is required on an ongoing basis to ensure that the demand plan is updated at the detail level. He asks the group to remember that the demand plan for sales and operations planning is expressed in product families or groupings. Someone from the demand side of the business needs to convert that demand to individual product items or whatever level of detail the master schedule requires, or the level that feeds master scheduling.

"This requires a full-time demand planning function," Ross says. "This function logically falls within the demand side of the business, in the sales or marketing organization." He mentions that a more detailed discussion of the demand planner or demand manager's responsibilities is included in the book *The Marketing Edge*.

In Ross's experience, attention to demand planning at the management and executive level in actuality is sales and marketing management. Sales and marketing management is needed to fulfill a critical role — understand what is happening with customers and the marketplace, the products being sold, and the product forecast to be sold. This understanding is needed for sales and marketing management to effectively do its job.

Ross pauses and looks first at Sam, then at Mark, and then back at Sam. "To make sure my message is clear, Sam," he says, "you need a full-time demand planning function. Start with one person. That person should work for you directly in developing the demand planning process and operating the process for the first year. Also, you must chair the monthly demand review process."

"I think I have the picture," Sam replies. "I will follow your direction unless overridden by Mark."

Mark wants to be sure that Sam and the rest of his management team understand the message. "Sam, you and I are in sync with Ross's recommendations. We should discuss privately who would be the best person to perform the demand planning job."

Ross is not sure that Ray Guy, the final assembly manager, and Jim Simpson, the manufacturing director, have heard Mark's message. During the last few minutes, they have been whispering, heads together.

"Ray and Jim, why don't you share with the rest of the group what you have been talking about," Ross says.

They pull their heads up. "If we let Sam change his forecast continuously, how do we know whether or not the forecast accuracy is improving?" Jim asks.

Ross and Nolan look at each other knowingly. The concern Ray and Jim are expressing is common. They are uncomfortable with allowing the forecast to change, largely because they perceive, rightly or wrongly, that this would be the status quo. It is always a challenge to get people to understand what it is like to operate with best practices.

"One of the issues we have not discussed yet is schedule stability. Isn't that what you are concerned about, Ray and Jim?" Ross asks.

Ray and Jim nod their heads in agreement.

Ross puts the slide presentation on index and scrolls down, looking for a particular slide. He speaks while searching for the slide. "We have talked very little about the stability of manufacturing and engineering schedules," he says. "Remember our discussions about decoupling supply and demand? One of the reasons to decouple is to provide some stability to schedules for manufacturing, engineering, and purchasing — even when demand is variable and changes."

Jim and Ray intently listen, but their facial expressions show skepticism.

Ross decides to take another tack. "The overriding principle is that the company will build to schedule," he says. "Please note that I did not say build to order or build to forecast, which we referred to before as make to order and make to stock."

He explains that, in practice, the company should build to schedule, and the schedule should be based upon a strategy of make to order or make to stock. What this scheduling approach means for people in manufacturing, final assembly, or engineering is that the planning group determines the schedule, in collaboration with each functional department, and those departments will produce to that schedule.

"Susan Callahan and her planners need the ability to keep the schedule firm, with minimal changes for some number of hours, days, or weeks, depending on the product. Do you agree?" Ross asks Jim and Ray.

They nod their heads in agreement.

"Keeping the schedule firm within an agreed-upon time period is one of the functions of master scheduling," Ross says. He explains that a stable schedule minimizes changes to work in process and allows the supply side to start work on an item or order and complete the work without changes and interruptions to work flow.

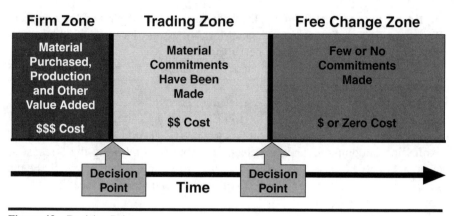

Figure 43   Decision Points

"This in turn should increase quality and lower costs," Ross adds. He turns toward Jim and Ray. "Are you two tracking with me?" he asks.

"This sounds good so far, but how is the schedule stabilized in the agreed-upon time period, as you called it?" Jim asks.

"Aah," Ross says, "that's where decision points come in. Let me show you." He finds the slide he has been looking for (Figure 43) and displays it on the screen.

"Decision points are used to define zones of stability," Ross says. "Decision points are also sometimes referred to as time fences." He points to the chart and the lines designated as decision points and explains that the chart shows three zones: firm, trading, and free change. The point of time between the zones creates decision points, or time fences.

He tells the group that the most immediate time frame is the firm zone. "This is where most of you focus presently and is, I think, Ray and Jim, where you are expressing concern," Ross says. "We want to minimize changes in the firm zone because significant value has already been added to the product, and change is costly."

Ross explains that the second zone in time is the trading zone. Material may have been purchased to support the products in this zone. Thus, the volume to produce may be fixed, but there is often flexibility to change the mix of the products within the volume.

The free change zone is the farthest away in time and, therefore, the most flexible for accommodating change. Both production volume and product mix can be changed with little financial impact from a product and production cost point of view.

"I want to emphasize that these zones are *guidelines* for change," Ross says while tapping the laser pointer on each decision point demarcation. "They are not absolute fixed rules unless you choose to make them absolute fixed rules. As guidelines, flexibility is increased and costs may increase as well. The decision to be flexible may not be the most cost-effective approach. Flexibility always involves a trade-off between cost and customer service. Using the zones as absolute fixed rules minimizes flexibility but provides the opportunity for reduced cost."

Anita Cooper, the purchasing manager, raises her hand. "Are the zones defined by supply lead times, the time it takes us to make the product and procure raw materials?" she asks. "From my perspective in purchasing, the use of decision points should give me the ability to provide more stable demand to my suppliers. It could also potentially enable me to give suppliers more visibility of what will be needed farther out into the future."

"Time zones and decision points are very useful for purchasing," Ross replies, "but let's also consider Sam's point of view." He turns to address Sam Wente, the sales director. "Sam, when do you want to be able to change the manufacturing schedule? How many weeks do you want to keep firm?"

Before Sam can answer, Ray Guy jumps in. "Sam wants to be able to change the schedule right now, in any volume and in any mix. He wants to be able to make changes as we load the product on the truck."

"And you supply guys would like me to keep the schedule firm for a year," Sam answers back. "Hell, anyone could make the stuff with that kind of stability."

Mark quickly interrupts. The discussion of decision points is a very useful revelation from his point of view as general manager, but he does not want a bloodbath in determining the length of time for each zone. "The setting of the time periods for each zone seems to me to be a key issue from a customer service and operations cost and efficiency point of view. This is a key point of integration," Mark says to his group.

He turns to Ross. "Because this is a key issue for integration, Ross, shouldn't we collectively agree as a management team on how much stability for how long we wish to provide in our schedules to manufacturing and engineering? Also, how much flexibility for how long do we wish to provide to our customers?"

"That's correct," Ross replies. "The establishment of these zones must be addressed from a strategic and tactical point of view — for manufacturing, engineering, purchasing, sales and marketing, and for the company overall. The zones must be collectively agreed upon by your management team."

"So what are the determining factors?" Mark asks.

"Anita pointed out one determining factor," Ross replies. "That is your supply lead times." He explains that supply lead times are physical realities. When changes are made within supply lead times, it increases costs and can have an effect on quality.

"I assume this is one of the reasons why so many companies are striving to shorten their cycle times," Mark states.

"Absolutely," Ross replies. He tells the group that the physical realities, such as supply lead times, can be mitigated with inventory strategy, flexible manufacturing methods, supplier scheduling, and flexible capacity strategies. For example, companies may choose to keep higher inventory for long-lead-time raw material. This inventory tactic allows more flexibility in the schedule to respond to customer demand.

"These are all subjects that are beyond the scope of this session today, but they will be part of the process design and other education and coaching that we will do," Ross says.

"Which brings us back to the original issue," Susan Callahan, the planning manager, says. "How do we know if Sam is doing well with his forecasting, his demand planning?"

Ross smiles and points to Susan. "Thanks for the reminder, Susan," he says as he brings up the next slide (Figure 44) and then uses the laser pointer to point to the end of each zone. "If you have established decision points or time fences," he says, "then you have also established a reference point for measuring forecast accuracy."

He tells the group that the decision points are important in order for the supply side of the enterprise to operate effectively and efficiently. To satisfy customer demand and simultaneously operate effectively and efficiently, demand forecasts need to be as accurate as is practical at the decision points.

"Save the demand forecast as it passes the decision point and compare the actual demand to that forecast," Ross says. "This brings us to the next subject, measurement."

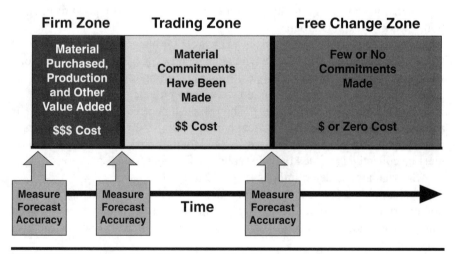

Figure 44   Forecast Accuracy Measurement Model

Ross notices Nolan at the back of the room pointing at his watch. We must be getting behind again, Ross says to himself. He realizes that he will need to pick up the pace.

"I'm not going to spend time today on the details of forecast accuracy measurement," he says. He tells the group that a paper on measuring forecast accuracy is included in the class material. It is also available on the EMI Web site. The paper goes into the detail of measuring forecast accuracy and should be used as a guideline during the process design and during implementation.

Ross tells the group that demand planning is a process. As such, it has inputs and outputs, all of which can be measured. "According to an old axiom, if you want something to improve, measure it," he says.

Ross reminds the group about the discussion on measuring forecast accuracy at decision points. "Measurements should be tied to the way companies choose to manage, which is what measuring forecast accuracy at decision points accomplishes," he says. "At whatever time point you choose to measure forecast accuracy, forecast accuracy or inaccuracy measurement is a key measure of the effectiveness of demand planning and the demand management process."

"But let me make a key point to control expectations," Ross continues. "There will always be inaccuracies. Let me repeat that. There will always be inaccuracies." He tells the group that the demand planning process should strive to minimize the inaccuracies. Whenever forecast accuracy is reviewed, tactics to deal with the inaccuracies also need to be reviewed.

"They go hand in glove," Ross explains. "They are like two sides of the same coin, or put another way," he says as he advances the computer to the next slide (Figure 45), "the greater the accuracy, the fewer tactics that are needed to deal with the inaccuracy. The greater the inaccuracy, the more tactics that are needed to deal with the inaccuracy."

Anita Cooper, the purchasing manager, raises her hand. "What do you mean by 'tactics'?" she asks.

Figure 45 Forecast Accuracy and Tactics

"May I respond to that?" Susan Callahan, the planning manager, asks.

Ross motions for her to proceed.

"The tactics would include choices to deal with the forecast inaccuracy. If we are going to meet customers' expectations all of the time, then we must deal with the anticipated inaccuracies. The tactics would include inventory management, capacity management, customer lead-time management, make-to-order versus make-to-stock choices, and other decisions."

"Thank you, Susan, for highlighting that we are striving to meet customer expectations," Sam Wente, the sales director, says from the back of the room, where he has gone again to stretch his aching back. "As I see it, you have listed a possible number of choices to deal with the inaccuracies. Those choices would be made in sales and operations planning."

Mark notices Ross and Nolan nodding to one another. They recognize that Sam and the rest of the team are beginning to truly understand the implications of the sales and operations planning process.

"Sam and Susan, you are right," Ross says. "Now let's move on to a favorite subject of mine: assumptions."

9

DEMAND MANAGEMENT TECHNIQUES

"Assumptions is one of my favorite subjects," Ross tells the group, "because the process for documenting assumptions and occurrences greatly influences forecast accuracy and the effectiveness of your demand management process."

He explains that there are always underlying assumptions that are made whenever a plan is developed — whether it is the demand plan, the sales plan, the marketing plan, or even the supply plan. "However, at this point in time, we are going to focus on the assumptions of the demand plan," Ross says.

He explains that discussion about assumptions (what is assumed will happen in the future) and occurrences (what has happened in the past to impact performance and forecast accuracy) is a fundamental principle of sales and marketing planning. The assumptions frequently focus on the planned effectiveness or the targeted objectives of actions that will be taken to influence the market. Assumptions also focus on external factors, such as competitors and the economy, which affect demand and the condition of the marketplace.

Ross tells the group that in addition to being of tremendous importance for developing effective marketing and sales plans, the documenting of assumptions also has an added benefit. It provides an excellent means of communicating the thought process used to develop the demand plan. It stimulates discussion, allows different views to surface, and is the basis for "what if" simulations and contingency planning.

"Recall the demand dashboard from earlier this morning," Ross says as he displays the graphic (Figure 46) again and points to the areas that relate to assumptions and occurrences. "The fundamental notion is to capture what has happened in the past that influenced demand and the assumptions about those things that will influence demand in the future."

Sam Wente, the sales director, raises a question from the back of the room. "Ross, the example you show has the occurrences and assumptions broken into internal and external. Could you explain that, please?"

Ross explains that *internal* refers to those factors over which Universal Products has control. *External* refers to those factors over which Universal Products has no direct control. For example, marketing mix, commonly known as the 4Ps — product, price, promotion, and place — is made up of factors that can be directly controlled by Universal Products. Therefore, they would be covered under internal assumptions and occurrences.

Universal Products has no control over such factors as the economy, the price of oil, currency exchange rates, and competitive actions, however. Therefore, they would be covered under external assumptions and occurrences.

"Are you attempting to capture the expected timing of the internal and external events or activities?" Susan Callahan, the planning manager, asks.

"That's an excellent observation, Susan," Ross replies. "It is tremendously important to capture timing to the extent possible. In demand planning, most people find that timing is everything."

"This appears to be organized common sense, but it also seems like a lot of work," Sam comments.

"It does require effort and discipline, and that effort and discipline always pays off in my experience," Ross replies. He explains that documenting and communicating the assumptions and occurrences is one of the responsibilities of the demand planner. The design of the demand planning process should make it as easy as possible for members of the sales and marketing organization to communicate the occurrences and assumptions.

He reminds the group that the company will be operating based on the plan and assumptions agreed to during the last sales and operations planning cycle. Initially, as sales and operations planning is implemented, it will take more time to capture, document, and communicate the assumptions and occurrences.

When sales and operations planning is operational, the focus of the process is on managing changes to the plan, including changes to assumptions. The effort becomes more management by exception, and the amount of work required to document assumptions and occurrences is dramatically reduced — unless there are major changes in the market.

"How do you make it as easy as possible for sales and marketing people to communicate assumptions and occurrences?" Sam asks.

"There are tools and techniques that facilitate the communications process,"

Demand Dashboard

BU: COMM   Family: XXX
Inventory Strategy: _____
Lead Time Strategy: _____

Demand Plan

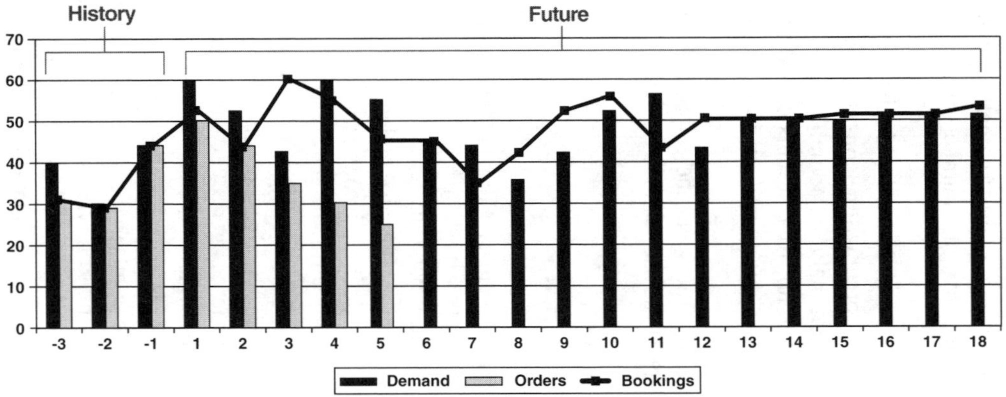

History   Future

Legend: ■ Demand   ▨ Orders   ◆ Bookings

- **Assumptions/Internal**
  Will add 1 salesperson in period 5.
  Promotion planned in periods 6 through 9.

- **Assumptions/External**
  Competitor will introduce a competing product in period 7.

- **Vulnerabilities/Risks**
  Product introduction delayed 3 months.

- **Opportunities**
  Customer A is increasing its volume by 20%.

- **Issues/Decisions**
  Resources for completing new product.

- **Occurrences/Internal**
  Shipment delayed in period 2 — quality problems.

- **Occurrences/External**
  Softening of economy in last quarter.

Performance Measures

Measure	-3	-2	-1
On-Time Delivery	90%	85%	85%
Plan vs. Actual	80%	80%	70%
Territory A	98%	95%	95%
Territory B	70%	60%	70%
Territory C	80%	75%	85%
Territory D	50%	60%	50%

Figure 46 Example of Demand Dashboard

Ross replies. "We will address this issue in detail during the demand management education and design workshop."

Mark Ryan, the general manager, is intrigued by the concept of documenting and communicating assumptions and occurrences. He wants to be sure he understands how to use this information in managing the company. "It seems to me that the occurrences and assumptions are mostly what I will want to talk about in the executive sales and operations planning meeting," he observes. "The performance numbers and measurements are presumably a function of occurrences in the past. The future numbers, or demand plan, are largely a function of the assumptions. If this information flows to me, I can concur or challenge the information, and a business conversation results. We can talk about something other than just the numbers. We currently seem to talk about the numbers without significant substance behind them."

"And if I have the same information," Janis Novak, the controller, says, "my reporting and communication to corporate will be considerably simplified. I will already have answers to the questions that are inevitably asked."

"And if I provide the information up front to Janis and Mark," Sam says, "I reduce the number of phone calls and questions I get from them. I have already given them the answers."

Ross smiles. "You all seem to understand the importance of documenting occurrences and assumptions," he says. "Let's move on to the next demand planning best practice: multiple views.

■ ■ ■

"One of the best ways to ensure the most accurate plans for the future is to get multiple perspectives or multiple views from different individuals," Ross tells the group. He explains that textbooks commonly refer to the process of obtaining multiple views as consensus forecasting. It is also called collaborative forecasting, especially when customers provide input into the process.

In its most simplistic form, a company will get a view from the marketing organization and a view from the sales organization. The marketing view is generated by marketing department representatives, product and market managers, and long-range planners. The sales view is generated by sales management and involves getting input from the sales organization.

"Here's an example of the multiple views of the future," Ross says as he brings up a new slide (Figure 47). He points to the different columns in the table. "Not surprisingly," he says, "when multiple views are developed regarding an uncertain future, there will be different perspectives and opinions."

He explains that the different views stimulate discussion and justification, and this is where the documented assumptions and occurrences become vital to

PRODUCT FAMILY/BRAND A							

Period	Statistical Forecast	Sales Plan	Customer Forecasts	Marketing Plan	New Product Plans	New Demand Plan	Previous Month's Approved Demand Plan	Annual Budget
1	1000	1500	2000			1000	1000	1500
2	2500	3000	3500			2500	2500	3000
3	4500	5000	5500			4500	4500	5000
4	1000	500	1000			1000	1000	1000
5	1000	500	1000			1000	1000	1000
6	1000	500	1000		10000	1000	1000	1000
7	3000	4000	5000	10000	10000	3000	4000	5000
8	3000	4000	5000	10000	10000	5000	4000	5000
9	4500	5500	6500	2500	10000	6000	5500	5000
10	6500	7500	8500	2500	5000	7000	7500	8000
11	7500	8500	9500			8000	8500	8000
12	5000	3000	4000			5000	3000	4000
13	1100	1725	2000			1100	1100	
14	2750	3450	3500			2750	2750	
15	4950	5750	5500			4950	4950	
16	1100	575	1000			1100	1100	
17	1100	575	1000			1100	1100	
18	1100	575	1000			1100	1100	

Consensus Plan

Figure 47   Multiple Views Model

understanding the different perspectives. The sales and marketing management is responsible for bringing the discussions to a consensus.

"What if the marketing people and the sales people can't agree?" Sam Wente, the sales director, asks.

"As the leader of sales management, it is your responsibility to bring them to consensus, Sam," Ross replies. "Remember, I did not say agreement; I said consensus."

Ross explains that consensus does not necessarily mean agreement. Consensus means that the individuals involved consent to support the plan at least until the next planning session.

When disagreement threatens the ability to come to a consensus, it is important to emphasize that demand planning and sales and operations planning are *replanning* processes. All the individuals will have the opportunity to present their case again during the next cycle. They can use the time between planning cycles to gather additional information and to validate their assumptions.

Ross turns toward Sam. "I need to emphasize, Sam, that the result of the process will be one plan with one set of numbers. By implementing the sales and operations planning process, you will have agreed to be accountable and responsible for developing and communicating one demand plan to the rest of the organization."

Mark Ryan decides that this is an excellent time to state the general manager's expectation. "From my perspective, Sam, you will bring to the executive sales and operations planning meeting one recommended plan that you and your team believe is most likely to happen."

"But suppose we are bidding for a large contract, which we will either win or lose. That can have a big impact on the forecast," Sam says.

"It is entirely appropriate, and desirable, to present alternative demand plans for 'what if' simulations and analysis," Ross replies, "but it is still incumbent upon you to provide the most likely scenario. The supply and finance organizations can use the 'what if' scenarios to develop alternative plans to support the business if it is booked or if it is not booked."

"The point I want to emphasize," Mark says, "is that we will be able to develop alternative plans *in advance,* rather than reacting after the fact. This is dramatically different from what we do today."

"Let me explain another nuance of multiple views," Ross says. He tells the group that, in his opinion, the use of multiple views is more than consensus forecasting. Other views should include:

- The result of demand stream analysis
- Top-down and bottom-up forecasting
- Input from individuals and organizations outside the company
- The results of market segment analyses

"I am often asked," Ross says, "whether a company should forecast top down, from aggregate to detail, or bottom up, from detail to aggregate. My answer is always yes to both."

He explains that the demand planner may do a statistical forecast from the greatest level of detail and add it up to product families. On the other hand, he or she may do a statistical forecast at the product family level and then break it down to the detail level. The sales force may provide detailed customer forecasts that will be added up by region, territory, or market segment. Forecasts can also be developed for a region, territory, or market forecast, and then these forecasts may be communicated to the sales force.

"This is the point," Ross says, "where more views are developed and considered, you achieve a better understanding of the marketplace reality, and this understanding provides a better basis for arriving at consensus."

"I think I understand what you are saying," Sam says. "There should be a critical analysis of the demand plans. This analysis is inherently part of marketing's job, but if you have multiple product and multiple market managers, someone still needs to conduct a critical analysis. I assume that someone is the demand planner."

"That's right, Sam," Ross replies. "At least the responsibility for the analysis is with the demand planner or demand manager. Some companies choose to outsource some of the analytical effort, but from your perspective, you want to make sure that you receive a 'polished and scrubbed' demand plan. Any obvious points of contention or unusual findings need to be reviewed as part of your demand review process."

Mark stirs in his chair. This subject interests him. He is glad to learn that there is clearly a body of knowledge and experience in demand planning which Universal Products will be able to draw upon. They won't have to fly blind.

Mark wants to emphasize one point. "It is apparent to me," he says to his management team, "that if we develop the multiple views well, we will have a much better understanding of the business. Sales and operations planning is obviously a decision-making process. With improved understanding of the business, we should be better equipped to make more effective choices and decisions."

■ ■ ■

Ross feels momentum growing. Mark Ryan and the rest of his team are beginning to understand the value of demand management. He decides to build upon that momentum and introduce other demand planning techniques.

"I mentioned earlier that collaboration is a demand planning best practice," he says. "Some people would include collaboration as part of the multiple views technique, but the term collaborative forecasting has become a buzzword recently, and I think we should discuss it separately."

Ross explains that many companies are attempting to establish closer relationships with their customers and suppliers. This relationship building has involved what is commonly referred to as "partnering" with customers and suppliers. As partners, they collaborate in developing the product forecast.

"A couple of our key suppliers have asked us to collaborate on the forecast," Anita Cooper, the purchasing manager, says. "Is this what you're talking about?"

"Yes, it is," Ross replies. He explains that collaboration on the product forecast involves both demand planning and communication with customers and suppliers. The customer and the supplier share information to provide visibility of future demand for the supplier.

The subject of collaborative forecasting usually comes up in discussions about supply chain management. In a broader sense, supply chain management utilizes demand information to develop supply chain tactics, such as the level of inventory to carry and the optimal timing and quantity for product replenishment.

Those companies that practice supply chain management inevitably consider the implementation of a process, such as vendor-managed inventories, continuous replenishment, process simplification, intercompany cycle-time reduction, and other activities. These processes and activities strip waste and add efficiency and value to the supply chain.

Sam interrupts Ross. "In your discussion of multiple views," Sam says, "you referred to consensus forecasting. Is this the same thing except between the customer and the supplier?"

"It is similar," Ross answers, "but here is a caution. Suppose our customer insists upon a forecast of demand that you believe is simply beyond the realm of possibility. Further, suppose you have done everything practical to convince your customer of the error of his or her judgment. What do you do? Do you take action based upon the customer's forecast, or do you use your own numbers?"

"It seems to me that this is not dissimilar to what we have inside the company as well," Mark says. "Should manufacturing and purchasing use the numbers from the demand plan, or should they second-guess and use their own numbers?"

"The way I see it, there is one big difference," Susan Callahan, the planning manager, replies. "Since we are one organization under one general manager, we should be able to communicate and come to consensus on decisions because, Mark, you control the entity. In the example Ross gave, the supplier does not control the entity, which is the customer."

Janis Novak, the controller, jumps in. "There would be a measure of control if the relationship is so strong that the equivalent of the sales and operations planning process exists between the supplier and the customer. Through that process, the issues and the consequences of the decisions could be fully understood by both parties."

"But if you have an ongoing replanning process, big differences between the customer's view and the supplier's view should rarely be the case," Ray Guy, the final assembly manager, says. "Maybe if you have a new product, the views would understandably be wider apart. Even with differences in views, the consequences should be understood and agreed upon by both parties, just like in sales and operations planning."

Ross attempts to regain control of the conversation. "I think you all understand the issue," he says. "I also believe you are realizing that the issues are the same, but the organization and decision-making process potentially become more complicated with collaborative forecasting."

He tells the group that when companies practice collaborative forecasting, it is important to define the regular and routine planning and communications process. It is also vital to define the process for dealing with significant differences of opinion. "Inside your company, that process is called sales and operations planning," Ross says.

He tells the group about a client that received weekly forecasts from its largest customers. The client company had a market share of 80 percent for one particular market segment and was the single-source supplier to all of its large customers, all of which competed for the same marketplace. These customers bought different products from the company.

"Here was the problem," Ross says. "When the company received the forecasts from its customers, they added up to 120 percent of the projected market. Clearly, some of the company's customers were not going to attain their forecasted level of business. The question, of course, was which customers were going to win in the market."

"What did your client do?" Jim Simpson, the manufacturing director, asks.

"The client hired an outside expert who specialized in the customers' market to provide another view," Ross replies. "The consultant's input into the process enabled the client to make a more informed choice."

"Did your client ignore the forecasts from its customers?" Mark asks.

"Ignore is too strong a word," Ross replies. He explains that the client worked with its customers to establish agreement on decision points that clearly defined the consequences of changing demand inside the decision points. The decision point agreements were handled as a business issue and were included as part of the contractual agreements between the client and its customers.

"The bottom line is that the supplier was required to honor the demand inside the decision points," Ross says, "but the supplier had the ability to use its own demand plan outside the decision points."

"This sounds extremely interesting," Mark says. "How many companies are doing this type of thing?"

"In industries where there is a regular, recurring demand, collaborative forecasting and the use of decision points are becoming the norm rather than the exception," Ross replies. He tells the group that this topic will be discussed in more detail in the demand management class and workshop.

"Before you move on," Sam says, "I want you to know that I appreciate what you are sharing with us. We have been so inwardly focused working on our problems that we have been missing what is going on around us. I am looking forward to tomorrow's education session on demand management."

■ ■ ■

Ross decides he should reground the group in what they have been learning and discussing. He explains that collaborative forecasting and multiple views are part of the broad subject of demand planning best practices.

"We have discussed process, attention, measurements, assumptions, multiple views, and collaboration," Ross says. "We still need to discuss two other best practices, customer linking and tools."

He explains that customer linking flows logically from the practice of forecast collaboration. He notes that there are few manufacturing standards for vocabulary, and thus customer linking is also known as customer networking, supplier scheduling, and vendor- or supplier-managed inventories.

It is important to understand the difference between collaborative forecasting and customer linking. Customer linking takes the process of collaboration one step further. It adds automation of the communication between the customer and the supplier and typically replaces the traditional order entry process. Automation is used as well to communicate forecasts, firm commitments, and shipping schedules. Customer linking also involves formalized agreements that define inventory tactics and commitments, lead time tactics, and the process for agreeing upon and approving schedule changes.

"Is the difference between collaboration and linking mostly in the automation of the process?" Susan Callahan, the planning manager, asks.

"Yes, along with the definition of and agreement on the operating rules," Ross says. "Customer linking handles the ongoing, day-to-day, week-to-week business."

He notes that another issue in customer linking is agreeing on the planning horizon for forward visibility. Some customer linking agreements define the planning horizon as twelve months or more, but most agreements define a much shorter planning horizon.

"We have some suppliers that ask for a twelve-week forecast," Anita Cooper, the purchasing manager, says. "Other suppliers ask for a forecast that covers eighteen to twenty-four months."

Ross smiles at Anita. "Those suppliers are trying to proactively get collaboration from you on their forecasts. Are any of your suppliers talking to you about automating the communication?"

"Not yet," Anita says. "I tell them I wish *we* had a useable twelve-week forecast! As for eighteen to twenty-four months, I just laugh."

"If the sales and operations planning process were up and working," Ross asks, "do you think you could provide the information your suppliers are requesting?"

"I'm sure I could," Anita replies. "The reliability of the forecast remains to be seen."

"What if you find that the reliability of the forecasts for some of the purchased parts is poor or demand is still unpredictable? How would you respond to your suppliers then?" Ross asks.

Before Anita can respond, Susan Callahan, the planning manager, answers. "Just like in our own company, demand for some products is more predictable than for others. We must establish tactics through inventory, lead time, or flexing of capacity to handle the less predictable. In working with suppliers, we would have to do the same thing. The concepts and principles are the same. The participants in the process are just different."

"You're right, Susan," Ross says. He adds that there is another key difference between customer linking and collaborative forecasting: the degree of cross-functional effort required by both the supplier and the customer to make the automated process work.

When implementing customer linking, the inevitable result is that the processes by which orders are placed, products are scheduled, and goods are shipped, invoiced, and paid for will change. These processes usually become much simpler, with less paper and less people intervention. Because the processes will change, sometimes dramatically, many functional areas must participate in implementing the customer linking process.

Ross looks around the room. "If there are no more questions," he says, "I will move on to tools, which is a very short and simple discussion."

"I have one question," Mark says. "Customer linking appears to apply to customers that do ongoing, week-to-week business with a supplier. Does it apply in a business that is more project oriented?"

Ross explains that customer linking is used less in project-oriented businesses than in businesses with ongoing, high-volume demand for product. Project-oriented businesses still largely use competitive bidding to communicate demand and determine the suppliers of choice. The quantity of items purchased in a project-oriented business typically is fewer, and changes to demand tend to fluctuate less frequently. Those changes often have bigger effects, however.

More projected-oriented companies are moving toward partner relationships with their customers and suppliers. Some customer linking techniques are being used as well.

The tools used for partnering and customer linking are different for project-oriented companies. Project schedules are automatically communicated between customer and supplier, instead of a stream of numbers representing demand which are communicated by high-volume businesses.

"The principles are the same, however," Ross says. "The first issue, of course, is to build the relationship and remove competitive bidding from the ongoing business activities."

Sam Wente, the sales director, raises his hand. "Are you implying that companies use customer linking to help build stronger relationships with their key customers or potential customers?"

"Yes, I am, Sam," Ross replies. He explains that there is a major difference in how companies implement the principles and practices that have been introduced in today's education session. Some companies' motivation in implementing sales and operations planning is to fix their delivery or inventory problems. Other companies see how the principles, processes, and practices of sales and operations planning can be applied proactively with their customers and suppliers.

"From my perspective," Anita says, "if I have credible information, I should be able to turn that into lower prices from my suppliers."

"Exactly!" Ross replies. "Now, let's move on to demand planning tools. For today, the subject of tools is an easy discussion," he says.

Ross explains that software tools are needed for performing statistical forecasting and statistical analysis. Automated sales planning tools are also very helpful to the sales force. These tools reduce the amount of administrative time and provide a platform for communications to the demand planner or demand manager.

At a minimum, the demand planner needs a software tool that utilizes history to forecast the future, unencumbered by any intimate knowledge of marketing and sales plan. He or she also needs a software tool to develop correlation between factors affecting the business and business volume.

These types of forecasting and analysis tools are readily available, and they provide another view of the future based upon history. They also may provide a place for the forecast assumptions and occurrences to be saved for measurement purposes.

"Do you have any tools in particular that you recommend?" Sam Wente, the sales director, asks.

"The list of forecasting tools is long," Ross replies. He tells Sam that the tools range from simple to complex, stand-alone for personal computers to modules that are part of enterprise resource planning systems, and moderately priced to high priced.

Ross recommends waiting to select forecasting and sales planning tools until the design of the demand management process is completed. The process definition will be valuable input in defining the tool specifications and requirements. "That way, you will be less likely to overspecify or underspecify the tools," he notes.

Ross glances at his watch. "We've been sitting a long time," he says. "How about a ten-minute break?"

As the group leaves the room, Nolan approaches Ross. "Ross, we are all but out of time. What more do you expect to cover today?" he asks.

"We should present an overview of the implementation process, ending with the next steps the team should take. We need to briefly cover methods for coping with inaccurate forecasts," Ross replies.

"I would not drag out the presentation too long. It has been a long day. The group has learned a lot, and people are demonstrating that they understand the principles," Nolan says. "Remember, everyone will not absorb all the material presented and discussed today. The purpose of today was to gain understanding, get commitment to go forward, and prepare them for the work that follows. They will learn as they implement."

Ross smiles at Nolan. "Points well taken," he says. "I guess my mentoring and coaching you is working. One measure I have is when my words come from you. You are correct, and I am pleased you are giving me such quality advice."

Ross and Nolan both chuckle. Their relationship has been push and pull. Nolan has learned from Ross's experience, and Ross has learned from Nolan's enthusiasm, curiosity, and challenging the status quo.

"I will finish up fairly quickly," Ross says. "You start the session tomorrow with the middle management team. Are you all prepared?"

Nolan looks at Ross with a straight face. "Am I prepared?" he says. "Does the sun rise? Is Pavarotti a tenor?" Nolan and Ross break into laughter.

"Technically, the sun does not rise," Ross says. "But seriously, we need to hit it hard the next two days. The managers are ready. If we want to get them results quickly, we need to help them move firmly and quickly."

Mark's attention is drawn to the laughter of Nolan and Ross. He suspects they are discussing the material yet to be covered and the amount of time left. He walks to the front of the room. "How much more do you plan to cover today? I think the management team is starting to run out of steam," Mark says.

"We were just discussing that," Nolan replies. "I wanted to make sure that Ross wasn't going to keep us overtime."

"Good. Let's wrap it up," Mark says. "I think we have accomplished what we set out to do today."

As people are in the process of being seated, Ross begins speaking. "One last thought on the best practices of demand planning," he says. He explains that it is important for everyone in the company to know that there will continue to be forecast and demand plan inaccuracies, even with the most effective demand planning process. The better the demand management process — including overt efforts to influence demand, the better the forecast accuracy.

Even with the most effective demand planning processes, there will still be errors in quantity and timing, in addition to variation in demand. Demand is rarely linear, especially day by day, week by week.

"As a result, every company needs tactics to deal with forecast error and forecast variation," Ross says as he clicks the mouse to display another slide (Figure 48). "These tactics should be not decided upon informally by the planner, or the people in the shipping department, or the salesperson who yells the loudest," he notes. "The tactics should be agreed upon by you, the management team. That is one of the purposes of the sales and operations planning process. Now, let's briefly address each tactic."

Ross explains that shorter cycle times and customer lead times help to create more accurate forecasts as well as respond to forecast error. As a rule of thumb, it

1. Shorten Cycle Times and Customer Lead Times
2. Carry Inventory
3. Flex Capacity
4. Reschedule Production
5. Reprioritize Customer Orders
6. Standardize and/or Rationalize Product Lines
7. Periodically Review Tactics by Product Line

Figure 48   Tactics for Coping with Forecast Errors

is usually easier to forecast closer in time than farther out in time. In other words, it is easier to forecast what customers will buy this month than it is to predict what customers will buy twelve months from now.

With shorter cycle times, the need to provide an accurate detailed forecast farther out in the planning horizon is reduced. Shorter customer lead times also help customers reduce their forecast error for the same reasons. In an engineer-to-order environment, the number of engineering changes is reduced with a shorter cycle time for the same reasons.

Advocates of lean and agile manufacturing readily embrace the tactic of shorter cycle times. They aren't as enthusiastic about the tactic of carrying inventory. However, inventory quantities can be reduced when the following occurs:

- Forecast error is reduced
- Demand variability is minimized
- Cycle times become shorter
- The ability to flex capacity increases

"Inventory management includes managing the inventory in the supply chain as well as in your factory," Ross says. "Determining how much inventory should be kept within the supply chain is of significant importance in achieving your objective to regularly and routinely meet customers' expectations."

He pauses for a moment and points to the third item in the list projected on the screen, flex capacity. "Let's discuss the need for flexible capacity for a moment," he says.

Ross tells the group that in some industries, the key to responsiveness is the ability to flex capacity. This may be done within the organization by carrying sufficient capacity to cover the peaks in demand. It may be done externally through contracting work to suppliers.

A logical extension of shortening cycle times is the ability to make supply match demand, even when there are variations in demand. This requires the ability to flex capacity.

"As for rescheduling the factory," Ross says, pointing to the fourth item in the list on the screen, "often the best thing to do to satisfy a demand opportunity is to reschedule work in the plant. Hopefully, the master scheduling processes and tools are in place to enable this to occur with minimal interruption to engineering and manufacturing — and at minimal cost."

Ross explains that, in his experience, most companies miss a tremendous opportunity for improvement by not master scheduling properly. If a company has a good demand planning process, most demand plan errors tend to be timing errors. Some demand materializes earlier than planned, and some comes in later than planned.

"One of the greatest tools for maximizing flexibility is de-expediting. In fact, in my opinion, the greatest expediting tool is de-expediting," Ross states. He glances around the room and sees puzzled expressions.

"Let me explain," he says. "When we de-expedite, we decide what we are not going to do in a particular time period. This frees up resources to work on what we really need to do. A quality master scheduling process strives for as many de-expedites as there are expedites. It strives for a balance. This subject is covered quite well in John Proud's book on *Master Scheduling*."

Ross points to the fifth item in the list, reprioritize customer orders. He explains that most companies realize that their backlog of orders includes orders with ship dates that do not necessarily match their customers' need dates. For example, a ship date can be one week earlier than the customer required delivery. In this case, when unexpected demand occurs, often the backlog of orders can be rescheduled to fulfill the unexpected demand and still meet another customer's real delivery requirement. This approach is known as reprioritization.

Sometimes, however, reprioritizing customer orders will not meet all the customers' real delivery requirements. When this happens, the only alternative is to determine which customers will receive product when they have requested it and which customers will not. Some planners and salespeople call this the "some customers are more equal than others rule."

"I had a client once who was a vice-president of sales," Ross says. "He called this process 'pick a victim.' This has a negative connotation, but at least sales management made the decision rather than someone on the supply side of the business."

Ross waits to see if anyone from the supply organization will take the bait and challenge why sales management should choose who receives product and who does not. Surprisingly, there is silence. He is pleased. They recall earlier discussions about the decisions that sales management should make because it is closest to the customers and ultimately responsible for demand.

Pointing at the presentation screen, Ross tells the group that standardizing or rationalizing product lines is a longer term issue. Over time, product lines become cluttered with products that no longer truly support the value proposition for the market. Products and product options should be reviewed frequently. The review should be used to identify opportunities to simplify the product offering and to ensure that the products continue to meet the needs of the marketplace and the business strategy. A fun and interesting book that relates to this subject is *Clutter's Last Stand* by Don Aslett, who writes about the benefits of simplicity.

Two significant benefits result from product rationalization and standardization. First, there are fewer items to forecast and plan. Second, the resulting product offering is usually a higher volume, which also is more accurate to forecast and plan.

"The final way to cope with forecast errors," Ross says, "is to periodically review the tactics for each product line." He explains that tactics should be periodically reviewed to make sure that the availability and delivery lead-time strategy still matches the market's expectations. If the strategy no longer meets customer needs and expectations, the manufacturing and inventory tactics will need to be refined.

The mismatch of customer expectations with availability and delivery lead-time strategy is often incorrectly interpreted as forecast error. "You may not have a forecast error problem at all," Ross says. "You may have a problem with where you meet the customer, which we discussed this morning."

Ross pauses and looks around the room. The expressions show both understanding and interest in the techniques for coping with forecast errors. "Let's move on to one last subject — how to approach the implementation of sales and operations planning," he says.

Susan Callahan, the planning manager, raises her hand. "Before we move on, I'd like to make a comment first," she says. "I know we need to wrap up for the day, but I feel we need to emphasize that coping with forecast error is extremely important. Sam may implement an excellent demand management process, but we still need tactics to deal with the errors and variations. I presume that the need to develop tactics will surface as we go through each sales and operations planning cycle."

Ross begins to respond to Susan, but Mark Ryan interrupts. "That's right," he says. "What I like about the options that Ross presented is that the tactics are a conscious choice and decision that the entire management team participates in making. I think it will reduce the firefighting that we do now."

"You're right!" Ross says.

10

COMMITMENT

"Let me discuss our experience in implementing sales and operations planning. After more than fifteen years helping companies to implement, we have found what works and what doesn't work," Ross says. He explains that the approach that has been most effective involves the following steps:

1. Education
2. Process design
3. Getting started
4. Learn by doing

"This is not a long-winded implementation. It is not like when you implemented enterprise resource planning or other information systems," Ross adds. "We are talking about getting started within months, not years. We are seeking benefits from the process as quickly as we can get them."

Ross tells the group that a fundamental principle, which he and Nolan will emphasize during the implementation, is that time is the enemy. The longer it takes to implement, the more it costs, the more benefits are missed, and the greater the potential that management will lose interest.

"We always find a few key business areas that require improvement early in the implementation," Ross says. "We also find areas where it is difficult to improve without additional processes and tools. However, we discover the need for these improvements by doing sales and operations planning. You do not want a big expensive study from some consulting firm, including ours, to help you get started in sales and operations planning."

Ross shows the group a diagram (Figure 49). "These are the key elements of the implementation, which will be reviewed in detail in the managers' session.

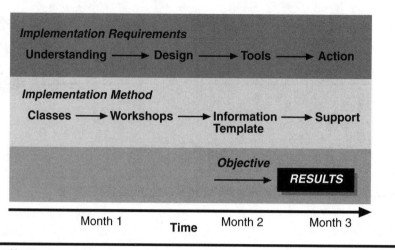

Figure 49   Implementation Approach

Nolan will be reviewing the process elements and timing with each of you independently as well," he explains.

Ross looks around the room and makes eye contact with every person. "The keys to a successful implementation are in this room," he says. "If you, collectively and individually, decide to make this work, it will work. If you do not give it the appropriate amount of attention, it will become just another mediocre effort of Universal Products."

Ross walks directly in front of Mark Ryan and speaks directly to him. "Mark, if you make this a high priority, if you give it proper attention, if you insist that your management team members do the same, it will work. If you choose to delegate the implementation process and only participate once a month in the executive sales and operations planning meeting, the implementation is at risk. In short, be involved. This is *your* process."

Ross walks back to the front of the room while still addressing Mark. "Mark, one or more people in this room will not give it the proper amount of attention. When that happens, it is incumbent upon you as the leader of this enterprise to communicate that lack of involvement is an unacceptable behavior."

Ross again makes eye contact with every person. Addressing the group, he says, "If you do not appropriately participate, my message to Mark is that you are not interested in being part of the management process in this company — because sales and operations planning is, or will be, *the* management process of the company. This is serious business."

Ross pauses again to allow the group to think about what he has just said. The room is quiet. After a few moments, he says, "All we need today is for each of you to tell Mark that you will support the effort. The next step is the middle management seminar scheduled for tomorrow. This will be followed by process design. During the design, we will utilize the output of your conversations and discussions today. The first sales and operations planning cycle will be next month."

Janis Novak, the controller, raises her hand. "Do you expect us to include all of the product lines in sales and operations planning next month?"

"No," Ross replies. "After the process design is completed, we will agree upon one or a few families to cover in the first cycle." He explains that the purpose of the first cycle is to test the process design, find sources of information, develop a standardized information presentation based on the template that will be provided, and learn the process. As part of the learning, Ross and Nolan will expect at least one management decision to result from the first cycle. The rest of the families will be added in future cycles as quickly as is practical.

"I need to get my demand manager assigned quickly if we are starting next month," Sam Wente, the sales director, says.

Ross turns to Mark. "See, we're shortening the implementation time already."

■ ■ ■

In planning today's session, Ross had told Mark Ryan that, as the general manager, it was his responsibility to get commitment to implement sales and operations planning from his management team.

Mark stands up. "Ross, I would like to address the group," he says. Mark moves to the front of the room. Ross moves to the side of the room and sits down.

"We have covered a lot of ground today," Mark says. "I am only beginning to know what I don't know. The principles we learned about today are fundamental to any business and are, indeed, organized common sense, but there is more to sales and operations planning than that."

Mark paces as he talks. "This is about changing the way we work, about changing the way we communicate, about dealing with issues that have not been dealt with before. My expectation is that more issues that will need to be addressed — issues that we may be unaware of today — will surface through implementation of the sales and operations planning process. In short, this implementation is about changing the way we manage this business. That is no small task."

Mark pauses and takes a deep breath. "This morning, which right now seems like long ago, I talked about the need for this process in our company. I want you all to understand that I was committed this morning, but that commitment was based on instinct. After hearing about sales and operations planning, I thought it was the right thing to do. Now, after all I have learned today, I am committed with a higher level of understanding.

"What was it that Ross or Nolan said? Commitment without understanding is a liability. We are going to implement sales and operations planning, and not in a mediocre manner. I want this division to be a showcase. A showcase for us, our employees, prospective employees, our customers and suppliers, and the whole corporation.

"What I want from each of you now is your support and commitment. If you feel you cannot commit to the effort and the behaviors required to make the process work, I want to know it now. If you have reservations, I want to know it now. If you believe that we should not implement sales and operations planning, I want you to tell me now, not later."

Mark stops speaking and looks at each member of the team. "I am going to go around the room and ask each of you for your commitment or your reservations. If you think sales and operations planning is the right thing to do, a simple response of 'yes, I am committed' is sufficient. If you have reservations, please explain them."

Mark walks in front of where Sam Wente, his sales director, is seated. "Sam, let me start with you," he says.

"Yes, I am committed," Sam replies, in a strong, firm voice.

Mark begins his journey around the room.

"Yes, I am committed," Susan Callahan, his planning manager, says.

"Yes, I am committed," Anita Cooper, his purchasing manager, says.

"Yes, I am committed," Peter Newfeld, his product development/engineering director, says.

"Yes, I am committed," Ray Guy, his final assembly manager, says.

"Yes, I am committed," Jim Simpson, his manufacturing director, says.

"Yes, I am committed," Janis Novak, his controller, says.

"I am also clearly committed," Mark says. "*We* are committed."

Mark turns to address Ross and Nolan, who are sitting side by side in the back of the room. "Ross and Nolan, I expect you to keep your commitment to us, as members of our team. You will coach us to become excellent in sales and operations planning in as short a period of time as is practical."

"We are committed," Ross and Nolan say at the same time.

The tone of the discussion has been serious. Jim Simpson breaks the mood. "I am committed," he says, "but I reserve the right to back out if Sam screws up the forecast."

Sam jests back. "If you will only begin doing what you say you are going to do, you will never see me lose my commitment."

Mark claps his hands. "Alright, everybody. Let's have some beverages and dinner. Ross, is that okay?" Mark asks.

"Okay? It's great!" Ross replies. "Today's session is officially closed."

Mark watches the members of his team boisterously file out. He feels relief.

For the first time since he started as general manager with Universal Products, he feels the future is within his grasp and control. He knows that implementing sales and operations planning won't be without its challenges. But he now has a path to follow to solve Universal Products' business problems and improve the company's performance to customers and shareholders.

As he closes the door behind him, Mark thinks to himself that he and his management team have turned the corner. They have been struggling to keep their sales and profits from diminishing. Now, they have the means to help grow the business.

GLOBAL SALES AND OPERATIONS PLANNING

It has been nine months since Universal Products, Inc. started its sales and operations planning effort, and Mark Ryan, the general manager, is looking forward to his meeting today with Jack Baxter, Global Products corporate president.

Mark chuckles to himself. What a difference a year makes. One year ago, he dreaded conversations and meetings with Jack. He knew that Universal Products' poor customer service and financial performance were eroding Jack's confidence in his management abilities. He feared that he would lose his job.

Today is much different. Universal Products has gone from the worst-performing division within Global Products to the best-performing division. He and Jack both know that the catalyst in this turnaround was sales and operations planning.

Jack called Mark last week to tell him he wanted to visit Universal Products. He told Mark that one of the main purposes of his visit was to discuss how to implement sales and operations planning in other Global Products divisions.

Sheri Waterman, Mark's assistant, interrupts his reminiscing. "Mr. Baxter is here," she announces.

Jack pushes the door open and strides into the room. "Mark, how the heck are you?" he says and pumps Mark's hand.

Jack and Mark have worked together for more than fifteen years. Their bantering has an ease about it, and their chitchatting is comfortable.

Mark knows Jack is on a tight schedule. He has stopped by to visit en route to another Global Products division in California. Mark offers Jack a seat and takes one himself around the round table in the corner of his office.

"So, what's up?" Mark asks.

"There are two or three subjects I want to discuss," Jack replies as he settles his six-foot frame into the chair. "First, I want to talk about Universal Products' improved performance. Second, I want to talk about the sales and operations planning process you have put in place."

"Those two subjects go hand in hand," Mark replies.

"What interests me is how you have improved performance in such a short period of time. Nine months is not long to achieve such a dramatic change," Jack comments. He pulls out the financial numbers from a notebook and points to the revenue, operating expense, inventory, and profit lines.

"There is more to be gained from sales and operations planning," Mark comments. He tells Jack that during the initial education session for his management team, the consultants from Effective Management, Inc. said it would take six monthly planning cycles before sales and operations planning would become a solid, repeatable process. They also said that there were four implementation phases that typically take two years to complete.

"What are the four phases?" Jack asks.

Mark opens his sales and operations planning notebook. He flips to the section on implementation and shows Jack a diagram (Figure 50).

"We're in the third phase now, problem prevention," Mark says, pointing to the diagram. "And our efforts in the problem prevention area are pushing us toward making more tactical and strategic decisions."

"In all honesty," Jack says, "when you called me to discuss whether you should implement sales and operations planning, I looked at it as a last-gasp effort to right a sinking ship. I was already beginning to make contingency plans to possibly sell off the division. Mark, the progress this division has made is remarkable. You are to be commended."

"Thanks for the compliment," Mark replies, "but I don't deserve it. It was the people in this organization who made the difference. The only thing I really did

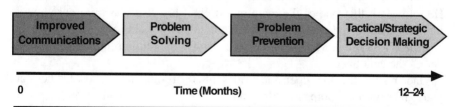

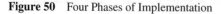

Figure 50   Four Phases of Implementation

was make sure that the regular and routine discipline of the sales and operations planning process remained intact."

He tells Jack that the sales and operations planning process enabled his team to identify problems, prioritize the solutions, and eliminate the constraints to getting the work done. This required improved communication and problem solving.

"We now have developed the skills to tackle any opportunity or problem quickly and effectively," Mark says. "Excuse me, Jack, have I told you the difference between effectiveness and efficiency?"

Jack laughs. "Several times," he says. "Let me see if I remember. It is more important to be effective than efficient, and sales and operations planning is all about being effective. Only after the organization becomes effective should management prioritize and tackle efficiency issues."

Mark glances at his watch. Jack will need to leave for the airport in less than one hour. "What specifically did you want to discuss about sales and operations planning?" he asks.

"We are already talking about what I wanted to discuss," Jack replies. He tells Mark that he has been doing some independent research on sales and operations planning. He has talked to executives in a number of corporations that he respects. He has found that sales and operations planning is a standard company practice across all divisions in these corporations.

"One CEO of a corporation much larger than ours told me that Class A sales and operations planning is not an option; it is the way his business is run," Jack says. "While I haven't personally experienced the power of the process, I'm now convinced it is right for all our divisions. I want to extend Universal Products' success to all of our other divisions around the world."

A broad grin spreads across Mark's face. "Jack, you have made my day. I take what you said as an 'atta-boy' and a compliment. Ross Peterson, our advisor, predicted this would happen even before we had our first education session. He also cautioned me about thinking that our success could simply be duplicated in a cookie-cutter fashion in the other divisions around the world."

"What do you mean?" Jack asks.

Mark explains that Ross warned that once Universal Products was successful with the process, corporate executives would believe they could simply and easily copy the process in other business units or divisions. "It's not quite that easy," Mark says.

He flips through the pages in his notebook and shows Jack another graphic (Figure 51). "Where executives go wrong is thinking that the key to success is the tools or the process itself. But the real key to success is people," Mark says, pointing to the people circle in the diagram. "I found that it is easy to mandate the process and tools. It is entirely another thing to get people to use them."

Figure 51   Business Excellence Elements (Copyright Oliver Wight International. Reproduced with permission.)

He tells Jack that there were three keys to success:

1. Getting first his executive team and then managers and supervisors to agree to operate using certain best practice principles, sometimes called Class A behaviors
2. Encouraging open and honest communication and not "shooting the messenger" when bad news was delivered about a problem or constraint
3. Not making departmental efficiency decisions without considering the impact on the effectiveness and efficiency of the company as a whole

"Stated differently," Mark says, "we have learned the interdependence of all the elements that make a company run. In short, Jack, implementing a best practice, or Class A, process in all the other divisions will be more difficult than just mandating that all divisions implement the process. The people in the other divisions will have to *learn* the things we have learned. They will have to *behave* in the ways we have learned to behave."

Jack studies Mark for a moment. He has always respected Mark's insight and his ability to make sound recommendations. "I am a bit surprised, Mark," Jack says. "You have been such a strong advocate for the process. Are you backing off now? Are you saying we shouldn't do sales and operations planning in the other divisions?"

"No, I'm not backing off," Mark replies. "I truly believe in the benefits of sales and operations planning. And I believe that we should definitely implement the process in the other divisions. What I am trying to say is that you cannot mandate success simply by telling people in the company to use a particular process or software tool. You have to be willing to invest in the people who will be implementing the process and the tool."

"What do you mean by 'invest in the people'?" Jack asks.

It is Mark's turn to study Jack. How direct should he be in answering Jack's question? Should he risk offending him or making him angry?

He decides to risk it. "Jack, permit me to be very direct. You cannot continue to mandate head count reductions, mandate the reduction of the education budget, mandate expenditure cuts, and reduce the number of people and expect the remaining people to grow and improve the business. You and I have not talked seriously about the impact of these reductions for some time. I have serious concern about what appears to be the management approach of the corporation."

Jack replies in a soft, controlled voice. "That's a strong statement, Mark. Has a little success gone to your head?"

Mark does not respond to Jack's comment about success going to his head. He wants to stay on point. He does not want the discussion to become emotionally charged.

"I have learned much in the last nine months that I didn't understand before," he says. "I have learned about the desire of people to succeed and the ability of the people already here to do the job given a reasonable chance. I have also learned the many ways that management can, and does, screw up the natural flow of business. I have learned about management's ignorance about utilizing an integrated, synchronized management process — or the arrogance in thinking that an integrated, synchronized management process is not needed."

Mark looks Jack in the eye. Jack is tight-lipped and his face is red. He's seething.

Mark leans back in his chair. Still looking Jack in the eye, he says, "Jack, I am talking about *me*. I did not know the negative effects I was having on the business through the manner in which I was running, or attempting to run, the place."

Mark and Jack study each other for a long moment. Mark knows that Jack is angry. He decides to try a different tack.

"Jack, I'm concerned that you will try to dictate our process to the other divisions. If you do, the process will fail and the other divisions won't achieve the financial and operational results that you expect. You can't mandate the process unless you provide the proper education and support. The uneducated cannot operate the process. I'm convinced that we would have failed if we had not first learned the fundamental operating principles, how we were regularly violating those principles, and how sales and operations planning enables management to put those principles in practice. If you want to mandate this process, you're going to have to educate yourself and the other executives in corporate as well and invest considerable resources — time and money — in increasing the understanding of the management teams in the other divisions."

Jack visibly relaxes and smiles. He starts to laugh. "Mark, that's why I am here," he says. "I know that *you* know what will make sales and operations planning work in the other divisions. You know how to work with and talk to me."

Jack pauses. His expression becomes serious. "I want you to take the lead in bringing the sales and operations planning process to the rest of the corporation," he says. "I want your help full time in this effort. I also know that the continuous intervention, what some call micromanagement by the corporate staff, is not helping the business. In assigning you to this project, I want to make a statement to the other general managers that this is not the latest 'alphabet soup' initiative. This is a serious project!"

Mark is surprised. His first, gut reaction is resistance. He does not want to leave Global Products just when he and his team have gotten it on a firm footing.

"But, Jack, what about this division, *my* division? Who will run it?" he says. "We are just starting to make real progress in growing the business and increasing our market position!"

Jack waves his hand as though he is swatting away Mark's resistance. "You have a couple of candidates on your newly strengthened management team who can pick up from where you have brought this division. I am talking about a key corporate project and a task that has the potential to truly improve the *total corporate performance.*"

Mark holds up his hand. "Hold on, Jack," he says. "Before we have any more discussions about this role you're proposing for me, you need to understand what I believe will be the appropriate implementation process for the other divisions. If you have any heartburn with what I propose, then we may have an impasse before we even get started."

Jack looks at his watch. He needs to leave for the airport in a few minutes. "Tell you what, Mark," he says. "We need to spend enough time in discussions to make sure I understand what you think will be required of me and you understand what I think will be required of you. We are not going to have this conversation in fifteen minutes."

"You're right about that," Mark replies.

"Why don't you ask Sheri to come in here," Jack suggests. "We can have her reschedule my flight to late tomorrow morning. I'll call the California operation and delay my visit until tomorrow afternoon."

Jack gets up to use the phone, and Mark walks out of his office to talk to Sheri. When he returns, Jack is just hanging up the receiver. "Do you want to join Cheryl and me for dinner?" Mark asks.

"No, thank you," Jack answers. "I just called an old college buddy. We try to get together whenever either of us is visiting the other's hometown. It will be better to shelf the business talk this evening anyway. You have some thinking to do, and I have some thinking to do."

"You're right," Mark says. "I hope you don't expect an answer from me tomorrow on the role you're proposing."

"I would like an answer tomorrow," Jack replies. "And, Mark, if you think I need to spend more time here, even several days, to get a true understanding of what is involved in the implementation, I will. This is a priority for me."

"On that note, let's call it a day then," Mark replies.

Sheri is waiting in the doorway. "Sheri," Mark says, "can you help Jack book a room and rearrange his flight? His departure may not be firm yet, but at least you can work with him so he knows the options."

Mark picks up his briefcase. "I'll see the two of you in the morning," he says and strolls out of his office. As he walks down the hall, the sound of his heels striking the tile floor seems loud. Mark realizes that he is wired and anxious. He wonders if his future is cast and what impact that future will have on his family. Cheryl and Chad have barely become settled in Colorado. They truly enjoy their life-style there.

Mark wonders whether Jack has another move in mind for him or whether the job can be done from Colorado. After all, the implementations will take place in divisions all over the world. In theory, shouldn't that mean he can reside anywhere he chooses within reason?

■ ■ ■

Mark and Cheryl had an enjoyable evening. He decided not to tell Cheryl about the potential new assignment. He would wait until he and Jack have had further conversations.

Now, seated at his desk the next morning waiting for Jack to arrive, he wonders if he made the right decision in not telling Cheryl last night. He can't undo his decision today, but vows to definitely tell her tonight.

After some thinking during the early morning hours, Mark has decided to tell Jack that he is interested in the new role, but he does not want to relocate. He also will not accept the position if Jack is unwilling to become an educated, committed partner in the endeavor. That means Jack must be willing to adopt the same best practice behaviors in corporate that the divisions would be required to adopt.

As Mark lets his gaze wander out the window, he recalls the quote by the late Oliver Wight that Ross Peterson of EMI is fond of using: "Commitment without understanding is a liability." A corporate president who is ignorant about the process will not help it to succeed.

Mark hears a tap on his door. He turns to see Jack poke his head through the doorway.

As Jack pushes the door open, it is obvious to Mark that he is full of enthusiasm and determination. "Good morning, Mark. So what do you think? Are you up to the task?" he asks in his characteristic no-nonsense, assertive manner.

Mark is just as direct in his response. "Yes, I am up to the task," he says, "but I am not sure that you will be up to my terms."

Jack gestures for him to continue. "If I take on this project," Mark says, "you must be as passionately committed as I am. You cannot be passionately committed without a greater level of understanding. Once you truly understand the fundamentals and best practices of operating the business and you make the commitment based on an understanding of what implementing sales and operations planning entails, I will be ready to accept your new job offer. This, of course, assumes that I can continue to live in Colorado and that we resolve a few other issues, such as compensation and performance expectations."

Jack appears to be perfectly comfortable with Mark's comments. "How long has it been since you were in sales?" he asks. "It sounds to me like we have an agreement in principle and that now we are negotiating terms."

Mark smiles at Jack and then quickly becomes serious again. "You have assessed the situation correctly," he says, "but my terms are firm, especially the ones about your level of understanding and my not having to relocate."

"I will agree in principle to the relocation issue," Jack replies, "assuming you convince me that you can successfully oversee the implementations from here instead of corporate headquarters."

"Agreed," Mark says.

"So how do you wish to proceed with increasing my level of understanding?" Jack asks.

Mark moves from behind his desk and offers Jack a seat at the round table. He sits in a chair next to Jack and opens his sales and operations planning notebook. "Why don't I give you a high-level perspective of the process, principles, and best practices and then explain the key elements of our implementation," Mark says.

"Sounds good," Jack replies.

Mark picks up the phone and dials the intercom for Sheri Waterman, his administrative assistant. "Sheri, please hold all calls until 11:30," he says.

Mark pushes the notebook in front of Jack. "I had the class notebook and the key notes I made during the implementation copied for you this morning," he says. "I believe these same elements that we implemented at Universal Products will be needed at each division if we are to be successful."

Mark explains to Jack that his choice of the word *we* is intentional. He wants the global implementation to be *Jack's* project and process. He wants Jack to understand that achieving the same kind of performance improvements that Universal Products did will not happen just by mandating the use of a process. It will require operating the business in a different way than it is currently being managed. Sales and operations planning provides the forum to make that happen.

"Results will be achieved much more quickly if all the vice-presidents, directors, and managers recognize the initiative and process as *your* process," Mark comments. "You need to 'walk the talk.'"

"Okay," Jack replies. "So help me reduce the chance of my becoming a liability. Increase my understanding. Educate me."

Mark flips the pages of the notebook until he comes to the diagram of the basic model of the sales and operations planning process. "I'm going to give you a high-level, twenty-thousand-foot view of sales and operations planning," he says.

He describes the basic process and the fundamental behaviors required to achieve maximum results from sales and operations planning. He is careful to emphasize that every implementation requires application of the process to the specific business. He points out the difference between the process and the business choices management makes in the process.

"It took us a while to understand that the process does not dictate how a company chooses to sell its products, make its products, design its products, or manage its supply chain," Mark says. "What the process does is make sure that the choices are considered from a total business perspective, rather than from an isolated department or functional point of view."

He explains that the views of all the departments or functions must be considered when making business choices. These various views bring an understanding of the trade-offs that are part of any decision. This also eliminates being surprised when those trade-offs materialize.

To consider the views of all departments and functions, of course, requires open dialogue among *all* members of the management team. Ultimately, if the process is to survive the test of time, it must be product independent, organization independent, and technology independent.

Mark tells Jack that he has come to the conclusion that the sales and operations planning process must be robust enough to withstand organizational change and flexible enough to work in multiple business environments. It needs to be used in good times and bad times and all times in between.

As Mark proceeds to discuss the elements of the implementation, he observes that Jack is engaged and interested. Jack asks numerous questions and readily seems to grasp the fundamental process.

Mark introduces process steps and describes the roles and responsibilities in sales and operations planning. He stresses that an effective sales and operations planning process requires regular and routine discipline. The steps cannot be skipped, and the management team must actively participate in the process. He also explains the leadership and behavior required from the general manager.

After about two hours, Mark turns the pages of the notebook to the dashboards used to present the planning and performance information in the sales and operations planning process. He points out that the information presented during sales and operations planning is "need to know" information. The presentation of the information is designed to enable the executive team to manage change and make decisions on a management-by-exception basis.

Jack holds up his hand, and Mark stops. "This seems so straightforward that it borders on being simple," Jack says. "As president of this corporation, I simply assumed the elements of this process were in place."

"The EMI people call it organized common sense," Mark replies. "But remember, achieving simplicity is usually not easy."

Mark brings up the people issue again. "That has been the toughest part of the implementation," he says. He tells Jack that when they started the implementation, sales did not trust manufacturing, manufacturing did not respect planning, planning had no confidence in purchasing, finance did its own thing, and Mark, in truth, was just along for the ride.

"The key is to get the directors and managers to open up, to communicate openly and honestly, yet with respect for the individual; in short, to act as a team," Mark says.

"So, how did you go about making that happen?" Jack asks.

"I could not have done it by myself," Mark replies. "The coaching, advice, and support that the EMI consultants gave us were key." He explains that Ross Peterson and Nolan Drake had experience in many implementations of sales and operations planning. They had gone through enough implementations to be able to quickly identify where help was needed and improvement was required.

"Ross Peterson actually chaired the first executive sales and operations planning meeting," Mark comments.

Jack looks up in surprise. "Why?" he asks.

"It was a great way to quickly demonstrate what was expected of each senior manager," Mark replies.

He tells Jack that Ross and Nolan also coached the managers during the demand, supply, and financial reviews. Their coaching and support enabled Universal Products to have the process operating in three cycles. During the first three cycles, the management team found and fixed problems and issues that had gone unresolved for who knows how long.

"Did you let Ross make your decisions?" Jack asks.

"No, but he helped us learn how to look at the integrated set of information to identify the pertinent and critical issues," Mark answers. He tells Jack that when the management team learned how to interpret the information, the decisions that needed to be made were obvious, or at least the business choices were obvious. The decisions were made as a management team.

"There were a few times when the conflicts could not be resolved, and a decision could not be put off," Mark says. "When this occurred, Ross made sure that *I* made a decision."

He recalls the time during cycle four when Ross came into Mark's office, closed the door, and said, "Mark, I think I have found the problem. The problem is in this room, and it isn't me."

"Ross was right," Mark says. "I was avoiding some difficult decisions in an attempt to keep all my staff happy."

"Are you recommending that we use the EMI consultants for the other implementations?" Jack asks.

Mark tells Jack that every division will need outside help from experienced experts in sales and operations planning. A division may eventually be successful without outside help, but it will take longer to achieve the significant results that Universal Products accomplished. Use of experienced outside help will also provide consistency across the company.

"So, you're saying that in addition to you leading the effort, we are going to need consulting help," Jack comments. "I assume you personally can provide some of that help, but you cannot be in all divisions simultaneously. Does the EMI firm have the capability to help us internationally?"

Mark explains that EMI employs consultants around the world. He is certain that EMI can handle Global Products' coaching needs.

"Why do you refer to coaching rather than consulting?" Jack asks.

Mark tells Jack it is because of his own bias against consultants. When the enterprise resource planning system was implemented at Universal Products, consultants were used. The consultants were mostly experts in information technology or recent graduates with master's degrees in business. They had never really worked for a manufacturing company. When the consultants finished the implementation, the software was operable, but Universal Products' people did not know how to use it. The software was implemented without properly addressing the processes and people issues in Universal Products' operating environment.

The approach of EMI was different. The primary objective in Ross and Nolan's coaching was to make Universal Products self-sufficient in as short a time as possible. This approach cost relatively little compared to the implementation of the enterprise resource planning software. In addition, Universal Products achieved far greater performance improvements in about one-tenth of the time.

"I understand," Jack says, nodding his head. He pushes his chair away from the table and looks out the window for a moment. "You know, Mark, I am in much the same position as you were nine months ago," he says.

"What do you mean?" Mark asks.

"Nine months ago, you were extraordinarily concerned about whether you could turn around Universal Products," Jack replies. "Well, I am equally concerned about whether I can improve the performance of the enterprise. I am concerned about whether I can get significant improvement in the other divisions."

Jack tells Mark that he at one time questioned whether he had made the right choice in appointing Mark as general manager of Universal Products. He has the same concern about the general managers of the other eight Global Products divisions.

"After seeing your success with sales and operations planning, I came to realize that replacing all the general managers is not the answer," Jack says. "If implementing sales and operations planning in the other divisions is only one-quarter as successful as your implementation, it will be very well worth the expenditure."

Jack pushes himself back toward the table and flips the notebook back to the sales and operations planning model. "I understand how the process, in concept, works for a single division," he says, "but I would like to have a companywide view of the business. Is it possible to develop a corporate sales and operations planning process that I would lead?"

"Jack, I have only implemented sales and operations planning in one division," Mark replies. "We will need to get you and Ross Peterson together to discuss how to create a corporate sales and operations planning process. I know he has helped many large, worldwide organizations implement what he refers to as global sales and operations planning."

"Can you arrange for us to meet?" Jack asks. "I would like you to attend the meeting as well."

"We still need to address the other key personal issues for me," Mark says. "Assuming we address those issues, I most assuredly would want to be present for the discussion."

"Let's discuss those personal issues and see if we can put them to rest," Jack says. After relatively little discussion, he agrees that Mark can continue to live in Colorado. They agree that Mark's new role is short term and will probably last two years. The role Mark will take on after completing this assignment will be subject to future discussions.

Mark stresses to Jack that his goal will be to implement sales and operations planning in the other divisions as quickly as possible and to work himself out of a job. Travel to the other divisions will be essential. Mark will also need to spend some extended time at corporate headquarters, particularly during the education phase of the implementation.

Mark and Jack pause. They are both satisfied with their morning discussion.

Jack looks at his watch. It is noon. He can catch the early afternoon flight to Los Angeles.

As Jack prepares to leave, he stuffs the sales and operations planning notebook into his briefcase. "Let me know when Ross Peterson is available to meet with us," he says. "I'll plan to make my schedule flexible so we can meet as soon as possible."

■ ■ ■

"Honey, I'm home," Mark announces as he enters the side door from the garage. He hears the television and walks into the family room.

Cheryl, shoes off and feet tucked under her, is immersed in the six o'clock news. "Hi, sweetie," she says as Mark leans over the back of the sofa to give her a light kiss.

"I see that you have slaved over the stove all day and have dinner ready for me," Mark says.

Cheryl laughs. This has become a long-running joke between them. After years of cooking, Cheryl has all but retired from the kitchen.

"Where's Chad?" Mark inquires.

"Studying at his girlfriend's house supposedly," Cheryl replies.

"What does that mean?" Mark asks.

"He loves his girlfriend's mother's cooking," Cheryl answers.

"Better than yours?" Mark asks.

"I don't cook anymore, remember?" Cheryl says.

"Well, then, let's go out for a nice dinner," Mark suggests. "You pick the restaurant."

"You seem in a very generous mood tonight," Cheryl observes. "What's up?"

"I can never hide anything from you," Mark replies. "So you'll just have to wait until we get to the restaurant."

Cheryl picks a small, intimate Italian restaurant. Mark likes the choice. Not only is the food excellent, but they won't have to scream at each other to be heard over the other diners' conversations.

They order a merlot wine and clink their glasses together. "To us," they both say. It is a ritual they have been saying for more than twenty-five years now.

"So what's up?" Cheryl asks. "I know that Jack Baxter has been visiting, and you were awfully quiet last night."

"I should have talked to you last night, but I wanted to see how things played out today," Mark says.

"So where are we moving this time?" Cheryl asks.

Mark leans back in his chair and laughs. "It's impossible to slip anything by you, isn't it?"

"You married a woman with a brain, remember?" Cheryl replies.

"That's the type of woman I prefer," Mark says, smiling.

"Well, let's hear it," Cheryl says.

"First off, we're not moving," Mark tells Cheryl. "But I am going to take a new position." While eating ravioli with clam sauce, he tells her of Jack's job offer and his negotiations with Jack.

"So, you'll be traveling a lot," Cheryl observes. "But I'm glad we don't have to move again."

As the waiter clears their dishes from the table, Cheryl is thoughtful. Mark waits. He knows she will give him a succinct analysis.

"Here's the upside and the downside," she says after a few moments. "First, the downside. You will be out of a job in two years. That's a little early for retirement, so you'll need to be sure there's another position for you within Global Products."

"I agree," Mark says.

"Now the upside," Cheryl continues. "You will gain an intimate view of every division in Global Products. Jack could be grooming you for his position."

"Hold on, now," Mark says. "That may be a bit of a farfetched idea."

"Those are the possibilities," Cheryl replies.

■ ■ ■

Mark waits for Jack Baxter and Ross Peterson to arrive at the LeQue Hotel, his choice of a location for the education session for Jack. He makes sure that coffee, juice, muffins, and fruit are delivered to the meeting room.

He chose the LeQue for its quaint meeting rooms. This one has dark wood walls, and three sides of the room are filled with vintage books. The fourth side of the room is lined with glass windows that permit light to stream across the conference table.

Jack and Ross arrive at the same time. Ross is carrying his computer, which he will plug into the overhead projector. Jack is carrying the notebook Mark gave him two weeks ago. After exchanging pleasantries, the three men gather around the coffee urn to pour themselves coffee and juice.

"I've heard a lot about you and Nolan from the managers at Universal Products," Jack says. "They had plenty of good things to say about the job you did helping them implement sales and operations planning."

Ross smiles at Mark. "Thank you," he replies, "but the real effort came from Mark and his staff. They did a great job. I will say that it has been a pleasure working with someone who listens and acts upon the advice given. In so many companies, I find that considerable time and effort are wasted by arguing about issues that should be accepted as fundamental principles."

Jack, in an attempt to demonstrate some of his learning, says, "I understand that the people circle is the toughest."

Ross smiles again. "Mark told me that you two went over some of the material from the class. It sounds like Mark is a good teacher."

"Mark has reviewed some of the material with me. Plus I have reviewed it and his notes on my own twice," Jack explains, pointing to the notebook.

Mark, Ross, and Jack move toward the conference table. Still standing, Jack says, "I think I understand the concept of sales and operations planning. Today, I would like to learn about the implementation issues and problems, particularly from a global business perspective where a number of implementations will occur simultaneously."

Ross walks to the front of the room and begins advancing the computer through the slides. "The focus will be implementation from a global perspective," he says. "But before we get into implementation issues, I would like to spend an hour or two on the basics, just to make sure you and I are in sync on the fundamentals. After the overview of the basic fundamentals, next we will discuss *operating* sales and operations planning in a large company with divisions worldwide. We also will discuss the nuances of implementing the process in a global environment. Is this okay with you?"

Jack nods his head. "That's fine. Hopefully, you will find that Mark has done a good job teaching me so that we can move quickly into implementation."

"We will go at whatever pace is necessary — fast or slow," Ross replies. "The objective is to develop a solid understanding of the concepts, implementation issues, and leadership issues."

Mark is impressed with Ross's ability to work with Jack. He is able to maintain his agenda even with Jack's attempt to move him away from it. In talking with Ross to prepare for today's session, he recalls that Ross told him what he expected. He anticipated that Jack, like many other executives with whom Ross has worked, would be anxious to move forward.

"But they don't know what they don't know," Ross told Mark. "Without discipline, the danger is that the project moves forward with executive commitment without understanding."

As Ross works through the overview material, Mark observes that he is determined to make sure that Jack truly understands the concepts. Ross repeatedly asks Jack if he understands and agrees. He also challenges him with questions to check Jack's depth of understanding.

So far, Jack is up to the challenge. Jack also asks his own questions. Some of the questions are new; others are repeats of questions asked in their earlier discussions. Mark has worked with Jack long enough to know what he is doing. Jack is testing his own understanding. He also is testing Ross's knowledge of sales and operations planning.

Mark enjoys observing the give-and-take between Ross and Jack. He is surprised to glance at his watch and find that three hours has passed.

"You have demonstrated a solid grasp of the fundamentals, Jack," Ross says. "Let's take a break and then discuss how to operate sales and operations planning in a global environment."

■ ■ ■

Mark opens his notepad, ready to take notes. He is keenly interested in learning how to implement sales and operations planning around the world for Global Products.

He knows that Universal Products' implementation was fairly simple and straightforward. Every functional area reports to Mark as general manager. It is clear to Mark which managers are responsible for demand, supply, product development, finance, and the support functions. Each functional manager is responsible for his or her function on a global basis. Universal Products has one set of operating books for management. Of course, there are the necessary fiscal reporting requirements when doing business in other countries, but for all practical management purposes, Universal Products is a financial entity with one profit center.

Mark knows that the implementations in the other divisions will not be as straightforward. Some divisions operate largely on a regional basis, but with central support. In these divisions, a matrix-type organization exists. Some divisions have regional or geographic sales territories, but also have account managers whose areas of responsibility include more than one region. Some of the divisions sell and ship product directly to consumers. Other divisions have multiple channels to the market. Some divisions have regional sales efforts but global brand organizations. Some divisions manage their manufacturing on a regional basis; others manage it on a global basis. Many divisions have been changing their supply strategies from regional to global.

"It seems like Global Products has every possible combination of management organization," Mark comments to Jack and Ross. "It does not seem to me that it will be easy to operate sales and operations planning in some of these complex organizational structures."

Ross does not seem to be as concerned about Global Products' complexity. "The key issue in operating sales and operations planning in a large company with a more complex organization is to decide how you want to run the business," he says.

He explains that when helping a large company implement sales and operations planning to improve its performance, the first issue he must understand is the company's strategy. Key strategic questions often have not yet been answered or communicated. Some of these strategic questions include:

- Should the factories be focused centers of excellence, or should the factories be capable of producing multiple products for a particular geographic area (country, territory, region, or worldwide)?
- What should be the approach to the market?
- Should there be geographic regions for sales, marketing, and brand management, or should there be global sales, marketing, and brand management?
- What is the best method for managing product development and launch — locally, regionally, globally, or a combination? If an approach is selected that is not currently in place, what is the time frame to make the change?

Ross tells Jack and Mark that sales and operations planning can be implemented to fit *any* environment, simple or complex. It can also be changed as a company changes its strategies with the following caveat: *the company's management must commit to operate using the fundamental principles and practices upon which sales and operations planning is based.*

"Are you saying that the divisions can all have different operating strategies? That sales and operations planning will work effectively regardless of the organizational structure, strategies, products, and business environment? And we will see business benefits?" Jack asks.

"And if there is an open or pending strategic issue, that issue should surface during the implementation of sales and operations planning?" Mark adds.

"You are both correct," Ross replies. He explains that the sales and operations planning process operates independent of the business choices that need to be made. He has seen many companies attempt to solve product, customer, and market problems by implementing sales and operations planning as well as several other improvement initiatives. In many of these cases, their actions to solve the problems were too late.

Sales and operations planning always makes the current reality visible. Sometimes the current reality is that the company will not meet its previously agreed-upon and communicated goals. It is often too late to make up lost ground.

When this occurs, it is important to recognize that the sales and operations planning process did not create the current negative reality. Hopefully, however, sales and operations planning will enable the management team to identify issues and problems and stimulate changes to action plans. If the action plans cannot close the gaps between the current reality and the previously communicated goals, then it is necessary to communicate the reality.

"It is always better to communicate bad news early rather than bad news late," Ross comments. "One of the best practices, or what I call a Class A principle, is to change expectations when reality shows that the previously agreed-upon expectations will not be achieved."

Jack holds up his hand to signal Ross to stop. He turns to Mark. "I am starting to understand why you made such a fuss about me not simply mandating the process work without committing to investing in the appropriate support," Jack says.

"We're going to need to anticipate that strategic issues will undoubtedly surface," Mark replies, "and we'll need to be prepared to address the issues."

Ross reiterates that sales and operations planning does not create the strategic issue. The strategic issue usually has been bubbling just under the surface. Sales and operations planning makes it difficult to avoid making a decision about the issue. The consequences of not addressing the issue become highly visible through the sales and operations planning process.

"To implement sales and operations planning as *the* management process to run the business, the management team must agree on the fundamental strategic infrastructure of the enterprise," Ross says.

This issue concerns Mark, because he is certain that nearly every division will find strategic issues that have not been addressed. "During the implementations of sales and operations planning, should I be given the ability and authority to address these strategic issues with each division?" he asks. "Ross, what do *you* do when you encounter a company or division with these issues?"

Ross explains that he starts by recognizing that every company is operating to a set of strategies, stated or implied. These strategies are the company's strategies until changed. Ross has discussions with the president or general manager to determine whether he or she is implementing sales and operations planning for the current strategy or is attempting to use the implementation to change the strategy.

If he learns that the company is using sales and operations planning to change its current strategy, he works with the management team to define the desired change in strategy. If he learns that the company has no desire to change the current strategy, he guides the president or general manager to clearly articulate that operating to the current strategy is a criterion for implementing the sales and operations planning process.

Jack takes off his reading glasses and rubs his eyes. "So how often is the implementation of sales and operations planning used to change the strategy as opposed to support the current strategy?" he asks.

"More often than not, the sales and operations planning process is implemented in support of the current strategy," Ross replies. "Think about it. Usually a company implements sales and operations planning to help solve some current problems. The problems may simply be lack of synchronization, or the problems may result from a change in strategy for which the supporting infrastructure is lacking. In either case, management wants to get control of the *current* environment."

Mark sees where Ross is leading the conversation. "As a general manager, once I'm in control of my current environment with sales and operations planning, I can then use the process to help implement a change in strategy if that is what I choose to do," Mark observes.

"That's correct," Ross answers.

"I'm okay with the strategic implications," Jack says, "but I need to know how the basic sales and operations planning model changes in a larger, more complex company environment."

Ross brings up the slide index on his computer and locates the basic model (Figure 52). He explains that they should consider the basic sales and operations planning model, and then he will introduce some elements to it for a more complex, global environment. One of the first questions to ask when implementing sales and operations planning in several divisions or a complex environment is whether the company will operate with a single-level or multiple-level process. Most large, global companies tend to utilize a multiple-level process.

"What do you mean by multiple-level process?" Jack asks.

Ross answers that the most common model of a multilevel process consists of the following elements: Sales and marketing are managed and controlled in a regional business unit. Manufacturing or the supply of products is controlled both regionally and centrally. Regional manufacturing or supply control is provided for local manufacturing or supply management. There is also central control provided for *global* visibility and decision making about the manufacturing or supply of product.

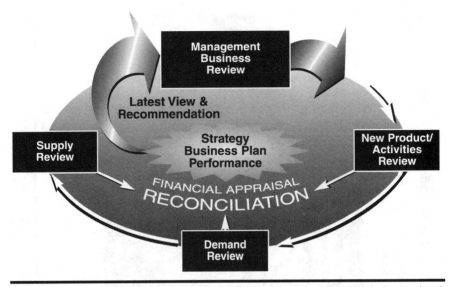

Figure 52   Integrated Business Management Model (Copyright Oliver Wight International. Reproduced with permission.)

"Why?" Jack asks.

"So that the company can utilize its total global resources in a most practical, cost-effective manner," Ross replies. He explains that in this environment, the regional general manager owns the sales and operations planning process for the region. The regional model looks very similar to the basic sales and operations planning process model. There is also a global supply review process that includes a roll-up of consolidated demand and total available resources. Often, a second global sales and operations planning process is conducted to review the business from a *total* global perspective.

"If this process is properly orchestrated," Ross says, "multiple, simultaneous views of the business will initiate business discussions about deployment of resources, leveraging of branding, leveraging of product development, and other opportunity issues." He shows Jack and Mark a model of a multiple-level sales and operations planning process (Figure 53).

"So the regional general mangers would have a complete view of their respective businesses on a regional basis, and corporate management would have a complete view on a global basis," Jack observes. "Corporate management would also have the ability to drill down to a region as may be desired or required. And the supply organization can see if one plant or region is overloaded while another is underutilized. This would potentially give supply management the ability to juggle production between plants or regions."

"That's correct," Ross replies.

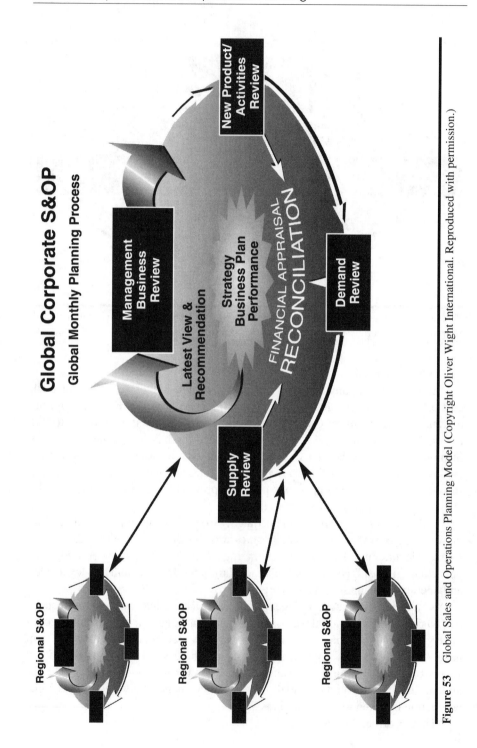

Figure 53 Global Sales and Operations Planning Model (Copyright Oliver Wight International. Reproduced with permission.)

"This multiple-level model would be particularly important when the regions share a common resource that is a current or potential constraint," Mark says. "The resolution of conflicts relative to the constrained resource could be done from a global perspective."

"You're right," Ross replies, "but I want to raise an issue." He explains that some executives in the divisions and central management will believe that they presently operate with an effective conflict resolution process. They will question whether sales and operations planning will create a redundant process.

The conflict resolution process employed by most companies is called an *allocation* process. There are several problems with most allocation processes, in Ross's experience.

First, the allocation takes place at too low a level in the organization. The wrong people make the allocation choices. Frequently, this may be people in the planning or shipping organization. In their defense, they make the allocations because no one else will take responsibility for making the allocation decisions.

The second problem with most allocation processes is that the choices are made by the supply organization, which has the least customer or market knowledge of the best opportunity to apply the scarce resource.

The third problem is that allocation decisions are typically made with less than complete information. Even if allocation is done by the right people at the right level, the information is often so poor that poor decisions result.

The fourth problem is that allocation almost always happens after a problem has occurred. Stated differently, many customers will not have their expectations met because the need to allocate has not been anticipated.

Finally, when allocation is done in advance of a problem occurring, it is almost always part of a flawed implementation of the annual business plan. Even when companies have a strong annual planning process, allocation in support of the business plan violates a key principle: For maximum flexibility, do not make a decision before it is necessary. When allocation purely supports the business plan and is not based on the need to address an imbalance in demand and supply, it strips away flexibility that may be needed in the future.

"One of my clients was a chemical company," Ross says. "Before implementing sales and operations planning, the company allocated globally based on an annual allocation of its traditionally constrained active ingredient or raw material. After implementing sales and operations planning, the company began utilizing decision points for making the allocation choice. During the first full year after implementing sales and operations planning, the company achieved its highest sales, lowest inventory, highest return on net assets, and best customer service ever. Mark, let me ask you why or how that was possible."

Mark hesitates for a moment, as he thinks through the answer. "When the company used an annual global allocation," he replies, "some regions ended the year with excess inventories while other regions did not have enough stock. This was caused by the allocations being based upon demand assumptions that changed during the year. When the company conducted its monthly reviews as part of sales and operations planning, it was able to replan more frequently and was, thus, able to more closely match the market demand. The regions ended up with the inventory at the right place so it could be sold. At the end of the year, there should have been increased sales, less inventory, better asset utilization, and better customer service because the inventory was where it was needed. In essence, the company made the decisions when it needed to, not early and not late."

"Ross, is this an actual case history, a true story?" Jack asks.

"Yes, it is," Ross replies. "As Mark knows, I hate the word 'allocation.' If we have a constraint that I make a business choice to live within, then I need to adjust my marketing plans accordingly to ensure that I properly create and then meet customers' expectations."

He explains that for a business to be successful, it must satisfy customer expectations. When choosing to live with a constraint, executives must be sure they have a replanning system that identifies the best utilization of the constrained resource.

"When sales and operations planning is properly implemented, it does just that," Ross says, adding that this is not an easy concept for many companies and many managers to grasp.

Ross returns to the subject of multiple-level sales and operations planning. He emphasizes that companies should strive to keep the sales and operations planning process as simple as possible. All the benefits of simplicity come with keeping the sales and operations planning simple.

"If you do not need a multiple-level process, don't implement it," Ross says. He explains that a more complex, multiple-level model usually results when a company chooses to manage its supply from a central location in order to maximize utilization of fixed assets. Rather than having one facility overloaded and another looking for work, a central master planning function is responsible for moving work from the overloaded facility to the underloaded facility. Many ramifications should be considered when making the choice to operate in this environment. Considerations include:

- The ability of multiple facilities to produce the same quality product
- Comparative manufacturing costs
- Standardization of products and manufacturing processes among facilities
- Transportation capabilities and costs

"I need to raise a caution flag," Ross says. He explains that some companies get so involved in figuring out the best, lowest cost way to produce the product that they lose sight of the original objective, which is to meet customers' expectations. A properly implemented sales and operations planning process always starts with determining what the company desires to accomplish in the marketplace. It is demand driven, and supply should be predisposed to be in a position to say yes to business opportunities.

"I have seen companies try to save a point or two in manufacturing costs and as a result lose major gross margin opportunities," Ross comments. "These opportunities were lost because there was no process in place to enable the decision to be made in the best interest of the company. Consequently, the decision was made in the best interest of manufacturing."

Jack and Mark are intrigued by Ross's insight and considerable experience. They do not interrupt his observations.

Ross points out another frequently used multiple-level sales and operations planning model. In this model, product development is a shared resource and is managed from a central location.

With this model, the challenge becomes how to best communicate regional customer and market requirements so that they are included in the product portfolio and are considered as part of product introduction decisions. Visibility of customer and market requirements is particularly important when the products offered must have significant local variation to meet the needs of particular market segments.

"It is important to design the sales and operations planning process to ensure that the needs of the market are reflected in the product development decisions," Ross comments.

Jack holds up his hand and turns to address Mark. "As I see it," he says, "the process must be designed for the particular division's management requirements. The process must provide the right information to the right people regularly and routinely so that the best decisions can be made."

"I agree," Mark replies. "Each divisional implementation will have its own specific application requirements. There is no one management model that works for every division. The fundamentals of sales and operations planning still apply, but the application will depend on the nature of the business and how management has chosen to manage the business."

Ross smiles. They truly understand the concepts and implications for the divisions. He is optimistic that they will provide the leadership and guidance needed to implement global sales and operations planning.

■ ■ ■

It is obvious that Jack is deep in thought. He pushes himself away from the table and begins to pace. Mark and Ross do not interrupt his thoughts. Mark gets up and refills his coffee cup. Ross advances the computer to the next visual he plans on discussing.

Finally, Jack turns to Ross. "We have a difficult issue," he says. "We share a common resource in many of our divisions. That resource is product development, or engineering. The basic development is done centrally, but enhancements are supported by the regional structure. How do we make sure that all product development resources are properly focused on what we want them to do?"

Ross's demeanor calms Jack. He acts as if this problem is not insurmountable. "This is a common problem with a common solution," he replies. "It is conceptually simple and straightforward, but do not confuse that statement with the notion that the solution is easy to implement."

Ross explains that the issue can be addressed by establishing a central planning process that works in conjunction with the regional planning processes. The central planning process is responsible for ensuring that the corporate and regional product development resources are synchronized.

This responsibility implies that the central planning organization and the regional planning organizations reach consensus on product portfolio, product development and launch, product exiting, and product rationalization every month. Monthly consensus is reached by conducting a product review meeting prior to the regional demand review meeting. These product reviews are conducted at the region level and central level.

"Let me explain the product review process," Ross says. He tells Jack that the inputs to the regional product review include:

- Marketing information from consumers and customers
- Strategic goals
- Business assumptions
- Competitive research
- Technology
- Price and cost assumptions
- Current product portfolio
- Current product development schedule and status
- Current product end-of-life schedule
- Current demand/supply/inventory synchronization plans

The output from the product review includes an update of *which products are available to be sold and delivered and when.* It includes assumptions on all significant new or exiting products.

The feasibility of product development and launch programs is tested, using rough-cut capacity planning or aggregate resource planning techniques. The results of these tests are reviewed to ensure the company has the capability to accomplish the task.

In essence, the output of the process is one product offering game plan updated for changes each month. The output of the regional reviews is communicated to the central planning organization so that central and regional reviews can be synchronized and reconciled each month.

"Let me make sure I understand," Mark says. "Once a month, all the key players agree upon what products are available to be offered inside the planning horizon. This is made visible for sales and operations planning. The primary difference for Global Products versus what Universal Products does today is that this model has multiple potential areas for management control. There's central control and some local control. However, there is a process for the central organization and regional organizations to reach consensus each month."

"That's correct," Ross replies.

"If I understand you correctly," Mark continues, "the output of this process defines our product offering, or portfolio, and timing. During each sales and operations planning cycle, demand and supply will be balanced to make sure all people in all locations are operating to the same product plan, agreed-upon introduction schedule, agreed-upon exit schedules, and agreed-upon volumes and margins."

"That's right," Ross says, "and each cycle will be based upon the most current product portfolio offerings and schedule."

Jack wants to be sure he understands the implications and opportunities from a corporate president's point of view. "So if I, as president, were to sit in on any divisional executive sales and operations planning meeting," he says, "I would get a clear view of what the product strategy and offering is for the next eighteen months, assuming that eighteen months is the agreed-upon planning horizon. And I could be reassured that the product plan is updated to deal with the normal changes in the business."

Ross nods his head in affirmation. "And if you require more detailed information, you could sit in on the regional and central product review meetings," he explains. "The inputs to your executive sales and operations planning are the plans and assumptions that are the output of the individual review meetings, including the product review."

"What I see as significant," Mark comments, "is that consensus is reached not just centrally and not just regionally, but both centrally and regionally together. There should not be any question about what the product game plan is."

"That's correct," Ross replies. He explains that once a company gets its demand, supply, and financial projections balanced and in sync with the business goals, the product review becomes perhaps the most significant area where management directs its primary attention. The rest of the process simply *works,* and the decisions are relatively easy.

Product development choices and priorities are almost always more demanding than simply managing the ongoing business. The product review is where marketing, customer, and demand strategies connect with product development, operations, and execution from a schedule perspective.

Executives find that the decisions made in the product review process directly impact growing the business, increasing market share, and increasing margins. One focus of the executive sales and operations planning meeting is to connect the product review decisions to the customers and the supply chain. The executive sales and operations planning meeting also focuses on a view of the total business, including the specific product road maps and project status. An output of the executive sales and operations planning meeting is an understanding of the financial ramifications of the most recent changes to the product, demand, and supply plans.

"When companies use this model for shared resources, such as product development, they gain control at the regional level, central level, and corporate level," Ross explains.

Jack is pacing again, hands clasped behind his back. Mark and Ross wait.

Jack walks behind Mark and taps him on the shoulder. He moves to the front of the room so he can see Mark's face.

"Mark, thank you for insisting that I get some education on sales and operations planning," he says. "I now understand what you have been trying to tell me. If I am any general manager of any division or region, I should truly know whether I was on plan to meet my strategic objectives. And I should be able to gain this knowledge in a few short hours each month."

Mark smiles at Jack. He understands how Jack is feeling because he went through it himself. When he realized the power of sales and operations planning, it was like a light bulb went on, and it has been burning brightly ever since.

Jack continues. "Because the process occurs every month, regularly and routinely, as a general manager I have the ability to identify problems or opportunities early," he says. "I can make sure that any changes are reflected in all the plans for all functional areas of the company."

Jack turns to Ross. "This may be organized common sense, Ross, but it seems to me it can be very powerful."

Before Ross can reply, Mark, who is grinning, says, "It really is just organized common sense. However, common sense is not necessarily so common. Ross has stated, and I agree, that doing sales and operations planning well often provides a significant competitive advantage."

"If I look at the results you and your team have achieved at Universal Products," Jack says, "I believe that Global Products will not only improve its operational performance but will also increase market share if we implement sales and operations planning to a best practice, Class A level."

"That should be the goal," Ross concurs.

12

EPILOGUE

Mark Ryan is restless. He looks around his office at corporate headquarters on this sunny autumn morning. This office was always a temporary place to drop his bags and meet with people when visiting corporate headquarters. The place still looks temporary. There are no pictures of his family on the desk, no photos on the wall. The office is a cubbyhole really, just down the hall from the office of Jack Baxter, the corporate president.

Mark is in a thoughtful mood and decides to buy a cup of coffee from the cafeteria. He reaches into his pocket to make sure he has his cafeteria card, in his mind a wonderful invention. About twice a month, he goes to an ATM-like machine, inserts the card and money, and the card is credited electronically. No need to worry about having cash every day.

Mark serves himself a cup of Starbucks dark roast and slides his cafeteria card through the slot at the pay stand. He decides to drink the cup of java in the cafeteria and looks for a table near the window, something his office does not have and essential for Mark to think well.

Today is a milestone in several ways. The implementations are complete in all eight divisions around the world. Today, Ross Peterson and Nolan Drake will present to Global Products a plaque to commemorate its operating sales and operations planning to best practices, or what Effective Management, Inc. calls a Class A level.

More important than receiving a plaque are the performance improvements that every division has achieved. Sales revenues and profits are up and operating costs are down in every division, some more than others. Mark knows from his experience at Universal Products that if every division continues to operate sales and operations planning effectively, the improvements will incrementally increase over time. So there is still more to gain, including increases in market share.

Today is a milestone for Mark personally as well. Thirty months after taking the assignment to lead the global implementation effort, he has worked his way out of a job. He does not know what his new assignment will be. It is something he and Jack Baxter are scheduled to discuss tomorrow.

Mark thinks back to the global implementation. At first, it appeared a daunting task. Most of the executives in the divisions had not heard of sales and operations planning. Education was the key to getting the general managers and their senior staff on board and committed to implementing the process.

Mark remembers some of the education sessions. First, he visited every general manager and then he brought Ross Peterson along to conduct one-on-one sessions, much like the session that worked so well in educating Jack. Then Ross Peterson and Nolan Drake conducted education sessions for the senior staff and middle managers. These sessions were similar to the ones held at Universal Products.

In thinking about the global implementation, Mark is appreciative that there was a proven implementation method that every division could follow. The steps in the implementation process were the same, and there was no need to reinvent the wheel.

The design of the process at each division and for corporate headquarters was more complex and took longer than at Universal Products. There were centralized and decentralized elements to consider. The corporate level oversaw global supply, product development, and branding. The divisions were responsible for sales, marketing, and production. The care taken in the design was well worth the effort. It was essential to ensure that the roles and responsibilities at the division level and corporate level were well understood.

Mark considers himself something of an organizational change expert now after overseeing nine implementations. He learned that one reason people resist change is not because they are comfortable with the status quo. Heavens, most people in most divisions were tired of firefighting and working endless overtime without ever truly satisfying the customers or improving their division's performance.

Mark is now convinced that the reason most people resist change is the fear of failure. This revelation was a surprise to Mark, but it became crystal clear during the design portion of the process.

Design workshops were conducted at every division. During the workshops, the inputs and outputs of each element of the sales and operations planning process were defined. In addition to accomplishing the design, the objective of the workshops was to get commitment to operate using that design. When it came time to truly commit to operating the elements the way they had been designed and set a timetable for doing so, some people began to show reluctance to operate the process.

Thankfully, Ross, Nolan, and the other EMI consultants knew how to guide people through what Ross called the natural course of change. For the most part, it was nonconfrontational.

It was also interesting, and sometimes surprising, to see who emerged as the risk takers. These were the managers who had less reluctance and less fear of failure. Mark, the general managers, and the EMI consultants utilized those people as the leaders and champions of the process. On a daily basis, they guided the rest of their team through the implementation. When obstacles presented themselves, they were the ones who found ways to resolve the issues and helped others to see that the solutions would be effective.

Mark looks around the cafeteria dining room. It is a large room with forty or so tables. Informal and formal meetings are conducted in the dining room throughout the day. It is a comfortable and well-lit place to sit, and you don't feel as hemmed in as when enclosed a meeting room. You also don't have to reserve dining room space. It is first come, first serve.

Mark listens to the conversations around him. The tone and tenor of the talk during meetings have changed. Mark has observed this change at corporate headquarters and at every division.

It used to be that employees openly criticized management for not knowing what it was doing or making poor decisions. Sometimes they openly questioned whether senior management would support their decisions, and often the priorities were not clear when decisions were made. Now, there is less criticism and little questioning as to whether management will change its mind about the direction and priorities that have been defined and communicated.

The criticism hasn't entirely disappeared, and Mark believes it never will. It is almost like a national pastime to second-guess our leaders, whether in business, politics, or sports.

Mark looks up to see Jack and two other people, obviously guests, serve themselves coffee. Jack waves to Mark, but doesn't stop by to talk. The trio heads back down the hall toward Jack's office.

Mark considers Jack for a moment. They have worked together for more than seventeen years. Jack has been Mark's mentor and leader for all of those years.

Mark admires Jack's willingness to change. Once the benefits of sales and operations planning were demonstrated at Universal Products, Jack provided the impetus to implement across all divisions. His support never wavered.

Mark remembers how skeptical he was about Jack's enthusiasm for sales and operations planning. He had been burned too many times by Jack and other senior executives. They would embrace the latest three-letter-acronym improvement initiative, only to drop it when another one came along.

He challenged Jack's understanding and commitment to sales and operations planning. During the one-on-one education session with Ross, Jack demonstrated a solid grasp of the concepts of sales and operations planning. He promised to "walk the talk," and he did, too.

Mark recalls the aftermath of the education session for the division general managers. Jack was obviously committed to the process, and all of the general managers voiced their commitment at the end of the session.

About one month later, the implementation process was not moving along in one division at the same pace as the other divisions. It became clear to Mark, Ross, and Nolan that the general manager did not believe the process would work and only paid lip service to the implementation efforts. He delegated the implementation to middle managers in the organization.

Learning of the general manager's resistance, Jack told Mark that he would handle the situation. Mark never learned what Jack said to the general manager, but the implementation effort was reorganized. The general manager and senior managers carried out their proper roles and responsibilities in the implementation, and the general manager turned out to be a good leader of the process.

Jack utilized other motivational methods that worked well. He repeatedly emphasized that sales and operations planning was a key priority at Global Products. He visited every division at least three times to observe its sales and operations planning meetings. He added an implementation status report as a standing agenda item in his monthly executive staff meeting, and he asked every general manager to report his or her status. He did not want Mark to present the status; he believed that would prevent the general managers from becoming accountable for the success of the implementation. To back up his words and actions, Jack included the successful implementation and operating the process to a Class A level in the annual performance measures of all his key executives.

Mark looks around the room for a moment. He sees the sales and operations planning coordinators for the Europe and Asia divisions across the room. He is pleased that all of the coordinators from every division were invited to today's ceremony. They were the linchpins during the implementation and still are today in ensuring that the process continues to operate well.

The role of the coordinator, Mark sees now, is a great way to train managers to advance in the division. The coordinators work shoulder to shoulder with the executive staff. They learn how to communicate with the senior staff. They learn how decisions are made and how the business is run. Mark wishes he had that advantage when he was a young, ambitious junior manager.

Mark looks up and studies the television monitor, which is turned to CNN. He strains to listen to Alan Greenspan, chairman of the U.S. Federal Reserve, testify before a congressional committee on the health of the U.S. economy. Greenspan refers to manufacturing capacities, inventory, demand, costs, and profits in explaining the strengths and weaknesses of the economy.

It strikes Mark that these are universal indicators to guide decision making, whether for the U.S. economy or the health of a manufacturing company. Before implementing sales and operations planning, however, the division managers never had clear-cut projections of what their position would be with regard to capacities, inventory, demand, costs, and profits. Most attempts by the financial organization to develop these projections were challenged within the divisions and tinkered with by the general managers prior to communicating the projections to corporate headquarters.

Little or no time, in all honesty, was spent in utilizing the projections to understand the condition of the company and identify opportunities in the marketplace to improve the company's position. They were merely reported with the hope that the report would satisfy corporate management.

Everyone, general managers and corporate president included, was too caught up in making sure that the crisis of the moment was being properly addressed. Mark remembers the daily pressures he felt from customers and corporate to ship back orders. There was no time to think about anything else.

Mark ponders this revelation for a moment. What enabled the general managers and corporate management to truly manage often highly complex divisions into a healthy, profitable position? In his mind, certainly sales and operations planning as a process was key. But that process would not have been successful without what Mark can sum up in four words: *standard information formats* and *consensus.*

By agreeing upon a basic template of how the demand, supply, inventory and backlog, capacity, finance, and performance measurement information would be presented, it was possible to get a much clearer picture of the problems and opportunities. That clear picture enabled the senior managers to reach consensus and make decisions very rapidly. Consensus and decisions did not take months to reach with fruitless after fruitless meeting.

Mark decides the genius was in the information templates that EMI introduced. Those templates were modified slightly to accommodate the nuances of Global Products, but the templates have changed very little over the course of two years.

It is interesting to Mark how the general managers in particular guarded against "mucking up the information," as one general manager put it. It must be human nature to want to create the complex from the simple. People tried to introduce more detail to the basic information. Those attempts were fought off by permitting additional detailed information to be presented when the information was necessary to reach consensus and make decisions. Use of the detailed information was more the exception than the rule.

Mark sees Ross Peterson and Nolan Drake in the line to buy coffee. He waves at them to join him.

"I've just been thinking about you two," he greets them. After spending more than two years traveling and working together, there is an ease and informality to their conversations.

"Hopefully, the thoughts were all good," Ross replies.

"I was thinking about the implementations and what really made them work for every division," Mark says. "It was the information templates and then the education you provided in understanding the meaning of the information. That's what enabled us to make the decisions we needed to make about the business. It gave us a good handle on the health of the business."

"That's funny. Nolan and I were talking about the implementations while driving here today," Ross comments, "and we said the keys to the success were you and Jack. Jack had the wisdom to appoint you as the leader of the global implementations. You had successfully implemented the process yourself. It gave you credibility and the ability to quickly identify those who were 'walking the talk' and those who were not. And Jack 'walked the talk' better than most presidents in other companies with which we have worked. When he attended the division sales and operations planning meetings, he would turn the conversations toward the business. He had the ability to review the information, accurately interpret it, and make sure that the meetings were focused on reaching consensus and decision making, not merely reporting."

"Speak of the devil," Nolan says.

Jack strolls across the dining room, stopping to say a few words to the sales and operations planning coordinators, now gathered in full force, and other employees. When he reaches Mark's table, he shakes hands with Ross and Nolan.

Turning to Mark, he says, "Did you see the two fellows I was with thirty minutes ago? I would like you to meet them after the presentation this morning."

"Sure," Mark replies. "Who are they?"

"You've heard we are considering the acquisition of another company. They are with that company," Jack says. "I want you to run it. And you'll be pleased to know that the company is located in Colorado."

Jack briefly clasps Mark on the shoulder and continues to greet employees in the dining room.

Mark turns to Ross and Nolan and says, "I guess we have our next assignment."

BIBLIOGRAPHY

American Production and Inventory Control Society; *APICS Dictionary,* 9th Edition.

Aslett, Don; *Clutter's Last Stand,* F&W Publications, 1984.

Correll, James G.; Edson, Norris W.; *Gaining Control: Capacity Management and Scheduling,* John Wiley & Sons, 1990.

Cross, Robert; *Revenue Management: Hard-Core Tactics for Market Domination,* Broadway Books, 1997.

Drucker, Peter F.; *The Executive in Action,* Harper Business, 1996.

Goddard, Walter; Ling, Richard; *Orchestrating Success: Improve Control of the Business with Sales and Operations Planning,* John Wiley & Sons, 1988.

Hamel, Gary; Prahalad, C.K.; *Competing for the Future,* Harvard Business School Press, 1994.

Kaplan, Robert S.; Norton, David P.; *The Balanced Scorecard: Translating Strategy into Action,* Harvard Business School Press, 1996.

Katzenbach, Jon R.; Smith, Douglas K.; *The Wisdom of Teams,* Harper Business, 1994.

Kotler, Philip; *Kotler on Marketing: How to Create, Win, and Dominate Markets,* Free Press, 1999.

Landvater, Darryl V.; *World Class Production and Inventory Management,* John Wiley & Sons, 1993.

Miller, Robert B.; Heiman, Stephen E.; *Conceptual Selling,* Miller Heiman, 1987.

Miller, Robert B.; Heiman, Stephen E.; *Strategic Selling,* Miller Heiman, 1987.

Oliver Wight Companies; *The Oliver Wight ABCD Checklist for Operational Excellence,* John Wiley & Sons, 2001.

Palmatier, George; Shull, Joseph; *The Marketing Edge: The New Leadership Role of Sales and Marketing in Manufacturing,* John Wiley & Sons, 1989.

Porter, Michael E.; *Competitive Strategy: Techniques for Analyzing Industries and Competitors,* Free Press, 1980.

Proud, John; *Master Scheduling: A Practical Guide to Competitive Manufacturing,* John Wiley & Sons, 1994.

Strassman, Paul; *Information Payoff: The Transformation of Work in the Electronic Age,* The Information Economics Press, February 1985.

Treacy, Michael; Wiersema, Fred; *The Discipline of Market Leaders: Choose Your Customers, Narrow Your Focus, Dominate Your Market,* Addison-Wesley, 1995.

Wheelwright, Steven C.; Clark, Kim; *Leading Product Development: The Senior Manager's Guide to Creating and Shaping the Enterprise,* Free Press, 1994.

INDEX